Industrialization and the State:
The Korean Heavy and
Chemical Industry Drive

Harvard Studies in International Development

*Jointly published by the International Center for Economic Growth.

Industrialization and the State: The Korean Heavy and Chemical Industry Drive

Joseph J. Stern
Ji-hong Kim
Dwight H. Perkins
Jung-ho Yoo

Harvard Institute for International Development
and Korea Development Institute

Distributed by Harvard University Press

Published by the Harvard Institute for International Development
July, 1995

Distributed by Harvard University Press

Editorial management: Don Lippincott
Editorial assistance: Sarah Newberry
Design and production: Editorial Services of New England, Inc.

Library of Congress Cataloging-in-Publication Data

Industrialization and the state: the Korean heavy and chemical
   industry drive / Joseph J. Stern . . . [et al.].
      p. cm. — (Harvard studies in international development)
   Includes bibliographical references and index.
   ISBN 0-674-45225-9
   1. Industrial policy—Korea (South)   2. Industrialization—Korea
(South)   3. Steel industry and trade—Government policy—Korea
(South)   4. Automobile industry and trade—Government policy—Korea
(South)   5. Shipbuilding industry—Government policy—Korea (South)
   6. Aluminum industry and trade—Government policy—Korea (South)
   7. Chemical industry—Government policy—Korea (South)   I. Stern, Joseph J.
   II. Series.
   HD3616.K852I53 1995
   338.95195—dc20   95-15799
                                                                CIP

Printed in the United States of America

Contents

Contributors

Joseph J. Stern is an Institute Fellow and former Executive Director of the Harvard Institute for International Development, and a lecturer on economics at Harvard University. He has worked in a number of Asian countries, including Bangladesh, Brunei, Indonesia, Korea, Malaysia, Pakistan, and Sri Lanka. The main focus of his work has been on the relations between international trade policies and industrial development. His work in Korea has centered on the political economy of industrial policymaking and implementation. Stern holds a Ph.D. in economics from Harvard University.

Ji-hong Kim is a Professor of International Economics at Han Yang University in Korea and has worked as a Research Fellow at the Korea Development Institute. He has written several articles on Korean industrial policy. He received a B.A. in economics from Seoul National University, an M.B.A. from the Harvard Business School, and a Ph.D. from the University of California, Berkeley.

Dwight H. Perkins is the Harold Hitchings Burbank Professor of Political Economy at Harvard University and is a Faculty Fellow at the Harvard Institute for International Development, where he also served as Director from 1980 to mid-1995. He is the author, coauthor, or editor of eleven books and over eighty articles on issues of economic development, particularly on the economies of China and Korea. Much of his current work deals with the analysis of market-oriented reform efforts in Asia and the role of the state in Asian industrial development. Perkins received a Ph.D. in economics from Harvard University.

Jung-bo Yoo is Senior Fellow at the Korea Development Institute. He has worked as Senior Counselor to Korea's Deputy Prime Minister of Economic Planning. His area of research interest includes international trade and economic development and the related policy issues. Recently, he estimated the nominal and effective protective rates of Korea's industries. He graduated from the Law School of Seoul National University and received a Ph.D. in economics from the University of Wisconsin, Madison.

Preface

Fifteen years ago the Korea Development Institute (KDI) and the Harvard Institute for International Development (HIID) jointly researched, wrote, and published ten book-length studies on the first three decades of Korean economic development (1945–1975). Several years ago, the reception of these volumes encouraged the two institutes to think of a sequel. In considering that sequel, we decided to focus on a number of studies that went in-depth into several of the key features of the post–1975 period.

We chose three themes that dealt with central features of Korean development, which were either not present in the pre-1975 period or were present in only muted form. The first of these studies dealt with macroeconomic policy during the difficult period of the 1970s, when oil prices were rising sharply, and with the aftermath of these macro problems in the 1980s. This study deals with Korea's move away from generalized support for exports of manufactures to a policy of targeting specific industries, the heavy and chemical industry drive of the 1973–1979 period, followed by the retreat from industrial targeting in the 1980s. The final study will deal with some of the strains of rapid economic growth. Special attention in that study will be paid to labor relations and the labor market in the 1980s, when Korean democratization led to the end of government efforts to suppress the labor movement, and labor and management had to learn new ways of working together.

These three studies differ from the earlier ten-volume series in another important respect. The earlier series dealt only peripherally with the politics of the economic changes that were analyzed. The three recent studies include political economy issues as central themes. Technical economic analysis continues to play an important role, but many chapters are devoted to how and why key economic policy decisions were actually made, a process that involved more than purely economic considerations.

The starting point for this volume on the development of Korea's heavy and chemical industry drive is the announcement by President Park Chung-hee on January 12, 1973, that "the government hereby initiates a Heavy and Chemical Industry Policy that places heavy emphasis on the measure to promote the development of heavy and chemical industries."[1] At the time the HCI policy was announced, the economy was still at an early stage of economic development. About half of all workers were engaged in the agriculture sector, the manufacturing sector employed little more than 15 percent of the workforce, per capita incomes were relatively low, and exports were heavily concentrated in labor intensive products.

The chance of the policy's success was considered fair. The economy had, after all, achieved remarkable development in light industries and had made considerable progress in laying the basis for more capital intensive industries, such as cement, steel, and petro-chemicals. Industrial countries faced problems with their "smoke-stack" industries because of rising labor costs and popular demand for a cleaner environment. Korea had the advantage of a "late industrializing" country that could import the latest technologies from abroad.

Because Korea achieved a large measure of economic and social success in the years that followed the initiation of the HCI drive, promotion of the heavy and chemical industries is often taken as a vindication of those who argued for a stronger role for government involvement in development policy. Various studies have used Korea's success in the development of a modern industrial state as evidence that successful government interventions are not only possible but desirable. And just as Korea looked to Japan as an economic role model, so other Asian countries today look to Korea as a role model for their development efforts.

Disentangling what impact the HCI drive actually had and to what extent its success and failures were due to external factors is a difficult process. The numerous studies that have focused on this period reach different conclusions. Some argue that without the HCI drive, Korea's economy would be less able to compete in today's world market. Others conclude that the HCI drive resulted in a considerable waste of resources,

[1]The Office of the Secretary to the President. *Collection of President Park Chung-hee's Speeches*. Vol. 5, p. 39, (1976). Seoul: Daehan Gornon-sa. (Unofficial translation).

an increase in foreign debt, and that by creating numerous monopolies under the guise of protecting new industrial ventures, the government laid the ground for the labor-management conflicts that marked Korea's development experience in the late 1980s and 1990s. This volume hopes to move the debate along.

In completing this volume on the heavy and chemical industry experience, the authors owe special thanks to David Lindauer, who managed the pre-production conferences for all three volumes. We also want to thank the four past presidents of KDI who helped initiate these studies and bring them to fruition, Dr. Park Yung Chul, Dr. Koo Bon Ho, Dr. Song Hee Yhon, and Dr. Whang In-Joung. Funding for these studies was provided from KDI funds and from the unrestricted income of HIID. Able research assistance was provided by Hiroshi Kato, Annette Kim, A. K. Shiva Kumar, Lora Sabin, and G. P. Shukla. The editorial process for this volume was under the overall direction of Donald Lippincott and Sarah Newberry of HIID's publications office.

DWIGHT H. PERKINS
Director, HIID

DONG-SE CHA
President, KDI

Industrialization and the State:
The Korean Heavy and
Chemical Industry Drive

1

Introduction _____

Governments in developing countries play an active role in the promotion of modern economic growth, and industrialization is an integral part of that growth. It follows, more or less automatically, that governments in these nations pursue an industrial policy, whether they recognize it as such or not. The Korean industrial policy experience since the early 1960s, which is analyzed here, therefore is part of a more general phenomenon. What makes Korea interesting is not just that the government had an industrial policy but the particular kind of policy that the government pursued. In fact, Korea pursued different industrial policies at different periods. In this study, the focus is on Korea's promotion of heavy and chemical industries in the 1970s, but the policies of that decade are contrasted with and evaluated in comparison with industrial policies pursued in the 1960s and the 1980s.

In the broadest terms, industrial policy is any action of government that is designed to promote the growth of industry, the efficiency of the industrial sector, or the equity with which the output of the industrial sector is shared. In general terms, therefore, much of the debate over industrial policy concerns the appropriate role for government in development. The discussion often takes place on an abstract level governed by economic theory and not a little ideology. This study attempts to bring that debate down to something closer to the reality that developing countries in general, and Korea in particular, face.

World Views: Economists and Others

In Korea in the 1970s, the debate over industrial policy took place between engineers and economists, and it was arbitrated by a general-turned-politician, President Park. Much the same sort of clash occurs between economists and engineers over how to foster more rapid industrial growth in a number of countries. In Indonesia, for example, the debate is between the technocrats—the economists who have managed the stabilization and reform process over the past three decades—and the technologists—the engineers and politicians who support a more active role for government in the development of high-tech industries. In Malaysia, politicians, notably Prime Minister Mahathir himself, have dominated industrial policy. In the United States, the debate is mainly between economists and lawyer-politicians.

Economists' views of industrial policy are rooted in an economic theory that is rigorous and, once the basic premises on which the theory is based are accepted, unchallengeable. Critics of this view who dispute the validity of conclusions derived from economic theory are rarely persuasive as long as they accept or fail to challenge the assumptions on which that theory rests.[1]

What, in essence, is the economists' view of industrial policy and the proper role for government in the economy? Economists start by assuming that markets for the products of industry and the factor inputs used in that industry exist. If information about the supply and demand conditions on those markets is known with certainty, and the number of firms in each industry is large, competition will exist and will ensure that the economy produces on the frontier of its potential. Firms will respond to market signals (prices) in such a way as to guarantee an efficient outcome. No intervention by government will be more efficient than this market-determined outcome. In these circumstances, therefore, there is no role for government intervention in the economy.

This picture of perfectly competitive, efficient markets, however, does not fit the real world and does not ensure a desirable outcome in all cases. In the real world, market failures do occur, and efficiency is not the only goal. The question of equity, not to mention national defense, also arises.

The market failures most discussed with respect to developing economies in the 1950s and 1960s were those involving oligopolistic and monopolistic control of particular markets by small numbers of firms and external economies or diseconomies. The presence of these latter externalities meant that private firms would not capture all of the benefits of their development efforts (on-the-job training, for example) or pay the full cost of those same efforts, due to pollution and the like. Another market failure believed to be prevalent in developing countries was the presence of surplus labor that resulted from the inability of labor markets to adjust wages down to the true marginal product of that labor. Government, it was argued, had to intervene to correct for these failures.[2]

Equity considerations provided a valid basis for intervention even where markets were working well. In the eyes of many, the very presence of so much extreme poverty in the developing world was itself grounds for rejecting market outcomes in favor of government intervention to help the poor.

By the 1970s and 1980s, however, economists and others increasingly realized that many government interventions were creating the very market failures and inequities they were designed to correct. Equity for the poor was too often turned into benefits for the well-off officials who designed government interventions. Monopolies more often than not were created by government trade policies designed to guarantee the domestic market for local producers. And too-high wages were sometimes created by minimum wage laws affecting a privileged urban minority of workers.

The political economy of how government interventions really worked in the developing world led a great number of the world's economists to conclude that market outcomes were preferable to those generated by government intervention. Markets may be second-best solutions, but government policies led to third-best outcomes. To economists who held these views, Korea was often seen as a case in favor of reliance on the market, although the most casual observer could not fail to notice the extensive nature of the Korean government's intervention in the economy.

The Role of Government

The attack on government interventions in its extreme form was no more realistic in the developing-country context than were the earlier efforts to justify all manner of government controls. There are externalities in the real world, particularly in developing countries. An industrial enterprise that puts large amounts of money into educating and training its workers is likely to see many of the benefits of the training lost to the enterprise when workers shift to other firms. Education is essential to industrial development, and all nations see some role, normally a large one, for the government in promoting education, even in market-oriented countries such as the United States.[3]

Critical industrial infrastructure in developing countries frequently involves both externalities and the presence of substantial monopoly power. Roads are a case in point. Even in Hong Kong, most of the roads are built and maintained with government funds. Electric power is another example. Whether private or public, electric power companies have a great deal of monopoly power if left unregulated. In advanced industrial economies, it is barely conceivable, although seldom tried, to use competitive pressures rather than regulation to limit monopoly power. In developing countries, an industrial enterprise has the choice of tapping into the national system or constructing its own generators.[4] The latter alternative is sometimes resorted to out of necessity, but no one argues that this route to large-scale industrialization is efficient.

Government also plays an essential role in the development of capital markets in the developing world. Small- and medium-scale enterprises seldom have access to funds from the organized capital markets during the early stages of national development. By taking steps to create appropriate financial institutions and an appropriate legal framework for those institutions, government can go a long way toward correcting this bias that exists against all but the largest and best-known firms. Banks left to their own devices, without even the refuge of last resort provided by a central bank, are likely to follow conservative and short-term lending policies. Industrial development, in contrast, is likely to be both risky and long-term.

These examples by no means exhaust the full list, but they illustrate the point that industrial development virtually requires an active government involvement in the process. Although it is conceivable in theory for capital markets and other infrastructure to be provided adequately without government intervention of any kind, there is no country in the real world of the twentieth century where a pure laissez-faire approach has been tried, although Hong Kong comes close.

The interventions discussed so far involve general support systems for all industrial firms. It is when one moves from these general forms of assistance to aid that is targeted at individual industries and even individual firms that real controversy erupts; here economists often part company with interventionist government bureaucrats and their political and intellectual allies.

Industrial Targeting

The Korean heavy and chemical industry (HCI) program of the 1970s is particularly interesting to students of industrial policy because it is a clear case of a government's determining which industrial sectors to develop and then taking steps to ensure that development actually took place. Furthermore, the Korean HCI policy took place in the context of an overall successful development program that achieved very high sustained rates of growth of gross national product. In many developing-country cases, industrial targeting has been one of numerous interventions whose overall impact on economic performance was disastrous.

The exception is Korea, where most policies were clearly supportive of rapid economic growth. The question thus becomes one of whether industrial targeting on balance was an additional positive force, or a negative or neutral one. If the answer is that it was positive, then Korea may provide lessons for when and under what circumstances industrial targeting is desirable. If the answer is in the negative, the Korean case provides important support for the view that industrial targeting is never likely to be fruitful economically in the real world.

Economists looking at the issue of industrial targeting usually start by implicitly assuming that there are private entrepreneurs or business interests who will respond to whatever the market signals. In an advanced industrial economy with tens of thousands of industrial enterprises and much larger numbers of experienced entrepreneurs and managers, this assumption is probably realistic. In a country such as the United States or Japan today, a failure to respond to a market opportunity more than likely signals a lack of an appropriate vision about the future development of new technologies and new products. Government officials and politicians are not likely to do better in judging these future developments than private business interests and researchers who have devoted their lives to the study of particular sectors and who will gain or lose a fortune depending on whether they guess right.

But the typical developing country is not operating on the frontiers of the world revolution in technology. Most are trying to catch up to the already industrialized world. By definition, follower countries have someone to follow. In the case of post–World War II Japan, it was most often the United States that provided the guidelines as to which new industries could fruitfully be developed.[5] In the case of Korea, the model more often than not was, and still is, Japan.[6] For countries further behind in the development process, such as China, Korea itself is a model.

Picking industries in a follower country is not easy, but it is a simpler process than deciding which altogether new technology is likely to be the wave of the future. Follower countries do not have to determine what the newest wave of computer technology is likely to be, a subject that even the best computer minds can only grope toward in an informed way. Korea in the 1970s did not have the computer scientists and entrepreneurs to participate in this kind of competition or in the next wave of telecommunications technology. In the United States and Japan, in contrast, thousands of highly trained people have devoted their lives to these subjects, and most of these people are in the private sector, although some are in public-sector agencies such as the National Aeronautics and Space Administration.

Deciding whether to develop a new textile factory or even a steel plant is not such a complex process. A judgment has to be made about whether technical and managerial personnel to run such a plant are available or whether they can be trained in a reasonable period of time. There is also usually a range of technologies to choose from, and not all technologies suitable for one country are equally suitable for another. Nevertheless, the technologies themselves do not have to be invented outright, only adapted to local conditions.

The skills required to make these decisions include a knowledge of the technologies involved and the skills required to make them work, an understanding of the economic conditions that will make the decision to develop an enterprise profitable, and the organizational skill and entre-preneurial vision to find markets for the product and manage the plant and marketing network efficiently. In a developing country, all of these skills will be in short supply, especially when altogether new industrial sectors are involved, such as those in Korea's HCI program. Furthermore, few individuals will have all of these skills. Any decision about whether it makes sense to build a 5-millon-ton integrated steel plant is thus likely to require engineers who have worked on such plants, economists who can calculate the likely costs and benefits or profitability of such an undertaking, and managers and entrepreneurs who know what it takes to build and run an undertaking of this magnitude.

Which is better qualified to bring these diverse skills together and reach a decision as to whether to go ahead: the public sector or the private sector? Managers and entrepreneurs familiar with operating in a market-oriented economy are likely to be few or even nonexistent in a government bureaucracy. The rules of a well-functioning bureaucracy are fundamentally different from those required in growing profit-oriented enterprises. Economists, on the other hand, can be found in both the public and private sectors, and there is no reason for thinking that the "best" economists are likely to be in the private sector, even if "best" is defined as those who can most accurately determine the likely future internal rate of return of an untried enterprise. The private sector will have most of the engineers even in a developing country, but not necessarily the right engineering minds for analyzing a technology new to the country.

If the private sector in a developing country is small in scale and financially weak, and firms are narrowly specialized, that sector might on its own have great difficulty bringing together the range of skills required to determine whether a new industrial sector that is large and complex makes sense. In these situations, the public sector may well have the superior capacity to organize the necessary talent. The public sector may have one other advantage as well: Government officials closely tied to the political process may be in a better position to judge which kinds of government support for the prospective industry are feasible and which are not. This knowledge, to be sure, can be a two-edged sword. Government officials may be in a position to mobilize government support for their own mistaken judgment, but this need not always be the case. In the best case, if government officials participate in the decision process, they can remove some of the uncertainties that government actions in developing countries often create. Government officials involved in developing an export-oriented steel industry may be less likely to push for an overvalued exchange rate or a high tariff on some critical input.

Another variation on this same theme starts from a realization that most governments in developing countries play an active role in licensing new investments, giving firms access to foreign exchange, and the like. Certainly this was the case in Korea. The first-best solution in economic terms might be, and probably was, to abolish all of these licensing arrangements and other controls, but only rarely is such a first-best solution tried. If government is to be heavily involved in the industrialization process, the industrial policy must allow the government to participate intelligently in the selection of targeted industries. When controls over new development are pervasive, the private sector on its own is unable to respond to market signals. Government assistance is required, and the challenge, often unmet, is to ensure that assistance serves broad development goals, not narrow bureaucratic ones or other special interests.[7]

Our point is to underline the obvious but often ignored fact that real people with a range of relevant skills in real countries must determine whether to go ahead with a new industry. Economists often talk as if the response to market opportunities is automatic. If the opportunities exist, private profit-maximizing entrepreneurs will always respond. One does not have to spend much time or energy in trying to understand who those entrepreneurs are likely to be and what it will take to get them to respond in the appropriate way. In the United States or Japan, a reasonable approach may be to leave these issues to the board rooms and management committees of private firms. Certainly there is little reason to think that the bureaucratic generalists or lawyer-regulators who populate the Washington bureaucracies are well qualified to make decisions about the new frontiers of technology.

But in developing countries, where the experience with setting up new firms is limited and the range of technologies involved may be unfamiliar to the existing private sector, the automaticity of the private-sector response cannot be taken for granted. Does anyone think that the Korean private sector in the 1970s would have developed the Pohang Iron and Steel Company, Ltd. (POSCO) steel complex or the Hyundai shipbuilding yard totally on its own? If it made sense to start these industries at that time, there is little reason to think that the Korean private sector would have responded to the opportunity on its own. Chapter 2, on the history of the HCI decision-making process, makes that point clearly. Much of the rest of this book is devoted to trying to answer the question whether it made sense to start HCI development in the 1970s. Our conclusion is that no single answer applies to each and every industry. All that will be said here is that no a priori case can be made for the proposition that, if the profitable opportunities are there, private entrepreneurs in a developing country context will always respond. In the Korean HCI case, the public sector, and only the public sector, took the lead, and there were, with the benefit of hindsight, opportunities to make large profits in some HCI industries.

Measuring the Effectiveness of Industrial Targeting

Whether the government should make decisions about developing new industries, therefore, is first of all a question of whether there is a private sector willing and able to respond to the opportunities that exist. In a system of Soviet-style central planning, no enterprises exist that will respond to market opportunities. There are also reasons to believe that in the developing world, characterized by imperfect information, limited financial markets, and the presence of widespread bureaucratic controls over the economy, the private sector may not be in a position to respond. Here, the public sector might step in as a substitute for the private sector in the decision-making process.

But whether the decisions are public or private, what criteria should be used in evaluating whether a particular set of industrial decisions was a benefit to the economy? Answers to the following questions are vital to this evaluation:

1. Were the industries targeted under the industrial policy regime activities that would have been considered appropriate if they had been evaluated using such standard neoclassical guidelines as economic cost-benefit analysis?[8]
2. If so, did the industries become financially viable? If not, why not?

3. If the targeted industries would not have passed the cost-benefit test, did they nevertheless become successful? And if so, why?

An industrial targeting policy concerned primarily with the development of projects that would have passed the cost-benefit test (projects that fall into category 1 above) may be defined as a market-conforming industrial policy. Measures to promote such projects are sanctioned by traditional economic theory, which suggests that if the economic rate of return on a project exceeds the opportunity cost of capital, the project is worth implementing and is in line with the economy's long-run comparative advantage. If, for a variety of reasons, the financial rate of return for this project is below the market cost of capital, private agents will not undertake the activity. In this case, government measures can serve to bring the private returns in line with economic returns and ensure that economically desirable activities are undertaken or that the government can undertake the activity itself.

Admittedly, many governments attempt to play this role but fail to achieve their goals efficiently, providing excessive incentives that often encourage economically poor projects to be started and sustained. As a result, all too often the institutional framework that is designed to move private returns closer to economic returns degenerates into a system of political payoffs.

A broader and more challenging definition of successful industrial targeting includes economic policies that promote industrial activities whose economic rates of return were below the opportunity cost of capital but that eventually became economically and financially viable.[9] Here, industrial policy can be said to be nonmarket conforming. If industrial policy fostered the development of industries that would not have passed the neoclassical cost-benefit test while creating an environment in which those activities eventually became internationally competitive, then industrial policy has indeed picked the winners. In such instances, it is possible to argue that industrial policy significantly helped develop important externalities, which, in turn, contributed to improved productivity and growth throughout the economy.

It remains to ask why selected industries succeed or fail. Obviously, many factors determine the success or failure of an activity. To simplify the analysis, we classify these factors as either technical factors internal to the firm, or exogenous changes in the external environment. Among the technical reasons for failure are an inability to handle the chosen technology, lower-than-expected levels of output and quality, and the inability of the domestic economy to support the project by providing the necessary inputs, such as an ensured supply of electricity or transport services. On the other hand, a better-than-expected performance regarding such technical factors will contribute to the success of the activity. Only detailed industry studies will be able to shed light on the precise extent to which various factors contributed to the actual outcome.

Among the exogenous factors affecting the profitability of an activity, the most common are sudden changes in output or input prices, which can occur for any number of reasons, including the sudden introduction of a new technology. Thus a project that might have been successful at the world prices prevailing and forecast in the base year may have failed because a sudden shift in world demand or supply sharply lowered international prices. The opposite may also occur: A project that was expected to be financially and economically unsuccessful may become successful because of unforeseen price changes. When unforeseeable exogenous factors, especially changes in input and output prices, affect the success or failure of an activity, one would not necessarily want to credit industrial policy, whether it was market conforming or not, with either the success or the failure of the chosen investment projects.

In some cases, however, unforeseen exogenous influences are more than just happy or unhappy accidents. Uncertainty about the future is inherent in all industrial development, and any prudent maker of industrial policy will take the risks entailed in this uncertainty into account in deciding which sectors to promote. A successful industrial policy can mean positioning oneself to be able to take advantage of exogenous changes when they occur. For example, if Korea had not begun developing the automobile sector much earlier, when international market conditions were unfavorable, then that industry would not have been poised to take advantage of the opening in the North American automobile market that was created when quotas on Japanese automobile exports led Japan to abandon the low-cost end of that market.

Clearly, however, industrial policymakers cannot position their industries to take advantage of all positive exogenous shocks that might occur. The cost of simultaneously promoting every conceivable industry where price and other market changes might someday turn a poor investment into a good one would be enormous. Prudent industrial targeting, done by the public or private sector, involves judgments about which industries are most likely to achieve higher-than-originally-forecast rates of return. Formally, the process is one of estimating the probability distribution of possible alternative rates of return for a particular industry rather than a single best guess of that rate of return. More realistically, industrial policy under uncertainty involves some judgment about future developments in international markets that are not now apparent, or hunches that enterprise managers in the end will prove to be more successful in cutting costs or raising quality than they now believe is possible.

Put differently, any appraisal of an industrial targeting strategy should look at the effort as a whole, not just at each industry one by one. In a world of uncertainty, some sectors will do better than expected and others worse. What matters is that the overall effort had a net positive rate of return at or above the level achieved in the rest of the economy. If unforeseen exogenous changes account for this higher rate of return, some analysts will still be inclined to attribute the result to luck rather than policy. But intelligent risk takers to some degree create their own luck, and an outsider may not be able to differentiate between these people and pure gamblers. Certainly President Park, when he undertook the HCI program, knew he was taking major risks.[10] The question we are concerned with in this study is whether that was a calculated risk intelligently undertaken and ultimately successful, or an unwise gamble against heavy odds that ultimately lowered Korea's overall economic performance.

A full analysis of the factors contributing to the success or failure of a project, or of an industrial targeting strategy as a whole, would carefully construct a cost-benefit analysis, using base-year information, and compare it to a similar analysis based on the actual values for various factors. The ex-post cost-benefit analysis would adjust not only for current input and output prices but also adjust the technical coefficients to reflect changes or shortfalls in such variables as labor productivity, capacity utilization, and the overall efficiency in plant operations. Such an analysis would shed considerable insight into the factors that make for successful industrial targeting. A more modest analytic approach would hold the technical variables that define a project constant while substituting current prices for base-year forecast prices. The result would be to eliminate those cases of success, or failure, that primarily reflect exogenous changes.

The concept of current prices cannot be precisely defined without entering into a lengthy methodological discussion. The year chosen as the current-price year may well affect the outcome of the analysis. For example, Korea's shipbuilding industry was considered highly successful some years ago when demand for new ships was high. Several years later, depressed market conditions made the decision to develop a shipbuilding industry seem less wise. Presumably the current prices appropriate for the analysis should reflect long-run expected values, which may well differ from the actual prices observed in any one year.

The classification scheme shown in Figure 1-1 summarizes this framework. The columns refer to outcomes at current prices, and the

		Current Prices	
B a s e Y e a r P r i c e s		ERR > P_k	ERR < P_k
	ERR > P_k	Quadrant I: Successful	Quadrant II: Unsuccessful
	ERR < P_k	Quadrant IV: Successful	Quadrant III: Unsuccessful

ERR = economic rate of return; P_k = opportunity cost of capital.

Figure 1-1. *Classification of Industrial Projects*

rows deal with the economic rate of return at base-year prices. Activities that are market conforming fall in the top row; nonmarket-conforming projects are shown in the bottom row.

Industries that fall into quadrant I would have been selected using the standard neoclassical selection criteria and would remain successful at current prices, either because there has been little change in relative prices affecting the activity or because the project is so robust that it remains economically attractive even when prices have changed. If a large number of projects promoted during Korea's HCI drive fall into this quadrant, it nevertheless remains an interesting case of successful industrial promotion in that the instruments used to support new industries do appear to have been successfully used without becoming captives of special interest groups.

Quadrant II activities are projects that would have been selected under a market-conforming industrial policy but are nevertheless considered unsuccessful. Their failure should not be viewed as a failing of industrial policy but as the result of unforeseen changes in the external environment. It may be that a fertilizer project would have passed a standard cost-benefit test at the prices prevailing and forecast in the early 1970s but today would be considered economically unsuccessful because at current prices for its inputs and products, it no longer earns a sufficiently high rate of return.

Quadrant IV activities are of greatest interest. These are projects that would not have been selected if the neoclassical acceptance criteria had been applied. If they were nonetheless implemented, they may have become economically successful for one of two reasons. The first is that changes in input and output prices were favorable. Such industries in quadrant IV and those in quadrant II do not support the argument that industrial policy was either successful or unsuccessful, although these are usually the examples cited in discussions of Korea's industrial policy. Second, quadrant IV projects may have become successful for reasons other than exogenous price changes. Only such projects provide evidence for nonmarket-conforming industrial targeting.

Finally, industries in quadrant III are activities that should have been rejected: They did not pass the cost-benefit test at the time they were proposed, and nothing has changed to make them successful. Unfortunately, it appears that many developing countries tend to support activities that fall into this quadrant. The fact that Korea seemingly managed to avoid this outcome is noteworthy.

In sum, a successful industrial targeting policy would have supported primarily activities that are market conforming. To the extent that this was effectively done, Korea's industrial policy was successful. A stronger measure of the success of industrial targeting comes about when the industries that were targeted would not have passed the classical cost-benefit test but have nevertheless become viable activities. If their current success is not merely due to changes in exogenous factors, such as the prices they face in the international market, then a case has been made that industrial policy generates externalities that are not captured by the neoclassical metric of success. Without industrial targeting, such economically successful industries would not have been undertaken. This is the clearest measure of a successful targeting industrial policy.

Outline of this Study

The next two chapters set the context in which Korea's HCI policy was made. Chapter 2 traces the history of those who actually put the HCI policy together, the criteria they used in deciding between one industry and another, and how their thinking changed over time in response to their perception of evolving economic and political conditions in Korea. Chapter 3 is an overview of the Korean economic system in which the HCI program was implemented. Was Korea basically a market economy where private entrepreneurs responded to market signals, or was the economy riddled with bureaucratic commands where government policy primarily shaped the outcome? Was the HCI policy, which without doubt was the creature of government policy, as Chapter 2 makes clear, an aberration from the way the Korean system worked, both before and after the HCI program, or was it typical of what went before and after?

The following chapters appraise the impact of the HCI program on the Korean economy. Chapter 4 looks at the impact of the heavy and chemical industries on the aggregate indicators of Korean economic performance. It asks whether the structure of the Korean economy was fundamentally altered by HCI investments in the 1970s, and if the change in structure that did occur reflected what one would have expected for a nation with Korea's per capita income and factor endowment. Chapter 5, in contrast, examines the performance of the HCI industries themselves. It is a microevaluation of these industries, in contrast to Chapter 4's macroevaluation. For a select group of industries for which data were available, a detailed cost-benefit calculation is attempted. The results of these estimates are calculations of the rate of return on various HCI investments and judgments about whether these investments were market conforming or nonmarket conforming. Chapter 6 deals with a set of industries—steel, automobiles, shipbuilding, aluminum—where cost-benefit calculations could not be carried out, so more impressionistic methods are used. These cases make it possible to include many of the specific elements that influenced the development of particular sectors, specifics that are lost when looking at the program as a whole.

NOTES

1. Many of the arguments in favor of industrial targeting are flawed. P. Krugman, "Targeted Industrial Policies: Theory and Evidence" (paper presented at Industrial Change and Public Policy, Symposium Sponsored by the Federal Reserve Bank of Kansas City, Jackson Hole, Wyoming, August 24 – 26, 1983), gives a relatively complete listing of the arguments in favor of industrial targeting and discusses their theoretical soundness or lack thereof.

2. A further, and somewhat different, argument in favor of industrial targeting is the concept of strategic export promotion. Proponents of strategic trade policy contend that world markets are far from competitive and are characterized by imperfect competition, barriers to entry, and the presence of pure profits. Hence, it is reasonable to ask whether a national government can do anything to ensure that its own participants in the competition win a large share of these profits. The arguments in favor of strategic export promotion are set forth in B. J. Spencer and J. A. Brander, "International R&D Rivalry and Industrial Strategy," *Review of Economic*

Studies 50 (1983): 707–722. However, Grossman and Dixit provide a more skeptical view of this rationale for policy interventions. See G. M. Grossman, "Strategic Export Promotion: A Critique," and A. K. Dixit, "Trade Policy: An Agenda for Research," both in P. R. Krugman, ed., *Strategic Trade Policy and the New International Economics* (Cambridge: MIT Press, 1986).

3. The relationship between educational policy and industrial productivity in the United States, is a major theme in the MIT study led by M. Dertouzos, R. K. Lester, R. Solow, and the MIT Commission on Industrial Productivity, *Made in America: Regaining the Productive Edge* (Cambridge: MIT Press, 1989).

4. The national system in almost all developing countries, including Korea, is publicly owned.

5. By the 1980s, Japan had evolved well beyond the point where it was catching up with the West, and the role of industrial targeting by the government had declined substantially in importance. See T. Pepper, M. Janow, and J. Wheeler, *The Competition: Dealing with Japan* (New York: Praeger, 1985).

6. See the discussion in Chapter 2.

7. As E. Tower points out, "Private markets do not work well in LDC's, so there generally is room for all sorts of positive economic policies to promote general economic welfare. But apparently the real problem is how to create political incentives to implement them." See E. Tower, "Industrial Policy in Less Developed Countries," *Contemporary Policy Issues* 4(1) (January 1986): 33.

8. We are not suggesting that governments in fact submit every project included in its industrial policy to a cost-benefit analysis. In reality, few governments consistently apply this analytic tool. All that is suggested here is that it is necessary, ex post, to differentiate projects that would have passed this test from those that would have failed.

9. An important question here is, What is the appropriate length of time over which we should expect a project to become financially viable so that the discounted value of its future net earnings will exceed the cost of the subsidies provided? There probably is no clear economic answer. Note, however, that the longer it takes for an activity to become viable, the less likely it is that the discounted future value will ever equal the cost of the early-year subsidies.

10. Interview. See Bibliography.

2

A History of the Heavy and Chemical Industry Program

South Korea's heavy and chemical industry (HCI) policy was formally launched on January 30, 1973, with the publication by the Blue House of the *Declaration of Heavy and Chemical Industrialization*. For the next six years, this brief document, supplemented by numerous additional studies and directives, guided Korea's efforts to build a modern, self-reliant HCI sector. The leaders of this effort were President Park Chung Hee, who devoted 30 to 40 percent of his time during the early years of this period to HCI matters,[1] and Oh Won Chol, an engineer by training who built and headed the secretariat that produced the plans that guided the development program for this sector.[2]

By late 1978 and early 1979, however, President Park was increasingly concerned with stabilization and social welfare policies as resistance to his eighteen years of authoritarian rule intensified. Oh Won Chol left the government, and the stabilization plan announced in April 1979 was put together by a group of economists who were not supporters of the HCI effort. President Park's assassination on October 26, 1979, by the head of the Korean CIA ended the Blue House's focus on heavy industrialization. When Chun Doo Hwan became president in a coup a year later, he turned for advice on economic matters to some of these same architects of the 1979 stabilization effort, notably to Kim Jae Ik, a Stanford Ph.D. in economics, who moved to the Blue House as economics secretary. The development of the HCI sector continued in the 1980s but no longer as the central focus of government policy.

Antecedents to the HCI Policy

The January 30, 1973, declaration marked a significant departure in policy toward the HCI sector, but it was a departure with antecedents.

President Park and his advisers did not suddenly decide in the early 1970s that Korea needed more heavy industry. In many ways, efforts to promote the HCI sector had begun in the mid- to late 1960s.

The experience of the machinery, chemical, and steel sectors, discussed in greater detail in later chapters, illustrates the main points about this earlier period. The emphasis in Korea's first five-year plan (1962–1966) was primarily on export promotion. The policies put in place to promote exports were not, for the most part, industry specific. All exporters, regardless of what they exported, were eligible for preferential access to foreign exchange and to preferential interest rates, for example. For the most part, exports in the 1960s came from the light industrial sector, and the government did not target specific industries. Even in the 1960s, however, the approach to heavy industry was somewhat different from that to light industry.[3] Efforts to accelerate development in such sectors as automobiles did involve a modest degree of targeting. On May 31, 1962, for example, the government introduced a law designed to promote and protect the domestic automobile industry and established the New World (Sae Na Ra) Auto Company, which in 1964 merged with Shinjin and assembled passenger automobiles. In 1964, Hankuk Machinery began to produce 125-horsepower diesel engines. Generally, however, these were modest efforts and involved little more than the assembly of imported parts for a handful of vehicles. In 1966, for example, only 3,268 passenger cars and 761 buses were produced in this manner.[4]

The machinery sector received more attention in the second five-year plan (1967–1971). In the words of the plan document, "It will be necessary to expand key industrial sectors in order to expand the degree of self-sufficiency of the capital goods industry. The construction of such key industries as chemicals, iron and steel, and machinery will be undertaken in order to establish the foundation for heavy industry, which will provide for balanced development of industrial growth in the future."[5] In March 1967, a machinery industry promotion law was passed, and a long-term plan for the promotion of the machinery industry was formulated in late 1967. Specific industries were targeted for promotion, and a fund was established to promote the domestic content of locally produced machines. Subsidies to the machinery sector rose from 2.4 billion won (US$8.5 million) in 1968 to 10.7 billion won (US$35 million) in 1969.[6] Despite this increased emphasis, the output of general machinery stagnated throughout the second plan period, and the percentage of rapidly increasing demand for machinery that was supplied from domestic sources fell from 23 percent in 1966 to only 6.5 percent in 1971.[7]

The chemical industry sector was, in some respects, ahead of machinery in the 1960s. Korea had some domestic production of chemical fertilizer in the 1940s, and production expanded rapidly in the 1960s, with domestic supplies of nitrogenous fertilizers accounting for 23 percent of total demand in 1963 and 56 percent in 1967. From 1968 on, supplies exceeded domestic demand, and Korea became a regular exporter of chemical fertilizer.[8] Domestic petroleum refining began later, in 1964. From that point on, however, domestic supplies accounted for almost all domestic consumption of petroleum products.[9] As for petro-chemical products more generally, domestic supplies expressed in terms of value accounted for 11.1 percent of total demand in 1968, rising to 30.6 percent by 1972.[10] The real push on the petrochemical industry, however, did not begin until the 1970s after the HCI declaration.

Korea's problem in getting the steel sector started in the 1960s is an illustration of the limitations of its heavy industry capacity as it existed in the 1960s, as well as an example of the determination of President Park to get an HCI sector going even before the January 1973 declaration. The first five-year plan in 1961 included an effort by the Ministry of Trade and Industry (previously the Ministry of Commerce and Industry) to build a 300,000-metric-ton steel plant, but financing for the project fell through. Several similar efforts in the late 1960s also came to naught when both the countries whose firms were designated to build the steel mill and the World Bank refused to provide the funds required. The economists pointed out that domestic demand for steel, based on the use of the Korean input-output table, was far too small to justify a plant large enough to achieve adequate scale economies. In 1962, for example, domestic demand for steel products of all types amounted to only 291,000 tons.[11] Others pointed to the fact that Korea had no history of steelmaking, no skilled workers, and no raw materials.[12] Not until the Korean government pressured the Japanese government in 1969 to provide a portion of its reparation funds to the proposed mill was financing finally secured. Construction on the by then million-ton plant began in April 1970, nearly three years before the HCI declaration. By that time, domestic demand for all steel products was approaching 2 million tons a year.[13]

The history of shipbuilding is much like that of steel. The original idea for building Korean supertankers arose in one of many conversations between Chung Ju Yung, chairman of Hyundai, and President Park, sometime in 1970 or 1971. At the president's urging, Chung toured the world looking at shipbuilding and searching for financing for a Korean yard, but without success. Only a veiled threat to Chung from President Park kept the effort to find financing going, until a deal with a Greek shipowner was finally signed in April 1972 to build two 250,000-ton tankers. Production on these ships began in March 1973.[14] Other plants set up prior to 1973 included the Ulsan petrochemical complex (ten plants) started in 1970 and completed in 1972, the Aluminum of Korea company plant completed in 1969, and the Young Pung Zinc company whose plant was completed in 1970. More generally, the third five-year plan, published in 1971 and designed to cover the years 1972 through 1976, set specific goals: to increase the share of HCI in manufacturing from 35.9 percent in 1970 to 40 percent in 1976 and to increase the share of HCI in exports from 14 percent in 1970 to 33 percent in 1976.[15]

Thus, there was development activity in the HCI sector in the latter half of the 1960s and into the first years of the 1970s. Most such development was done in various forms of collaboration with foreign firms, principally Japanese and American ones. The technology in many cases, particularly in machinery, was not very advanced, and the scale was small. The larger-scale plants, notably Pohang Steel and Hyundai shipbuilding, began only at the end of the second plan period or during the first year of the third five-year plan. Still, Korea's HCI base was growing. Industry as a whole grew at 17 percent a year in the decade after 1962, for a 4.7-fold rise overall, and the HCI sector rose from 25.8 percent of that total in 1962 to 41.8 percent of the much larger total industrial output of 1972, an annual rate of increase of over 22 percent.[16]

It is difficult to reconstruct the motives that led to the early heavy industry promotion efforts in the 1960s. The principal decision maker, President Park, is dead, and it has been a long time since, in any case. The government in the 1960s was made up of military figures, career civil servants, and a few economist-technocrats. Most of the decision makers of the 1960s had spent their formative years under Japanese occupation and in Japanese-language schools and had been heavily influenced by the Japanese development model, which allowed for a substantial role for government allocation of resources, however negatively they felt about Japanese colonial rule itself.[17] The dominant goal of the 1960s was to reduce Korea's dependence on declining foreign aid, which meant vigorous export promotion, mainly of light industry products, and import substitution, where most of the HCI promotion in the 1960s fits.[18] It is also likely that the military component of the leadership in particular, the influence of the Japanese model, and the strong nationalism of Koreans in general led many to the view that comprehensive industrialization, including HCI, was an essential ingredient of any truly independent and sovereign nation. How else could Korea hope to defend itself against North Korea and the People's Republic of China, both of which had been vigorously pursuing heavy industrialization since the end of the Korean War in 1953?

Although discussion of motivation for an HCI policy in the 1960s is somewhat speculative, there is little doubt about what caused the sense of urgency toward HCI development in the early 1970s. South Korea's government perceived that it had a heavy stake in the success of American efforts in South Vietnam, and officials backed up that perception with the commitment of Korean combat forces. But by the late 1960s, America's involvement in that war had begun to sour on the American people, and Richard Nixon became president of the United States with an increasingly clear mandate that somehow America had to reduce its open-ended commitment to its allies in Asia. On July 25, 1969, in Guam on his way to the Philippines, President Nixon outlined the underlying principles of U.S. foreign policy that came to be known as the Nixon Doctrine. From the Korean viewpoint, the critical component of that doctrine was that "in cases involving other [nonnuclear] types of aggression we shall furnish military and economic assistance when requested and as appropriate. But we shall look to the nation directly threatened to assume the primary responsibility of providing the manpower for its defense."[19]

When combined with statements about America's firm commitment to its treaty obligations, the Koreans had nothing to worry about since the United States would continue to supply its treaty partners with weapons. But below the surface in Korea and elsewhere in Asia, debate focused on whether the Nixon Doctrine and America's trauma in Vietnam marked the beginning of a withdrawal from America's Asian commitments. Nothing that happened throughout the 1970s was to allay Korean concerns. Early in 1971, for example, the Nixon administration withdrew the U.S. Army's Seventh Division of about 20,000 soldiers, reducing the U.S. ground forces in Korea by a third. Jimmy Carter in 1976 made a further withdrawal of troops part of his foreign policy platform during his campaign for president and implicitly tied the withdrawal to Korean human rights issues. In the spring of 1977, in the first months of his presidency, he announced that the Second Division of the U.S. Army would be pulled out by 1982. Some 3,400 troops were actually withdrawn before the Carter administration revoked the withdrawal plan in July 1979. The collapse of the South Vietnamese government without an American response in 1975 was also part of the picture, reinforcing earlier interpretations of the Nixon Doctrine. The Koreans in the early 1970s had only M-1 rifles, and they could not repair their World War II–era cannon because the United States no longer produced the necessary spare parts. Military stocks on hand in Korea were good for only three days of operations. There were no antitank mines that could deal with North Korea's T-62 tanks.[20] In short, Korea's military concerns were real and immediate. When combined with a desire for greater economic independence from the United States and general notions about the need for a more balanced growth strategy, the case for an HCI program appeared strong to the Korean leadership.[21]

Oh Won Chol was brought to the Blue House in 1971 to begin working on what was to become the HCI program. Formally, he was one of two economic secretaries, but he had more or less exclusive authority over micro-project-related activities. He immediately began pulling together a staff of specialists who were to become the secretariat of the government's HCI committee. The staff was drawn from the Ministry of Commerce and Industry and other ministries, and many, like Oh himself, had an engineering background. Oh also had ten years of factory experience, particularly in the machinery sector.[22]

Decision making on HCI policy throughout the initial years, when the policy had been developed and first promulgated, was almost exclusively in the Blue House and in the hands of President Park and Oh Won Chol. For example, the HCI plan was announced without consulting the minister of finance, Nam Duck Woo, despite Nam's central role in most other economic policies of the time. The minister of commerce and industry at the time was perceived by his colleagues as being weak, and he played no role in the process.[23] Heavy and chemical industries were mentioned in the third five-year plan, and it was anticipated that the various industries in this sector would play an increasingly important role within the manufacturing sector. But these industries were mentioned along with many other priorities and did not receive special emphasis.[24]

Despite being out of the loop, most of the high-ranking economists concerned with macroeconomic policy in the early 1970s were supportive of the HCI policy. In some cases, the support may have been lukewarm, but in other cases it was enthusiastic. The economists who resisted the plan at the beginning were mainly foreigners working for institutions such as the World Bank.[25] This attitude is especially notable given the fact that five or six years later, the attack on the HCI strategy was led by a group of economists concerned with the way in which that strategy was destabilizing the economy.

That decision making rested exclusively in the Blue House in the early phases does not mean that no one else had any idea what was going on. President Park held a monthly meeting with his economic ministers, leaders of the ruling party, and a few academics during which the economic situation and the progress of particular projects were reviewed. He also held regular meetings on export promotion with business leaders, heads of financial institutions, and the economic ministers. Views of a wide range of people on many issues were sought, but the HCI policies were not determined in these forums. There was no attempt at a ministerial consensus. The decisions were those of President Park.

HCI Policy: The Decision Criteria Used

In preparing the January 1973 declaration, several of those involved toured various parts of the world, from West Germany and the United Kingdom to Japan, and from Taiwan and Israel to Finland, looking at the way these countries had developed their heavy industries. Although the architects of the January 1973 declaration visited many countries, the main one referred to in the declaration itself is Japan. The Japanese long-term development plan of 1957, with its emphasis on the HCI sector, had a particularly strong influence.[26] Having looked at the experience of Japan and the others, the HCI secretariat then initiated studies of particular industries, which were carried out by secretariat staff or by groups within the Ministry of Commerce and Industry or other ministries.[27]

The approach taken by the HCI secretariat was to analyze whether it would be feasible for Korea to undertake the development of one or another industry given the overall level of development achieved by Korea at that time. The government would then take steps to ensure that the required infrastructure was in place. In many cases, the move to provide infrastructure was well underway before the January 1973 declaration. Development of the Changwon Industrial Estate, where much of the heavy industry was to be located, for example, began in 1971.

The government did not attempt to provide detailed designs and feasibility studies for the individual plants themselves. That was left to the private firms designated by the Blue House to implement the particular program. The Blue House secretariat would analyze these private sector studies and give the signal to go ahead or to do further study. If the decision was to go ahead, a wide range of government support facilities were made available to the private company. More will be said about the nature of this support in the next chapter.

How did the Blue House HCI secretariat determine whether it made sense for Korea to begin development of a particular industry in the early 1970s? As best as one can reconstruct the process, the appraisal techniques involved a combination of technical feasibility studies, an appraisal of whether the sector was appropriate given Korea's stage of overall development, and an analysis of how those industries would contribute to particular strategic military and economic goals.

The strategic military components of the criteria were straightforward. Petrochemicals and nonferrous metals such as zinc and copper could be used to produce ammunition and other explosives. Shipbuilding drydocks could be used as repair facilities for the U.S. Navy, and the machinery sector could make rifles, cannons, and tanks. But the HCI program was not focused on military security. Efficiency criteria did enter in, but not through the conventional cost-benefit route of the typical economic appraisal.

From the beginning, there was recognition of the desirability of taking advantage of the scale economies present in the HCI sector.[28] In industries such as steel, automobiles, shipbuilding, and petrochemicals, potential scale economies are very large, so a plant built on too small a scale is never likely to be competitive internationally. Yet domestic demand in Korea for civilian and military needs combined was often nowhere near sufficient to justify large plants. In the automobile sector, for example, an efficient scale of production was around 300,000 vehicles a year, but the total stock of passenger cars in Korea in 1973 was only 165,000 plus an unknown number in the military. To take advantage of these scale economies, therefore, the Korean HCI planners had to assume that the surplus over domestic demand in each of the sectors could be exported. The only other choice would have been to build a smaller plant behind more or less permanent protective barriers. The protective barriers were put in place, but the basic strategy was to move as quickly as possible to exports and to a level of efficiency that made these enterprises internationally competitive.

This early emphasis on economies of scale ensured that some plants produced efficiently in later years, but the sometimes extreme desire for very large-scale plants was to become a major problem. The enormous Changwon heavy machinery plant and Okpo shipbuilding yard operated way below capacity throughout the first decade of their existence. The losses that resulted from the operation of these two plants alone had much to do with the decision to reverse the HCI policy in 1979.[29]

Related to the concern for achieving scale economies was the decision to limit the number of entrants into an industry. Often only one firm was allowed in initially, to be followed by others when the market had expanded enough to make a second large-scale plant feasible. The Blue House also favored building completely integrated plants in which the eventual objective would be to produce Korean-brand autos, ships, and machinery primarily with domestic components. The Taiwan strategy of producing components rather than whole products was consciously rejected. In part, this decision reflected the fact that the large *chaebol* firms already had experience with huge, complete projects of this sort. But the decision of the Blue House to move in this direction also had more than a little to do with why the role of the *chaebol* so dominated Korean industry in the 1970s, unlike in Taiwan. Economists and politicians and later critics of this development strategy of the 1970s often dwelled on this bias in favor of large firms.

A third component of the appraisal was whether Korea had the technical skills to carry out a desired project. In some cases a project was rejected on such grounds. Jet engines, for example, were deemed too high tech for the first HCI phase.[30] The specific technical requirements of a particular project were often determined in consultation with foreign firms such as Bechtel or with the Korean Institute of Science and Technology. One critical issue was whether Korea had the necessary numbers of engineers and other technical personnel with the right kinds of experience. And if Korea did not have these personnel in sufficient numbers, how could they be attracted?[31] Numerous training institutes were set up by the government in such HCI development areas as Changwon, Ulsan, and Taejon, and these were supplemented by private firms' sending people for training.

Korea's insufficient number of trained personnel was in part a reflection of the early stage of the nation's development process, but it was also a result of the difficulty Korea had in attracting back Koreans trained abroad. One informal survey around 1969 by the minister of science and technology determined that some 1,200 Koreans had received Ph.D.s in the natural sciences in the United States and Europe, but only a few dozen of those scientists were working in Korea.[32] Some of these scientists could not be attracted back because of a general preference for life in the United States based on both political security and economic criteria. But others were willing to return if they had the research facilities needed to make use of their skills and if the economic sacrifice was kept within acceptable limits. To meet the requirements of this latter group, the Korean government created the Korean Institute of Science and Technology, an already-going operation in 1968, and later the Korean Advanced Institute of Science. In 1971, the Korea Development Institute (KDI) was established to attract economists. It succeeded in persuading a dozen economists with Ph.D.s to return, thereby roughly tripling the number of economists with this degree then in Korea. The HCI training efforts, therefore, were built on a foundation that had been laid earlier. Korean universities and graduate schools were expanding in the 1960s, but the real boom in enrollments at these two levels did not begin until the 1970s and 1980s.

At the beginning of the 1970s, despite the earlier efforts to remedy the situation, the research level in Korea was still very modest. In 1971, for example, only 2,477 persons were classified as researchers in science and technology, and total R&D expenditures were 10.7 billion won (US$29 million) or 0.3 percent of Korea's gross national product (GNP). By 1975, the number of researchers had quadrupled to 10,275, and R&D expenditures had risen to 42.7 billion won (US$88 million).[33] R&D expenditures were still a minuscule share of GNP, but the upward trend continued throughout the rest of the 1970s and all of the 1980s. By 1987, there were 52,783 scientific researchers, and R&D expenditures were 1.8 percent of the GNP. Conceivably, the early stages of this development of a scientific base would have occurred in the absence of the HCI program, but it is more likely that the two trends reinforced each other.

A fourth critical element in deciding whether to go ahead with a particular HCI project was the availability of finance. Finding foreign financing had been the main cause of delay in the earlier attempts to get a steel industry started, and it was the critical barrier Hyundai had to overcome when it wanted to build supertankers. Development in each of the HCI sectors involved large-scale importation of equipment and technical support services, hence a serious drain on the country's foreign exchange reserves. Throughout the 1960s and 1970s, Korea had a large balance-of-trade deficit that had to be covered by either foreign aid or foreign loans. The situation appeared to be improving in 1971 and 1972, but OPEC's increase in the price of oil in 1973 could not have come at a worse time for the Korean HCI program. The deficit on the balance of trade in 1974 rose to 11.6 percent of GNP from only 3.1 percent the year before and was high in 1975 as well before falling sharply in 1976 and 1977.

Domestic financing was also a problem. It was not that the commercial banks were unwilling to cooperate. They were state owned, and the Blue House could exercise whatever control over their portfolios that it chose. But in the early 1970s many Korean firms were in a precarious financial condition. The curb market reforms of 1972 had been designed in part to alleviate the pressures on those firms.[34]

The financing problem was not solved by foreign aid from Korea's traditional sources. Both the United States Operations Mission to Korea (USOM), the American aid program, and the World Bank were opposed to at least the scale, if not all of the specifics, of the HCI program. In part, the solution was to order the Korean commercial banks to lend to the HCI sector and hope for the best elsewhere. One estimate is that 70 percent of Korean bank financing was directed to the HCI sector in the early years of the program.[35] In addition, the newly established National Investment Fund collected money from various public accounts and then used the funds to finance the HCI sector.[36] Foreign financing involved a vigorous search for funds wherever they could be found.

Taken together, therefore, the criteria used in determining the HCI strategy involved a combination of security considerations, an analysis of technical or engineering feasibility, a determination on whether financing was likely to be available, and economic analysis of demand conditions at this particular stage of development. Careful analyses of discounted social costs and benefits were not part of the Blue House decision-making process. Individual private firms did do their own analyses of the likely profitability of proposed projects, but these calculations do not appear to have played an important role in Blue House decisions on whether to go ahead. Chapter 5 in this study is devoted to analyzing whether the HCI program, undertaken using these engineering-security-demand criteria, produced results that were better or worse than what could have been achieved if social benefit–cost techniques had been used in their stead. The World Bank, for example, did on occasion make such calculations for selected HCI projects and generally concluded that the time was not ripe for such an undertaking.[37] Who, in retrospect, was right?

Domestic political considerations also appear to have little to do with why the program was started in 1973 or took on the particular shape it did. Outside of the military, which President Park controlled in any case, there was no large constituency for the heavy industry strategy. In many cases the large *chaebol* conglomerates did reap substantial profits, but these *chaebol* were heavily dependent on the government, not the government on them. And some of the new heavy industries, shipbuilding and certain parts of the machinery sector, for example, were taken on by the *chaebol* only after government pressure was applied. It is not that President Park never used domestic political considerations in deciding on economic policy, but his constituency, outside of the army, was in the countryside, not in the cities. This constituency cared about farm gate prices, which the president did raise after his near debacle in the election of 1971. In contrast, there were few votes among the beneficiaries of heavy industry.

The one area where politics may have played a significant role was in the location of the HCI projects. The dominant element in determining location was military security, which is why all of the projects were in the south. The private sector left to itself would have located many of the HCI plants around Seoul, as they did for industries whose location they did control, but Seoul is within twenty-five miles of the demilitarized zone. Politics probably played a role in the location of all of these projects in the two Kyongsang provinces of the southeast rather than the two Cholla provinces of the southwest. Kyongsang was President Park's home base and the home of a large number of high officials in his government. Cholla was the home of few government officials and of large numbers of opponents of the Park government, including Kim Dae Jung, who had nearly defeated Park in the 1971 election.

HCI: The First Phase, 1973-1978

Once the decision was made to go ahead with a particular project, President Park rarely wavered in his support even when the project ran into difficulties.[38] Nor for more than five years after the start of the HCI program did he waiver in his support for the HCI program as a whole. With the resources of the government mobilized behind the HCI effort, the January 1973 declaration was anything but a paper plan.

Nowhere else was the speed of this expansion more apparent than in the iron and steel sector. The second phase of POSCO was started in 1976 and raised capacity to 2.6 million tons a year; the third phase, designed to raise capacity to 5.5 million tons, began in 1978. Several smaller plants were started or expanded elsewhere. As a result capacity to make steel in 1977 was over 4 million tons a year, up from 1 million in 1972, even before the 1978 third phase of POSCO had begun.

Machinery production grew at an even faster rate than steel. Between the end of the years 1972 through 1978, this sector averaged an annual growth rate of 45.5 percent, and transport equipment output grew annually at 53.4 percent.[39] The qualitative changes were in many ways as great as the quantitative ones. In 1975, the Korean automobile industry reached a crucial turning point when it established the basis for building Korean standard model automobiles rather than simply assembling cars from complete knockdown kits. Many of the enterprises producing specialized machinery were small, and the government began subsidizing dozens of these smaller firms in 1976 and 1977. Electronic machinery took off in this period as well, with the production of color television sets and numerous other electronic items. The electronic sector as a whole grew at 53 percent a year. The year 1978, however, marked a temporary end to the machinery boom. The sector overall grew modestly in 1979 and then output fell sharply in 1980, not to resume rapid development until 1983.

The boom in shipbuilding was equally dramatic, but the end of the boom came earlier than in the case of machinery and the decline that followed was steeper. In 1972, Korea manufactured small, steel, cargo ships with a total gross weight of only 21,000 tons. Two years later the figure was 605,000; it peaked at 807,000 tons in 1975 before falling back to a little over 400,000 tons a year in the 1977–1979 period. By the end of 1976, however, Korea had the capacity to produce 2.6 million gross weight tons of ships a year, and the plan was to expand that capacity to 4 million tons by 1980. The problem was that the bottom had dropped out of sales after the first OPEC (Organization of Petroleum Exporting Countries) oil shock.

Despite the cutback in ship orders, the first and the biggest of the shipbuilders, Hyundai, was kept afloat, and may even have turned a profit, by two measures. When the oil shock led to the cancellation of orders, Hyundai formed its own shipping company and began, with the help of Korean government "persuasion," to carry petroleum from the Persian Gulf to Korea. In addition, Chung Ju Yung, chairman of Hyundai, had earlier realized that many of the welding and other skills involved in his construction companies were the same ones involved in shipbuilding. In the late 1970s he carried the idea a step further by turning his shipbuilders into builders of ship repair facilities and oil platforms for the Middle East.[40]

The 1973 HCI declaration marked a major expansion of the chemical industry beyond chemical fertilizer and petroleum refineries to a broad range of petrochemical products. In 1974 Korea for the first time began producing ethylene, polyethylene, and polyvinyl chlorides. The nonferrous metal sector was also pushed in the mid-1970s, with production increasing fourfold between 1972 and 1978.

In short, the years 1973 through 1978 involved an across-the-board effort to develop a heavy industry sector. During the third five-year plan period, 60.4 percent of all investment funds going to industry—a total of 1,693 billion won (US$3.8 billion), went to the HCI sector, and the fourth plan, beginning in 1977, called for increasing that amount over the next five years to 3,273 billion won (US$6.8 billion).[41] The 1972–1976 figure represented 16 percent of gross capital formation in those years for a sector that accounted for 10 to 12 percent of GNP.[42]

Was the Korean investment in the HCI sector unusually large? By way of comparison, China during its first five-year plan (1953–1957), when it was trying to follow a Stalinist development strategy, devoted 36 percent of all investment in capital construction to the heavy industry sector; that percentage was 38 percent over 1981–1985 when China was supposedly deemphasizing heavy industry.[43] By those standards, Korean investment in the HCI sector was still modest. But from a macroeconomic stability perspective, increased emphasis on heavy industry in Korea was not so modest. This investment in the HCI sector was being added on to continuing private and public investment elsewhere, causing the rate of gross fixed capital formation to rise from an average of 22.5 percent of GNP in 1970–1972 to 24.3 percent in 1973–1976, and then rising steeply to 26.9 percent, 30.9 percent, and 32.6 percent in 1977, 1978, and 1979, respectively. This is a very sharp rise for so short a time period, and it is not surprising that Korea's economists were wondering how to finance the HCI effort without either inflation or the rapid run-up of an already substantial foreign debt.

If the emphasis on heavy and chemical industries in the 1972–1978 period was putting increased strain on macroeconomic stability, it was also having a sizable impact on the production structure. This HCI sector, which had stabilized at 41 or 42 percent of total industrial value-added between 1968 and 1972, had risen to 53 percent of industrial value-added by 1978.[44] Somewhat more surprising, exports from the heavy industry sector rose from 21.5 percent of all exports in 1972 to 30.6 percent in 1976, although relatively simple consumer electronic products seem to represent a large part of this increase.[45]

The End of the HCI Program, 1979–1982

The announcement of the stabilization policy of April 1979 marked the effective end of the HCI program. The development of this sector continued, but never again was it to receive the priority treatment that it had since January 1973. What brought about this change in policy? The answer is in two parts, the first dealing with the period when President Park was still in control, the second with the period immediately after his assassination in October 1979.

Park Chung Hee's decision to deemphasize development of the HCI sector came about in part because of events that were external to that sector, although some of these events were partly caused by the HCI program. There were problems within the HCI sector to be sure—the lack of demand for Korea's supertankers, for example—but there were also marked successes, notably in steel. In other industries, it was too early to tell by 1978 whether they would be able to stand on their own feet and continue to grow. Five or six years, the period between early

1973 and late 1978, is not long enough to judge a program that involves the start-up of a great many new large-scale enterprises.

Leaving aside President Park, the principal advocates of HCI development had not changed their minds by 1978. Oh Won Chol and his secretariat remained firm believers in the program. As part of the effort to defend the program, the Heavy and Chemical Industry Promotion Committee compiled a two-volume, 1,500-page study detailing the accomplishments and future development plans for the sector.[46] Nor had the security situation improved so much for Korea that much of the earlier motivation for the HCI program had disappeared. Admittedly the Carter administration had begun to back away from its emphasis on human rights and the Korean troop withdrawal, but the trauma surrounding those efforts was still fresh in the minds of the Korean leadership. North Korea had certainly not changed its security stance in any significant way.

The direct cause of the deemphasis on the HCI program was the government's perceived need to stabilize the economy. The architects of that stabilization policy were the economists Kim Jae Ik, director general of the Planning Bureau; Kang Kyung-sik, assistant minister in the Economic Planning Bureau; and Kim Mahn Je, president of the KDI. Nam Duck Woo, who, despite reservations about some aspects of the HCI program, had generally been supportive, resigned from the government in September 1978 to take some of the political heat from the introduction of the value-added tax (VAT), a tax that was particularly hated by small and medium businessmen who were less able to avoid it than the previous business taxes.[47]

If one confines oneself exclusively to the macroeconomic arena, it is not easy to explain why the government felt so compelled to change the basic direction of its economic policies. The current account on the balance of payments did become a negative US$1 billion in 1978, after being in balance in 1977, but the current account deficit in 1974 and 1975 had been twice as large. Debt service in 1978 was 11 percent of the total value of exports, slightly lower than the 13 percent ratio in 1973 when the HCI program started, and a level not likely to cause problems of any serious kind for the economy.[48] The inflation rate also began to climb in 1978. Consumer prices rose by 14 percent in that year, as compared to 10 percent in 1977, but the rate in 1974 and 1975 had been, respectively, 24 and 25 percent a year, without leading to a decision to cut back on the HCI sector. In 1979, the balance-of-payments deficit worsened substantially, and the rate of inflation increased further, but it was OPEC's decision to raise oil prices, not HCI investment, that was primarily responsible for these changes. And the OPEC price increase was in the middle of 1979, several months after the stabilization plan had been launched. Furthermore, the 1973 OPEC oil price increase had led to some delays in HCI investment, but it had not derailed the HCI program for long. Why was the response in 1978 and 1979 so different? It is unlikely that the economists pushing for stabilization won the argument solely on macroeconomic grounds, however valid their analysis of the macroeconomic situation may have been. One of the problems that led to the policy reversal had to do with the state of several of the new HCI enterprises. A number of these new, large plants were heavily burdened with debt and in real danger of going under without large, continuing government subsidies. If several of these enterprises failed, possibly some of the *chaebol* would have been dragged down with them.[49]

The most plausible explanation for the shift toward stabilization, however, involves politics. From 1972 on, with the introduction of the Yushin Constitution, the Park government had become increasingly repressive toward its opponents, and those opponents were becoming more numerous. Whereas in the 1960s rapid economic growth had made it possible for Park Chung Hee to win a reasonably honest election, that was no longer the case in the 1970s. The government increasingly resorted to plebiscites, which it won easily, but opposition politicians, labor groups, and others became increasingly embittered.

In this context, the choice was to rest power entirely on the foundation of the army and the Korean CIA or to attempt to restore some degree of popularity among the population at large. Accelerating inflation, even if within the bounds of previous experience, could only make matters worse. Real wages were still rising in 1978 and 1979, for example, but the increase in prices led many wage earners to believe that they were falling.[50] Another problem was that the direct beneficiaries of the HCI policy were small in number. The government's increasing interest in investing more in social welfare policies in the late 1970s, after largely ignoring these sectors earlier, may have reflected little more than the view that the country could by then afford support for social welfare, but the concern may also have derived from the desire to shore up political support.[51]

After the October 1979 assassination of President Park, the shift away from the HCI strategy is easier to explain. To begin with, 1980 was a disastrous year on the economic front. Bad weather caused a major harvest failure, with grain output plummeting by 34 percent. Continued high oil prices ballooned the current account deficit up to US$5.3 billion from the already high level of US$4.2 billion in 1979. The 1980 figure was 8.1 percent of GNP. Manufacturing output that grew at 21 percent a year throughout the 1970s fell by 1.9 percent in 1980. GNP in 1980 dropped by 4.8 percent and remained sluggish through 1981 and 1982.

On the political front, the government of President Choi Kyu Hah proved a weak match for an army that, under Chun Doo Hwan, increasingly took charge of the country. In May 1980, not long after General Chun moved from indirect to direct control and was installed as president, there was the bloody suppression of the political uprising against the government in Kwangju that still poisoned Korean politics a decade later.

President Chun's economic concern during the first years of his rule was stability.[52] Most of his efforts were directed toward bringing the rate of inflation down, and in that he was largely successful. From rates of increase of consumer prices of 28.7 percent in 1980 and 21.6 percent in 1981, inflation fell to 7.1 percent in 1982 and 3.4 percent in 1983. Chun's principal economic adviser throughout this period was Kim Jae Ik, an architect of the 1979 stabilization policy. After Kim Jae Ik was killed in a bombing in Burma, the new minister of finance and later the deputy prime minister and Economic Planning Board head, became Kim Mahn Je, another architect of the 1979 policy. Shin Byung-Hyun, who became deputy prime minister immediately after the Burma bombing, was also an ally of Kim Jae Ik.[53] The Blue House economic secretary became Sakong Il, a former associate of Kim Mahn Je at the KDI.

Chun Doo Hwan had some antipathy toward the large *chaebol* conglomerates and was willing to back his ministers in confrontations with business.[54] Kim Jae Ik's strong desire to liberalize the Korean economy in order to create a more even playing field for small and medium enterprises fit well with this attitude of the president.

Chun Doo Hwan's Blue House therefore gave little support to the kinds of security-oriented large-scale investments that had characterized the HCI program. Not all of Chun's advisers agreed with Kim Jae Ik, particularly some of the political advisers, but their disagreements came from a very different direction than did the thinking of men like Oh Won Chol. The fact that by 1981 Ronald Reagan was in the White House and had begun a massive peacetime military buildup must also have reduced Korean fears of being abandoned to their own devices in the security arena. If the heavy and chemical industries of Korea were to continue or to resume growth, increasingly they were going to have to do it on their own.

HCI Performance in the 1980s

What was the impact of these policy shifts in Korea's industrial structure? Did the announcement of the HCI policy in 1973 lead to a marked acceleration in the growth rate of the HCI sectors, and did the 1979 stabilization lead to a comparable deceleration?

The growth rate in the HCI sectors did accelerate in the five years after 1973 as compared to the three previous years in five of the seven HCI sectors. The exceptions were the two machinery sectors. After 1978, the growth rate slowed in all seven HCI sectors.

But an observer unaware of the January 1973 HCI policy declaration would not necessarily see this acceleration in growth of those sectors as unusual or remarkable. Industry as a whole grew rapidly in Korea throughout the 1970s, and many of the HCI sectors were above the all-industry average growth rate even before 1973. In a sense, therefore, the HCI declaration was a formal announcement or recognition of something that had already been happening. The Korean government did not suddenly discover the HCI sector in 1972–1973. It had been pushing these industries for many years prior to that time.

In a similar way, the abandonment of the HCI policy in 1979 did not lead to the end of HCI development. The Korean economy went through a sharp recession in 1980–1982 when everything slowed or came to a halt. But after that difficult period, the Korean economy boomed once again, and the heavy and chemical industries joined in the boom. From the beginning of 1979 through the end of 1988, all of the HCI sectors, with the exception of industrial chemicals, grew faster than the average growth rate for all of manufacturing.

What changed in the 1980s was the role of government in the development of the HCI sector. Industrial targeting was no longer the order of the day. The rhetoric of the early 1980s explicitly called for Korea to abandon Japanese MITI-style industrial policies. The reality of industrial policy in Korea, however, was more complex.

To begin with, something had to be done about the HCI enterprises that were in deep financial trouble. The government in the 1970s had encouraged firms to enter these sectors, and many felt that the government had implicitly agreed to share the risks entailed in the HCI program. That opinion was also held by many in government, and it is they who carried the day. Throughout the early 1980s, the government helped several dozen companies by lowering the interest on their debt and stretching out their loans.

With one major exception, the government did get out of the business of industrial targeting. That exception was telecommunications. Ironically, it was Kim Jae Ik who was the most active supporter of this industry—the one exception to his otherwise free market approach.[55] Telecommunications was set up as a government enterprise and remained so into the 1990s. The enterprise was given a monopoly and a protected domestic market. With this kind of support, telecommunications became Korea's largest industry and generated large surpluses for the government.

By 1984, however, a consensus was beginning to form around an all-out effort at liberalization of controls over domestic industry, except for telecommunications. On July 1, 1986, all seven individual industry promotion laws were abolished and replaced by a general industrial promotion law that did not target specific sectors. Some 140 forms of government intervention stipulated in these laws disappeared. All twenty-seven laws limiting the way land could be used, for example, were abolished. Regulations governing the establishment of new financial institutions were relaxed so that venture capital firms could be more easily set up. These venture capital firms, it was hoped, would make it easier for small and medium enterprises to gain access to capital.

Although the direction in which the government was heading in the 1980s was clear, implementation of these liberalization measures did not proceed without resistance. The Blue House and the Ministry of Finance were most active on the side of liberalization, but many officials in the Ministry of Commerce and Industry resisted their loss of power, although the minister at the time was himself supportive of the liberalization effort.[56]

Liberalization with respect to foreign trade, and especially foreign investment in Korea, proceeded more slowly than did efforts aimed at domestic manufactures, but liberalization made substantial headway in these areas as well. Restrictions on foreign investment in manufacturing, for example, were largely removed in a formal sense in 1987 and 1988, although procedural obstructions sometimes took the place of formal limitations. This chapter, however, is not the appropriate point to begin a systematic discussion of how many trade restrictions continued to exist into the 1990s. The trend was clear. Partly because of foreign pressures and partly because the moves were consistent with the overall direction of Korean industrial policy, the Korean manufacturing sector became progressively more liberalized throughout the 1980s.

Whatever the merits and demerits of the HCI policy of the 1973–1979 period, therefore, the lesson the Koreans themselves drew from the experience was that industrial targeting and active government support for targeted industries were no longer appropriate for Korea's economy of the 1980s and 1990s. Our interest in Korea's HCI policy, therefore, is for what it reveals about the effectiveness of a particular kind of industrial policy during the early stages of a nation's development, not for what that policy reveals about how Korea's economy is run today.

NOTES

1. Interview. Please see Bibliography.
2. There is a consensus among all of the principal policymakers of that period whom we were able to interview that Oh Won Chol, with President Park, was the dominant figure and architect of virtually all of the major HCI initiatives in this period.
3. Much of this discussion of machinery and steel is based on Heavy and Chemical Industry Promotion Committee, *Chung hwa-hak kongop pal-talsa (A history of the development of the heavy chemical industry)* (Seoul: Heavy Industry Promotion Committee, 1979), vol. 1.
4. Economic Planning Board, *Major Statistics of Korean Economy, 1982* (Seoul: Economic Planning Board, 1982), p. 98.
5. Government of the Republic of Korea, *The Second Five-Year Economic Development Plan, 1967–1971* (Seoul: Government of Korea, 1966), p. 35.
6. Heavy Industry Promotion Committee, *History of the Development*, Table 164, 1:455.
7. Ibid., Table 166, 1:463.
8. Economic Planning Board, *Major Statistics*, p. 71. There were some exports even before the country was self-sufficient.
9. Ibid., p. 112.
10. Heavy Industry Promotion Committee, *History of the Development*, Table 245, 1:725.
11. Ibid., Table 89, 1:268.
12. Interview. Please see Bibliography.
13. Heavy Industry Promotion Committee, *History of the Development*, Chart 30, 1:302.
14. Interview. Please see Bibliography. Also L. P. Jones and Il Sakong, *Government, Business and Entrepreneurship in Economic Development: The Korean Case* (Cambridge: Council on East Asian Studies, 1980), pp. 119–120, 357–358.
15. Government of the Republic of Korea, *The Third Five-Year Economic Development Plan, 1972–1976* (Seoul: Government of Korea, 1971), pp. 13, 23.

16. These figures are derived from data in Economic Planning Board, *Major Statistics*, p. 123.

17. Interview. Please see Bibliography.

18. S. Haggard et al., *Macroeconomic Policy and Adjustment in Korea, 1970–1990* (Cambridge: Harvard Institute for International Development, 1994).

19. H. Kissinger, *White House Years* (Boston: Little, Brown, 1979), p. 225.

20. Interview. Please see Bibliography.

21. Much of the ex-post rationalization of the HCI strategy stressed purely economic arguments tied to the need for HCI during particular stages of growth (see Heavy Industry Promotion Committee, *History of the Development, vol. 1*), but interviews with secretaries in the Blue House at the time indicated that military security considerations were central, although they were not the only reasons for the HCI strategy.

22. Interviews. Please see Bibliography.

23. Interview. Please see Bibliography.

24. Government of Korea, *Third Five-Year Economic Development Plan*.

25. Interviews. Please see Bibliography.

26. *Chunghwa-hak Kongophwa chongchaek sonohe ttayuh kongop kujo kaepyollon (A theory of industrial structure reformation based on the declaration of the policies toward heavy chemical industrialization)* (Seoul: unpublished government report, 1973), pp. 18–19.

27. Interviews. Please see Bibliography.

28. Interview. Please see Bibliography. The January 1973 declaration is explicit on this point (*Theory of Industrial Structure Reformation*, pp. 18–19).

29. Interview. Please see Bibliography.

30. Interview. Please see Bibliography.

31. Concern about the training of scientists, technicians, and other skilled workers is a major theme of the January 1973 declaration (*Theory of Industrial Structure Reformation*, pp. 21–23).

32. Interview. Please see Bibliography.

33. Economic Planning Board, *Major Statistics of Korean Economy, 1989* (Seoul: Economic Planning Board, 1989) p. 244.

34. Interview. Please see Bibliography.

35. Interview. Please see Bibliography.

36. Interview. Please see Bibliography.

37. Interview. Please see Bibliography.

38. Interview. Please see Bibliography.

39. Bank of Korea, *Economic Statistics Yearbook, 1980* (Seoul: Bank of Korea, 1981), p. 141.

40. Interview. Please see Bibliography.

41. Heavy Industry Promotion Committee, *History of the Development*, 1:218. The dollar figures were obtained by dividing by the average exchange rate for the 1972–1976 period (449.6 won = US$1) and by the 1976 exchange rate (484 won = US$1) for the 1977–1981 period.

42. The HCI in 1972–1976 rose from 42 percent total industry value-added in 1972 to 49 percent in 1976 while the ratio of manufacturing to GNP rose from 21 to 28 percent.

43. State Statistical Bureau, *Statistical Yearbook of China, 1986* (Hong Kong: Economic Information and Agency, 1987), pp. 373, 375.

44. Economic Planning Board, *Major Statistics, 1982*, p. 123. The figures are in constant 1975 prices.

45. The figures for trade broken down for heavy and light industry do not appear to be available for later years. These figures are from Heavy Industry Promotion Committee, *History of the Development*, 1:185–186.

46. The two-volume work was not published formally until 1979. Material in those volumes has been cited numerous times in this chapter. See citations of ibid., vol. 1.

47. Interviews. Please see Bibliography.

48. Economic Planning Board, *Major Statistics, 1982*, pp. 219, 246.

49. Interview. Please see Bibliography.

50. As one of the interviews suggested, these perceptions mattered to the government more than the objective reality.

51. One of our interviews suggested that a concern with social welfare and income distribution was high on President Park's agenda by the late 1970s.

52. Interview. Please see Bibliography.

53. Interview. Please see Bibliography.

54. Interview. Please see Bibliography.

55. Interview. Please see Bibliography.

56. Interview. Please see Bibliography.

3

Implementation: The Role of Markets versus Commands

The decision to build a petrochemical plant, a machinery enterprise, or some other unit within the heavy and chemical industry (HCI) sector was only the beginning of the process of making the HCI strategy a reality. The next step was to select the company that would build the new facility. With the company selected, the question then became one of determining how much support the government would provide.

The Korean government had a wide range of models to select from in implementing its HCI decisions. The pure neoclassical market model, as found in Hong Kong, would have left all decision making to private entrepreneurs, responding only to the impersonal forces of the market. At the other end of the spectrum was the pure command model as found in Stalin's Soviet Russia or Mao's China. In that system, the government ordered the enterprise to meet certain output targets and not to use more than a certain amount of identified inputs in the process of trying to meet those targets. To make sure that enterprises followed the guidelines, intermediate products were controlled by the planning authorities and delivered to the enterprise through administrative rather than market channels.

The Korean model was somewhere in between these two extremes. But was the Korean system one of indicative planning, where the planners calculated desired sectoral targets but let the private sector determine whether to use those targets or ignore them? Or did the Korean method of implementation rely to a significant degree on government commands backed up by various kinds of carrots and sticks?

Levers for Implementing HCI Decisions

In the HCI sector in the 1973–1978 period there is no question that the government went far beyond reliance on market forces or indicative planning. A listing of some of the measures used to promote particular HCI industries makes the point:

1. The government, meaning President Park and Oh Won Chol, personally selected the company to be charged with the first phase of a particular sector. If that sector was likely to be highly profitable, the company might be required to take on another sector where profitability would be more problematic.

2. The company selected was protected from non-Korean competitors in the Korean market, sometimes with outright import bans of the product in question. As for domestic competitors, often only one Korean company was allowed to sell on the domestic market in the initial phase of a new industry. Lucky Goldstar had the inside track with many consumer electronic products, for example, and Samsung was allowed to start in this sector only by promising to produce solely for export. Two or three years later, Samsung was finally allowed to compete with Lucky Goldstar on the Korean domestic market.

3. The state-owned banking system was ordered to channel its loans to the favored companies. In addition, the government placed its guarantee of repayment on foreign loans destined for the HCI sector, thereby lowering the cost of foreign capital. In the critical start-up period for the HCI program in 1974–1976, state bank loans for such sectors as the machinery industry or for equipment destined for the export industry ranged from 10 to 12 percent per annum.[1] Consumer prices in these same three years increased at an annual rate of 21.6 percent, and wholesale prices rose even faster. Thus, real rates on these loans were sharply negative, implying a major subsidy to firms favored with such loans.

4. Corporate taxation was formally based on tax rates that applied to all firms. In practice, the amount of tax paid was arrived at through negotiations between the companies and the tax authorities. Companies that undertook developments in the HCI sector could count on favored tax treatment. In addition, in 1975 a tax exemption reduction control law gave five-year tax holidays, investment tax credits, and accelerated depreciation to industries designated as key.

5. Imports in Korea in the 1970s were typically subject to high tariffs and tight quotas. Investors in the HCI program could import inputs duty free and receive favored access to a share of the quotas.

6. Utilities, such as electric power, were provided to the HCI sector at subsidized rates, and land was sold at below-market prices. The government practice was to earmark property for industrial estates and sell that land at the price it would have received before anyone knew the parcel was being considered as an industrial site. Despite these low land prices, enterprises did not flock to such government estates as Changwon, which were relatively ill-served by rail and road and far away from the political and financial center of Seoul. Changwon's location in the south, from the point of view of many investors, more than offset the subsidies to the price of land.

7. Government support was not confined to the investment or construction phases of an HCI industry. For a number of years until the enterprise was established and profitable, the government was prepared to help smooth over difficulties. The support for Hyundai shipbuilding when its ships rolled into the water and right into a dearth of demand for supertankers is a case in point. The Korean government persuaded the oil-producing countries to allow oil to be carried on Korean-owned bottoms and provided low-interest loans, with only a 10 percent down payment required, to those Korean firms, including Hyundai itself, that were willing to set up a tanker shipping company.[2] More generally, President Park, in his regular meetings with leading businessmen, personally issued orders to government officials below him to solve difficult situations brought to him by these private sector leaders. Often a company's problem was with one bottleneck or another generated by actions of the government bureaucracy itself. The personal concern of the president in these cases could be invaluable in breaking such bottlenecks. But to continue to have access to this kind of support, men such as chairman Chung Ju Yung of Hyundai had to be willing to do what President Park had asked, and to do it well.

Government intervention in support of the HCI sector in the mid-1970s was, in many ways, a significant departure from the way the government had managed the economy in the 1960s. It is not that government controls were necessarily less pervasive in the 1960s, but these controls were administered with less bureaucratic discretion than was the case earlier. The critical industrial policies of the 1960s were those dealing with foreign trade, and the main objective, particularly in the latter half of the 1960s, was the promotion of exports. By 1967, exporters had

> unrestricted access to and tariff exemptions on imported intermediate and capital goods; exemption from payment of indirect taxes both on

major intermediate inputs, whether imported or purchased domestically, and on export sales; generous wastage allowances in determining duty and indirect tax-free raw material imports, which permitted the use of these imports in production for the domestic market; reduced prices for several overhead inputs including electricity and railroad transport, which were intended at least in part to compensate for payment of indirect taxes in the normal charges for these inputs; a 50 percent reduction of indirect taxes on income earned in exporting, along with accelerated depreciation; and immediate access to subsidized short- and medium-term credit to finance working capital and fixed investment, respectively.[3]

Clearly, these were not laissez-faire policies designed to let the market freely work its will with a minimum of government interference. But these policies were different from those in the 1970s in one critical respect: they were designed to encourage all firms capable of exporting their products, not just a few individual enterprises that the Blue House in its judgment thought could do the job best. A company that expanded exports received the benefits; if it produced only for the domestic market, it did not. Government discretion over the application of some benefits such as bank loans was not completely absent, but there was little real targeting of specific sectors and specific firms as during the height of the HCI policy.

The 1980s were also different from the 1970s. Industrial targeting was largely confined to bailing out troubled firms in the HCI and the telecommunications sectors. For the most part, the government reverted to the use of less discretionary or more general controls over the economy. In the early 1980s, most of the control mechanisms, ranging from licenses to tariffs and quotas, were still in place, even if they were no longer being administered at the discretion of the Blue House. In some instances there was still a degree of bureaucratic discretion, but it was exercised at lower levels of the Ministry of Commerce and Industry rather than as part of a systematic effort at command planning.

By the late 1980s, the economy as a whole became more liberalized, partly as a result of the dramatic improvements in Korea's balance of payments, and government levers used to direct the economy became much less potent. Tariffs were lower, and there were fewer and fewer quotas or outright bans. The inflation rate came down into the low single digits after 1981, and state bank loan interest rates went up substantially, becoming positive in real terms. Administration of the tax system became somewhat less informal. Still, with all of these changes in the direction of liberalization of the economy, the Korean government retained a considerable capacity to influence investment decisions throughout the

1980s, even if that capacity was no longer exercised in such a single-minded way as to target specific industries. With political democratization after 1987, government support for individual firms came increasingly under public criticism, further limiting the capacity of the government to intervene in a discretionary way.

The remainder of this chapter puts some quantitative flesh on the bones of this outline of the nature of the Korean government's intervention in the economy. Much of the data presented will be for the 1970s, because that is the period of greatest concern to the topic of HCI development strategy. Where data are readily available, however, an effort is made to compare the various measures of intervention for the 1970s with similar measures for earlier and later periods.

These quantitative indicators attempt to measure related but distinguishable elements in government intervention, the degree to which prices were distorted, and the degree to which government commands were substituted for market forces of all kinds. Distorted prices increase the likelihood of government discretionary intervention, but it is possible to have distortions without much bureaucratic discretion. In fact, what distinguishes the 1970s from the 1960s in Korean industrial policy was not so much the degree of distortion in the system as the discretion exercised in targeting particular firms. Unfortunately, it is easier to find measures of price distortion than it is of the level of bureaucratic discretion. Still, some data on the latter issue are available, and they are presented here.

Measuring the Influence of Command and Market Forces

Measuring where Korea falls along a spectrum between a market and a command economy is difficult because there are no agreed-upon criteria about what one is trying to measure. All we really have is an agreement about the ideal types at the two extremes. The first task, then, is to attempt to clarify what we are talking about.

Ownership is not the primary basis for judging whether an economy is dominated by market or bureaucratic command forces. In principle, it is possible to have a market economy where all enterprises are state owned, or a command economy where all enterprises are privately owned. In practice, state ownership usually means that that enterprise takes a great deal of direction from the government so that there is a considerable degree of correlation between state ownership and the use of bureaucratic commands. There is no comparable degree of correlation between private ownership and the predominance of market forces. A Hong Kong toy manufacturer operates in a laissez-faire world; a large private manufacturer in India is hemmed in on all sides by government regulations and licenses.

The critical difference between a market and a command system is whether enterprise success is determined primarily by the enterprise's response to market forces or whether that success, or lack thereof, is dictated by decisions of government implemented through hierarchical commands. Enterprise owners and managers have no trouble determining which is the case in their particular situations, and they gear their time accordingly. If discretionary decisions by government officials over the allocation of import quotas will make or break an industrial firm, top management will devote its time and energy to securing those quotas. If imports are readily available at competitive prices on the market, little time need be devoted to their procurement. The critical problem will be, when once they are procured, to see that these imports are used efficiently so a firm's costs remain competitive with the costs of other producers.

In the developing world, there are no measures of how top management spends its time, so indirect measures of the degree to which enterprise success is determined by market or bureaucratic command forces must be used. The indirect measures that we explore in the balance of this chapter are designed to give a picture of the degree of price distortion and bureaucratic control over the Korean economy. Korea will be compared with other developing countries along these various dimensions. The result of these comparisons will fall far short of a cardinal measure of the degree to which Korea is a market or a bureaucratic command-driven economy. Nevertheless, the assessment will achieve progress toward an ordinal measure that allows some judgment about the degree to which prices were distorted in Korea and whether Korean industry is more or less driven by commands than economies such as Hong Kong, Indonesia, or Bangladesh. Each of these measures will be taken up in turn with overall generalizations about the nature of the Korean economic system reserved for the conclusion of this discussion.

Indirect Measures of the Korean Economy

Ownership

The first indicator, for all of its flaws, is ownership. Data on the ownership of Korean industry have been collected by L. P. Jones and are presented in Table 3-1.[4] Korea's 119 public enterprises (as of 1971) accounted for

Table 3-1. Industrial Origin of Public Enterprise Value-Added, 1972
(in percentage)

Sector	Share of Public Enterprise in Industry
Agriculture, forestry, fishing	0.20
Mining	31.01
Manufacturing	15.11
Construction	5.44
Electricity, water, sanitation	66.19
Transportation and communication	30.51
Trade	2.35
Finance	86.95
Ownership of dwellings	0.40
Public adminstration	0.00
Services	1.70
All industries	9.09

Source: L. P. Jones, *Public Enterprise and Economic Development: The Korean Case* (Seoul: Korea Development Institute Press, 1976), p. 76, reproduced with permission.

87 percent of the financial sector; 66 percent of electricity, water, and sanitation; and 30.5 percent of transport and communication. Trade, construction, and most other services, in contrast, had little public ownership. Manufacturing, where the public share was 15 percent of value-added, fell in between. As Jones has pointed out, these shares are strikingly similar to those of India, a country that is widely perceived as having a high degree of public ownership driven by Fabian socialist ideals. Jones himself suggests that public ownership is driven more by the economic characteristics of particular industries than by ideology.

Economic characteristics no doubt do play an important role in determining the degree of public ownership. A high degree of monopoly power in a sector with critical forward and backward linkages is one reason that the government steps in, with either outright public ownership or close regulation of private owners. From the standpoint of the relative importance of the influence of markets versus government commands, it may not matter whether government control is through ownership or regulation. Either way, government commands, not market forces, determine enterprise profitability. Ownership therefore does not get us very far in settling whether Korea was a market or a command economy in the 1960s and 1970s. Most societies do not leave the operation of railroads and electric power to the unfettered control of market forces, so Korea is like most other countries in this respect. Korea's state ownership and state control of the banking system do, however, place it on the more controlled end of the economic systems spectrum.

Many nations function with privately owned banks and other private financial institutions, which, although regulated to some degree, are heavily influenced by money market forces.

Sources of Labor and Capital

More important than ownership for the purposes of this chapter is whether Korean industrial enterprises bought most of their inputs on open and competitive markets and sold their output on such markets or whether government allocated inputs or market shares, to favored enterprises.

Domestic labor was freely available to the highest bidder. In fact, the government made a considerable effort to ensure that workers did not form unions with enough monopoly power to influence wages. Financial resources, however, were not at all freely available. Banks allocated loans to activities favored by the government at highly subsidized rates, particularly in the 1970s, during the first phase of the HCI program. If distortions from equilibrium interest rates are a measure of the degree to which government was involved in allocating credit, then the data in Table 3-2 suggest that Korea fell somewhere in the middle of most developing countries. If Korea was in the middle, that suggests that most countries allocated credit by bureaucratic directives because that is certainly the way Korea did it. Only the existence of a large, well-functioning, informal credit market kept enterprises from being totally dependent on either government favors or their own retained earnings.

The government's role in the allocation of credit is particularly apparent during the height of the HCI drive. As the data in Table 3-3 indicate, credit from the state-owned banks to heavy industry jumped from 32.21 percent of total credit to manufacturing in 1974 to 65.75 percent in 1975 when the HCI drive came into full swing. Furthermore, the HCI sector received credit at substantially lower cost than that provided to other sectors. The average cost of borrowing for the steel sector in the mid-1970s was between 7 and 8 percent, while that for textiles and apparel was higher by anywhere from 2 (1975) to 8 percentage points (in 1978). These differences in cost continued into the early 1980s, in part, no doubt, because of the need to bail out the troubled firms in the HCI sector.

This picture of a highly distorted and discretionary credit market is substantially different from that portrayed in earlier studies of Korean financial markets. Korea's interest rate reforms of the mid-1960s in some of these earlier works are considered an important piece of evidence in support of the view that correct prices lead to high growth. In September

Table 3-2. Real Interest Rates

Country	Percentage per annum
1. Ethiopia	1.8
2. Thailand	0.5
3. India	− 0.3
4. Senegal	− 1.0
5. Colombia	− 2.0
6. Cameroon	− 2.5
7. Tunisia	− 2.7
8. Malawi	− 3.4
9. Sri Lanka	− 4.0
10. Kenya	− 4.1
11. Pakistan	− 4.3
12. Egypt	− 4.4
13. Philippines	− 4.9
14. **Korea**	**− 5.0**
15. Ivory Coast	− 5.5
16. Bolivia	− 7.0
17. Jamaica	− 7.5
18. Tanzania	− 7.7
19. Brazil	− 8.0
20. Yugoslavia	− 8.5
21. Mexico	− 10.7
22. Bangladesh	− 10.9
23. Peru	− 11.1
24. Nigeria	− 11.7
25. Turkey	− 14.7
26. Ghana	− 19.0
27. Uruguay	− 20.6
28. Argentina	− 31.2
29. Chile	− 38.6

Source: Ramgopal Agarwala, "Price Distortions and Growth in Developing Countries," World Bank Staff Working Paper 575 (Washington, D.C.: World Bank, 1983), p. 23, reproduced with permission.

1965 Korea, among other measures, raised the ceiling on nominal interest rates for time and savings deposits from 15 to 30 percent. The result, combined with a reduction in the rate of inflation, was that real interest rates became positive by a substantial margin where before they had been negative. The consequences for the Korean economy, in the words of one influential book, were that

> the banking system's role as an intermediary within the Korean economy expanded rather dramatically. The use of higher real rates of interest had the effect of sharply increasing household saving and drawing more existing capital through organized financial processes. The dependence of firms on self-finance and the traditional curb market was reduced correspondingly. . . . From our theoretical analysis, one would expect a rise in the quality and quantity of investment—which indeed seems to have been the case, judging from the marked overall increase in Korea's real output and international competitiveness.[5]

Table 3-3. Credit Allocation by Sector (percentage share of total bank credit to manufacturing)

Year	Heavy Industry	Light Industry
1973	35.60	64.40
1974	32.21	67.79
1975	65.75	34.25
1976	55.95	44.08
1978	55.65	44.35
1980	59.76	40.24
1982	68.38	43.74

Sources: World Bank, *Korea: Managing the Industrial Transition* (Washington, D.C.: World Bank, 1987), p. 41. The original data were from publications of the Bank of Korea, reproduced with permission.

Subsequent analyses of the Korean experience with financial reform have raised fundamental questions about this connection between high real interest rates in the organized financial sector and higher savings and economic growth. Inconveniently for the "getting prices right" school, Korean real interest rates on savings deposits returned to the negative side of the ledger in the 1970s, and yet the growth of Korean gross national product (GNP) averaged 9.5 percent annually through the 1970s up to the assassination of President Park in 1979. Private savings as a percentage of GNP rose from 11.9 percent in 1970 to 23.6 percent in 1978 before declining in the aftermath of the assassination and subsequent economic recession. It appears that the main effect of high real interest rates on bank savings deposits may have mainly shifted funds from the unorganized but fairly efficient curb market to the organized, government-owned and -controlled banking system, without much impact on either savings or growth.[6]

Sources of Intermediate Inputs

Equally important to capital is how Korean industry obtained its raw materials and intermediate inputs. Inputs obtained domestically were bought freely on the domestic market. The Korean government, for the most part, did not attempt to dictate to producers of intermediate goods to whom they should sell. Utilities such as electric power were an exception to this more general rule, particularly with respect to the HCI program.[7]

Imported industrial inputs, however, were not freely available to the highest bidder. Throughout the 1960s and 1970s foreign exchange controls were tight, and importers also had to deal with an elaborate system of quotas administered by government officials.

In the 1960s, to be sure, there were sporadic efforts to liberalize Korean imports, and the system that existed in the late 1960s was somewhat more liberal than that in the 1950s. The following passage gives the flavor of policies in the early 1970s, at the beginning of the first phase of the HCI program:

> Despite [the 1972 and 1973] attempts at further liberalization and reform, resort to the old price-distorting policies and controls was common. A number of factors were involved. First, any adverse trends in the balance of payments prompted a return to the old methods. For example, when import demand increased sharply in late 1968, the government placed additional import items on the restricted list and increased export incentives. . . .
>
> Finally, and probably most important, certain vested interests in the business community had much to lose from further liberalization and favored a return to price-distorting mechanisms. . . . For good measure, related business groups staged a sit-down protest against the [1967] tariff change in the offices of the Ministry of Finance.[8]

The data in Table 3-4 are a crude indicator of trends in Korean policy toward import restrictions. Numbers of items, however, do not tell the real story. Ideal for the purposes of this chapter would be figures on the value of imports subject to quotas and the value of domestic production in sectors for which imports were completely prohibited. Such estimates, however, do not exist. Information on how these trade restrictions were applied in practice would also be useful, but those kinds of data do not exist in any readily available form. As we know from the experience of Japan, formal steps toward trade liberalization are not always as liberal as they appear to be. Nevertheless, by the 1980s the quantity of imports subject to quotas and to discretionary government decisions on the allocation of quotas and other similar restrictions was clearly on the decline. Throughout the 1970s, however, a period of concern to this analysis, industrial enterprises depended critically on access to these quotas.

Some idea of the importance of imported goods to Korean industry can be gleaned from the data in Table 3-5. The figures in this table probably overstate the dependence of Korean industry on imported inputs because capital goods imports data could not be separated from intermediate-goods imports. Still, the basic message of the table is clear: Korean industry depended on imports for a third, and possibly more, of its intermediate inputs. If an enterprise could not secure the necessary foreign exchange or had no access to the quota for a critical input, that enterprise was out of business. Given the tightness of exchange controls

Table 3-4. Number of Importable Items Subject to Restrictions, 1961–1988

Year (January–June)	Prohibited	Restricted	Automatic Approval
1961	305	35	1,546
1963	442	713	776
1965	624	111	1,447
1967	362	132	2,950
1968	116	386	810
1970	73	524	715
1976	553		544
1978	385		712
1980	317		693
1982	1,769		5,791
1984	1,203		6,712
1986	668		7,247
1988	367		4,548

Source: C. R. Frank, Kwang Suk Kim, and L. E. Westphal, *Foreign Trade Regimes and Economic Development: South Korea* (New York: National Bureau of Economic Research, 1975), pp. 45, 59. In 1967 Korea shifted from a positive to a negative list system for controlling imports, making the figures before and after 1967 not comparable. In the case of a positive list, goods are allowed in freely only if they are explicitly designated as being freely importable. With a negative list, all goods can be freely imported except for those explicitly listed as being subject to restrictions. The totals of the three columns taken together vary from year to year, presumably because of changes in the way product classification was subdivided. The 1976-1988 data are from Office of Customs Administration and World Bank, *Korea: Managing the Industrial Transition* (Washington, D.C.: World Bank, 1987), p. 64.

and the fact that quotas were common for many critical inputs in the 1970s, it is clear that success for industrial enterprises in Korea depended fundamentally on discretionary government trade decisions. To the degree that this was the case, these enterprises lived in a world of bureaucratic commands rather than market forces.

In Korea, however, the role of government commands in determining success for particular industrial enterprises was tempered by another characteristic of Korean industry. Korean industrial enterprises often had to export in order to survive. In fact, access to import quotas was itself, to a significant degree, conditioned on an enterprise's export performance even when the imported good was used in producing goods destined for the Korean domestic market. The more Korean industrial firms exported, therefore, the more these enterprises were governed by market forces rather than by discretionary government commands. Governments, after all, have little capacity to control export markets for their country's manufactures.

Data on Korean exports of manufactures as a share of manufactured gross value output are presented in Table 3-6. Data relating these exports to manufactured value-added and to a crude estimate of manufactured gross value output for the developing regions of the world are given in

Table 3-5. Imports of Intermediate Goods as a Share of Total Intermediate
Inputs into Manufacturing

Year	Intermediate Inputs into Manufacturing	Imported Intermediate Inputs	Share
	(billion current won)		(percentage)
1965	315.6	103.6	32.8
1970	1,236.7	496.9	40.2
1975	7,252.4	2,946.0	40.6
1980	26,166.0	12,896.0	49.3
1985	49,665.0	25,114.0	50.6

Sources: The intermediate input figures were derived by subtracting value-added from gross value output as reported in Economic Planning Board, *Handbook of Korean Economy, 1980* (Seoul: Economic Planning Board, 1980), pp. 281–282, except for 1980 and 1985, where intermediate inputs were assumed to be 2.33 times value-added (70 percent of gross output value).

The import figures include some imports destined for agriculture and sectors other than manufacturing, so these figures are only crude approximations of imported inputs into manufacturing. The import figures were reported in current U.S. dollars and converted into Korean won at each year's official exchange rate. The dollar figures are from ibid. and Economic Planning Board, *Major Statistics of Korean Economy, 1988* (Seoul: Economic Planning Board, 1988), pp. 211–212.

Table 3-7. As the figures in these tables indicate, there is no question that as early as 1970, Korea was exporting a larger share of its manufactures than were other regions of the developing world. But does export of 14.5 percent of manufactures in 1970 mean that Korean industry was heavily dependent on export markets at that time? More Korean industrial profits probably came from the 85.5 percent of their output that was sold on the domestic market than from exports. The principal value of exports to many enterprises was that a successful export performance gave the firm virtually automatic access to government import quotas of goods needed to produce for the domestic market. To the extent that was the case, were Korean industrialists really ruled by market forces? Some of the government restrictions on the domestic market will be noted below. But for exports, did market forces determine enterprise decisions or did government-set export targets govern enterprise behavior? Business leaders knew that if they met those targets, they would gain ready access to government import quotas and other benefits available at the discretionary will of the government. One survey taken in 1976 makes clear that the firms themselves set the export targets. The government did make an effort to coordinate the targets but did not initiate them. In addition to coordination, the government allocated long-term loans in part based on these targets. Thus, the firm had an incentive to set the target as high as possible. Monthly meetings held by President Park and attended by the firms or their export associations also reinforced these targets, as did the daily computer printouts of progress toward the targets put out by the Ministry

Table 3-6. Share of Manufactured Exports in Total Manufactures

Year	Gross Value of Output of Manufactures (billion won, current prices)	Exports of Manufactures (billion won, current prices)	Share (percentage)
1965	459.4	30.5	6.7
1970	1,795.3	260.7	14.5
1975	9,842.8	2,318.9	23.6
1980	37,380.0	9,810.0	26.2
1985	70,950.0	25,708.6	36.2

Sources: The gross value output of manufactures are from Economic Planning Board, *Handbook, 1980*, p. 282, except for 1980 and 1985, where manufacturing value-added was assumed to be 30 percent of gross value.
  Exports of manufactures in current U.S. dollars are given in ibid. and in Economic Planning Board, *Major Statistics of Korean Economy, 1988*, p. 207. The U.S. dollar figures were converted into current Korean won using the official exchange rate for each year.

of Commerce and Industry. The export targets therefore were neither government commands nor simply reflections of the individual firm's views of its market opportunities. They were a halfway house between a command and an unfettered market system.[9]

By the 1980s, there is little doubt that the profitability of many Korean industries depended critically on reaching an efficient scale of output through reliance on exports. Such was the case in automobiles and steel. But in 1970, exports could not have been the primary vehicle allowing enterprises to achieve scale economies. Most output was destined for the domestic market, except in such sectors as textiles, where scale economies are not really very important. In the early 1970s, therefore, the markets that governed Korean manufacturing were domestic more than they were foreign.

Was the Korean domestic market an open, competitive market? Or was it, too, riddled with government controls that could make or break an industrial firm? In a truly competitive domestic market, imports compete on an even field with domestic producers, and there is relative ease of market entry for new domestic producers. But in Korea in the 1960s and 1970s, there was an effective prohibition on the imports of a wide range of manufactured consumer products and government-administered quotas for much of the rest. Only some intermediate products and capital goods not produced in Korea were allowed relatively unfettered entry into the country. Competition therefore depended on the existence of a large enough number of domestic firms in each industry.

But Korean industry is also known for its large conglomerates *(chaebol)*, which would seem to indicate that the Korean domestic market

Table 3-7. Exports of Manufactures as a Share of Manufacturing Value-Added and Gross Value of Output

Region	Share of Manufacturing in GDP (1)	Share of Exports in GDP (2)	Share of Manufacturing in Exports (3)	Share of Manufacturing Exports in Value-Added (4 = [3 × 2] /1)
Africa (Sub-Saharan)	13.2	22.8	14.6	25.2
Middle East and Northern Africa	15.4	2.3	9.6	13.9
Eastern Asia and Pacific	19.6	29.1	36.9	54.8
Southern Asia	13.6	5.8	45.2	19.3
Latin America	24.2	12.5	12.1	6.3
Southern Europe	22.8	15.2	51.7	34.5

Note: Share of manufactures in exports includes "machinery and equipment" plus "other manufactures."
Source: World Bank, *World Tables, 3d ed.* (Washington, D.C.: World Bank, 1983), pp. 502–519.

was controlled by oligopolistic enterprises with close ties to government. But here, popular perceptions are misleading. The top forty-six conglomerates in Korea in 1975 accounted for only 36.7 percent of manufacturing value-added and the top five conglomerates only 14.5 percent.[10] This degree of concentration is less than that found in either India or Pakistan, for example. Ideally, one would like concentration ratios broken down by industrial sector, but estimates of this type have not yet been produced for Korea. In the absence of these ratios, only a tentative conclusion is possible: there were more than enough firms in the various Korean industrial sectors to make vigorous competition possible. Few sectors were dominated by a single firm or only one or two firms, as is often the case in developing countries in the early stages of industrialization. Having enough firms to make competition possible, however, does not guarantee that it will take place. Import quotas can be, and often are, used to enforce cartel agreements, for example. Government can also restrict new firm entry into a field through licensing arrangements or through control over credit. Both forms of control existed in Korea.

Distortions in Relative Prices

We do not have any direct measures of the degree of government involvement in the domestic market, but two indirect measures give some information on this subject. The first of these measures looks at Korea's relative price structure in comparison with that found elsewhere in the world. The hypothesis is that if Korean domestic markets were relatively open and competitive, its price structure would resemble that found elsewhere, at least for traded goods. Major departures from world or international prices would indicate some kind of intervention in the Korean market, presumably by government, although private cartels could, in principle, cause distortions as well.

The data used to investigate this subject are taken from the United Nations studies of Kravis, Heston, and Summers.[11] This data set is not ideal for our purposes; all of its prices are domestic market or retail prices, and, as such, they contain not only the cost of the good when it left the factory but also all the costs entailed in bringing the good to market. In effect, all prices include a significant component of wholesale and retail services, and developing-country service costs are typically much lower than those found in a high-income industrial economy. This problem clearly introduces noise into our international comparisons but does not negate the value of the exercise.

Data comparing the price structures for traded goods of nineteen countries are presented in Table 3-8. The relevant figure is the coefficient of variation, which measures the standard deviation of the purchasing power parities of 103 individual categories of traded goods divided by the mean purchasing power parity of all traded goods. A coefficient of variation of 0.5, for example, would indicate that 30 percent of all prices (purchasing power parities) in the sample were more than 50 percent higher or lower than the average purchasing power parity. If all domestic prices were identical to the international price structure, the standard deviation and the coefficient of variation would be zero.

By this measure, the data in Table 3-8 indicate that price distortions in Korea were about average for the developing countries for which data are available. Specifically, Korea has about the same degree of distortion as India or Colombia. This table therefore appears to support the view that there was an important amount of intervention in Korea's price structure—intervention for the most part by government. If that intervention was on a nondiscretionary basis, say, by setting tariffs that remained fixed for long periods and were not subject to negotiation between business and government, then it is possible to speak of the Korean domestic market's being governed by market forces. To the degree that these distortions resulted from negotiated deals between government and business, as one suspects was frequently the case, particularly with respect to the HCI sector, then Korea's domestic market was interlaced with many of the features of a bureaucratic command economy.

Table 3-8. Deviation of Domestic from International Prices of Traded Goods, 1975

Country	Exchange Rate[a] (1)	Purchasing Power Parity[b] (2)	Coefficient of Variation[c] (3)
1. Zambia	0.644	0.999	1.042
2. Sri Lanka	10.600	9.585	1.028
3. Uruguay	2.299	2.763	0.813
4. Pakistan	9.931	8.826	0.797
5. Syria	3.700	3.134	0.777
6. Philippines	7.275	6.972	0.764
7. Colombia	30.869	27.134	0.713
8. **Korea**	**484.000**	**428.7**	**0.689**
9. India	8.653	6.854	0.688
10. Thailand	20.379	18.28	0.651
11. Rumania	12.000	17.63	0.642
12. Iran	67.639	71.10	0.635
13. Malawi	0.866	0.962	0.616
14. Malaysia	2.402	2.287	0.552
15. Mexico	12.500	13.35	0.530
16. Kenya	7.411	8.53	0.517
17. Brazil	8.204	8.90	0.484
18. Jamaica	0.909	1.145	0.430
19. Germany	2.461	3.46	0.377

[a]The official exchange rate expressed as the number of units of the local currency that were equivalent to US$1.00.
[b]The average numbers of local currency units, given prices actually prevailing in the domestic economy, that would be needed to purchase a basket of goods that would be worth US$1.00 in the U.S. economy.
[c]The variation of the purchasing power parity of all goods in column 2 divided by this same mean.
Source: I. Kravis, A. Heston, and R. Summers, *World Product and Income: International Comparisons of Real Gross Product* (Baltimore: Johns Hopkins Press, 1982), p. 10, with permission.

Korea may not have "gotten prices right" in the sense of making domestic prices equal to world prices, but it did make sure that its overall price level kept it competitive in international markets. Data in Table 3-9 have been arranged in a way that allows a judgment about the degree of overvaluation or undervaluation of the currencies for the same nineteen countries used in Table 3-8. By this measure, Korea had one of the more undervalued currencies. Undervaluation may not be a measure of the degree to which "prices were right," but it was certainly a boon to exports—though not a discretionary tool in the hands of the government.

This conclusion about the Korean exchange rate's being supportive of the country's export orientation is similar to that of a number of other studies using varying methodologies. The conclusion that Korean relative prices were highly distorted, however, is not shared by many analysts. The single most influential study on the subject, and also the one that attempted most systematically to measure the degree of price distortion, was that of Frank, Kim, and Westphal.[12] The problem with this study is

Table 3-9. Estimate of Exchange Rate Overvaluation

Country	Overvaluation Index	Average Purchasing Power Parity of Traded Goods, 1975	GDP per Capita at International Prices, 1975
1. Syria	−0.22135	0.847	1,794
2. India	−0.20088	0.792	470
3. Colombia	−0.18081	0.877	1,609
4. **Korea**	**−0.16468**	**0.886**	**1,484**
5. Thailand	−0.12244	0.897	936
6. Pakistan	−0.10772	0.892	590
7. Malaysia	−0.10193	0.952	1,541
8. Iran	−0.07728	1.043	2,705
9. Philippines	−0.05801	0.962	946
10. Mexico	−0.03985	1.068	2,487
11. Brazil	0.025676	1.095	1,811
12. Sri Lanka	0.060827	1.065	668
13. Uruguay	0.073795	1.202	2,844
14. Germany	0.099582	1.405	5,953
15. Malawi	0.124839	1.111	352
16. Kenya	0.158113	1.151	470
17. Jamaica	0.195692	1.260	1,723
18. Zambia	0.544837	1.553	738

Notes: The overvaluation index was derived by subtracting estimated purchasing power parity controlled for differences in per capita income from observed purchasing power parity for traded goods. The regression equation used to derive the estimated purchasing power parities was: PPP = 0.966097 + .000057 (1975 per capita GDP).

not with the calculations of subsidies, effective rates of protection, and the differences between world and Korean domestic prices. These were done with much greater care than is true of most such studies. The principal controversy is these authors' argument that their results suggest relatively small distortions in relative domestic prices compared to world prices. Part of the controversy may result from methodological assumptions made by the authors.[13] But it may also be the case that the three authors were making comparative statements about the degree of distortion without explicitly comparing their results to those of other nations. Subsequently, studies putting Korean data in an explicitly comparative context are more consistent with the conclusions reached using the Kravis, Heston, and Summers data than they are with the view that for all specific state interventions, Korea basically got its prices right.[14]

Inventories

The other indirect measure of the nature of Korea's economic system and the degree of government intervention are figures for inventories. The inventory figures for Korea are presented in Table 3-10. The data in this table measure the ratio of input inventories to output inventories,

Table 3-10. Inventories in Mining and Manufacturing, Korea (end-of-year totals in billion won)

Year	Finished Products (1)	Semi-finished Goods (2)	Raw Materials (3)	Fuel (4)	Ratios (A) (5)	(B) (6)
1968	44.7	16.3	43.8	N.A.	1.3	0.98
1970	107.8	77.4	N.A.	N.A.	N.A.	N.A.
1973	200.1	100.9	256.0	9.4	1.8	1.33
1975	729.1	635.0	N.A.	N.A.	N.A.	N.A.
1978	733.0	559.0	1,381.0	26.0	2.7	1.92
1980	2,002.0	1,198.0	2,670.0	108.0	1.9	1.39
1982	2,523.0	1,484.0	3,247.0	88.0	1.9	1.32
1984	3,428.0	1,967.0	3,827.0	132.0	1.7	1.17

Notes: Ratio A = [Col. 2 + Col. 3 + Col. 4]/[Col. 1].
Ratio B = [Col. 3 + Col. 4]/[Col. 1].

sometimes known as the Kornai Index, for Korea and for a selected sample of other countries. Underlying this index is an assumption that countries with a bureaucratic command system stimulate enterprises to accumulate large inventories of intermediate inputs in order to ensure their meeting planned output targets. Inputs not available in inventories usually prove difficult to obtain on a timely basis because one must fight one's way up the bureaucratic chain of command for each new allocation. Market economy enterprises, in contrast, can simply go to the market to buy what they need. An extreme version would be Japan's just-in-time method of inventory control. Market-oriented enterprises worry more about having enough final product inventory on hand to meet un-anticipated market demand and balance this off against the capital costs involved in maintaining such inventories.

As the data in Table 3-10 indicate, Korea's Kornai Index first rose, peaking in 1978, and then began to fall. These data should be used with caution, however, because there is more to a change in inventories than whether an economy operates through commands or markets. The business cycle and the level of inflation, for example, influence the level of inventories. But the pattern described by the data in Table 3-10 is broadly consistent with the earlier description of an increase in the role of commands over market forces, as Korea moved from an emphasis on the export of light manufactures in the 1960s to the HCI drive of the 1970s to the decline of industrial targeting in the 1980s.

The international comparisons with Korea are also instructive. Korea's highest Kornai Index ratio is comparable to or a bit higher than that of India or several Latin American countries; the lowest ratio is closer to that of the United States (if semifinished products are excluded). None of these ratios comes close to those of Hungary or China (where surveys suggest a ratio of perhaps 3.8 to 4.3). And the prereform economy of the Soviet Union, the quintessential command economy, had a ratio of 9.2 to 12.3.[15]

For all of their limitations, these inventory data suggest that Korean manufacturing remained somewhat market oriented even during the height of the HCI drive. Certainly Korea did not become a command economy of the Soviet type. On the other hand, Korea, prior to the 1980s, had inventory levels comparable to those of India and several large Latin American nations, nations known for their emphasis on import substitution and the government controls that go with such a policy.

Conclusion

What do all of these measures, pulled together, say about the relative strength of market and bureaucratic command forces in the Korean economy? The standard of comparison is other developing countries, and the average for developing countries involves a high degree of government intervention. Where does Korea stand relative to this average?

Ownership: Korea is similar to other developing countries, such as India, in the degree of public ownership of industrial enterprises and critical infrastructure services.

Degree of capital market distortions: These were about average for developing countries, as indicated by negative real interest rates prior to the 1980s, except for a brief period in the mid-1960s.

Importance of imports of intermediate inputs into industry and the degree of government control over these inputs: The Korean government in the 1960s and 1970s exercised a high degree of control over these inputs, which comprised, in turn, a large share of total inputs into manufacturing. In the 1960s, however, exporters had virtually automatic access to imported inputs, and this became increasingly true for all manufacturers in the 1980s.

Exports of manufactures as a share of gross manufactured output: Korea's share in the 1970s was high compared to other developing countries, but the greater share of manufacturing by far was still directed to the domestic market. This statement would also be true of the 1980s if the words *by far* were eliminated.

Degree of industrial concentration: Korea ranks surprisingly low on this index, relative to at least India and Pakistan (but almost certainly not Taiwan).

Degree of domestic price distortion: Korea is about at the median of developing countries for which data are available. This conclusion applies mainly to the 1970s, however. Data for the 1980s, when they became available, may indicate a decline in the degree of distortion.

Inventories and the Kornai Index: Korean inventory behavior is substantially closer to that of other market economies than it is to the full-blown socialist command economies, but the index rose significantly during the HCI drive.

In summary, Korea experienced a large degree of bureaucratic intervention in its economy that interfered with the free operation of market forces. The degree of intervention was substantial in the 1960s but was often used in a relatively nondiscretionary way. Virtually anyone who exported goods could take advantage of the government support programs. In the 1970s, however, this system of intervention became highly discretionary in support of the HCI drive. Highly discretionary industrial targeting in the 1970s led, in turn, to a reversal of these policies at the end of that decade. The move away from an activist government policy of industrial promotion continued throughout the 1980s, but some elements of intervention remained even at the end of the decade, particularly in the areas of foreign investment and telecommunications.

How does this degree of government involvement in the Korean economy influence our appraisal of the HCI program? To begin, it clearly does not make sense to treat the HCI effort as a deviation from free market pricing that inevitably led to a rise in inefficiency in the economy. The Korean economy of the early 1970s, just prior to the HCI drive, was already riddled with distortions from a free market ideal. The HCI drive involved more state intervention, and particularly more discretionary intervention, than previous government efforts, but the distortions that resulted were distortions in the world of the second best.

Two questions that can be asked about the HCI drive in the context of this chapter are whether that drive would have taken place in the absence of government support and whether the results contributed to Korea's high growth rate. Answers to the second question are addressed in the two chapters that follow. As to the first question, given the pervasiveness of government controls, it seems unlikely that the HCI drive would have been launched in the 1970s mainly on the initiative of the private sector's acting alone. The large capital requirements of such a drive, combined with state control of bank lending, would itself have made it difficult for the private sector to find financing. Nor were the highly leveraged *chaebol* in a position to sustain larger losses for several years before turning a profit in the absence of government subsidies of various kinds.

The Korean HCI drive is a reasonably clear case of a program that resulted from government initiative with cooperation, but not leadership, from the private sector. What remains in this study is to attempt to answer whether the HCI program contributed to, or detracted from, the overall development effort.

NOTES

1. These interest rate data are from Economic Planning Board, *Major Statistics of Korean Economy, 1977* (Seoul: Economic Planning Board, 1977), p. 139.
2. Interview. Please see Bibliography.
3. L. E. Westphal, "The Republic of Korea's Experience with Export-Led Industrial Development," *World Development* 6, no. 3 (1978): 350.
4. L. P. Jones, *Public Enterprise and Economic Development: The Korean Case* (Seoul: Korea Development Institute Press, 1976).
5. R. L. McKinnon, *Money and Capital in Economic Development* (Washington, D.C.: Brookings Institution, 1973), p. 111.
6. For a more systematic study of these issues, see D. C. Cole and Yung Chul Park, *Financial Development in Korea, 1945–1978* (Cambridge: Council on East Asian Studies, 1983).
7. Interviews. Please see Bibliography.
8. C. R. Frank, Kwang Suk Kim, and L. E. Westphal, *Foreign Trade Regimes and Economic Development: South Korea* (New York: National Bureau of Economic Research, 1975), pp. 56–57.
9. Yung Whee Rhee, B. Ross-Larson, and G. Pursell, *Korea's Competitive Edge: Managing the Entry into World Markets* (Baltimore: Johns Hopkins University Press, 1984).
10. Jones and Il Sakong, *Government, Business, and Entrepreneurship in Economic Development: The Korean Case* (Cambridge: Council on East Asian Studies, 1980).
11. I. Kravis, A. Heston, and R. Summers, *World Product and Income: International Comparisons of Real Gross Product* (Baltimore: Johns Hopkins University Press, 1982).

12. Frank, Kim, and Westphal, *Foreign Trade Regimes,* esp. chap. 10.

13. See, for example, R. Leudde-Neurath, *Import Controls and Export-Oriented Development: A Reassessment of the South Korean Case* (Boulder, Colo.: Westview, 1986), pp. 79–87.

14. See the estimates of effective rates of protection reported in B. Balassa, *Development Strategies in Semi-Industrial Economics* (Baltimore: Johns Hopkins University Press, 1982), pp. 28–29, and B. Balassa et al., *The Structure of Protection in Developing Countries* (Baltimore: Johns Hopkins University Press, 1971), pp. 66–67. The data presented in these studies can be used to calculate the standard deviation of the effective rates of protection for Korean goods that is sixth highest among the thirteen nations for which data are presented and at the same general level as the Philippines, Colombia, and Argentina.

15. B. Reynolds, ed., *Reform in China: Challenges and Choices* (Armonk, N.Y.: M. E. Sharpe, 1987).

4

Overview of Results

Throughout the 1970s, until the spring of 1979 when it announced the Comprehensive Stabilization Program, the Korean government carried out the heavy and chemical industry (HCI) policy to promote the development of certain important or key industries, which included iron and steel, nonferrous metal, shipbuilding, general machinery, chemicals, electronics, and others as designated by the president. Tax and trade policies, as well as credit and interest rate policies, were mobilized to promote the development of the heavy and chemical industries.

The tax system provided numerous incentives for the qualified firms in these industries, among the major ones tax holidays, special depreciation rates for fixed capital, and temporary investment tax credit. The legal bases for the preferential treatment were provided by various laws promoting the development of important industries that were already in place at the beginning of the 1970s, and the Tax Exemption and Reduction Control Law that underwent a major revision in line with the HCI policy in late 1974.

The effective tax rates on the marginal return to capital for firms in various industries, estimated under the assumption that firms take full advantage of the major incentives provided by the tax system, clearly shows the substantial differences in the tax treatment afforded between the industries favored by the HCI policy and other manufacturing industries.[1] From the mid-1970s until the early 1980s, the effective tax rate for the "favored" industries taking advantage of tax incentives was below 20 percent on the marginal return to capital, while the effective tax rate for other industries remained close to 50 percent (see Table 4-1 and Figure 4-1). Although these estimates are not the actual tax rates, they clearly illustrate the large bias the tax incentives gave to the favored industries. Subsequent to the reform of the tax system in 1981, the preferential tax treatment had nearly disappeared by 1982.

Table 4-1. Effective Corporate Tax Rate (in percentage)

Industry	1970	1971	1972	1973	1974	1975	1976	1977	1978	1979	1980	1981	1982	1983
Policy favored	39.2	34.9	27.7	33.5	29.9	15.9	18.0	17.5	16.9	18.3	18.3	20.6	47.1	40.4
Chemicals	38.3	34.2	29.5	33.6	33.8	16.9	19.1	19.3	18.2	21.6	17.2	19.5	47.0	41.0
Primary metals	39.9	33.1	24.8	30.8	33.7	12.4	11.9	11.9	11.0	10.6	15.0	16.4	47.5	40.0
Machinery/transport equipment	39.5	37.3	28.8	36.1	22.3	18.3	23.1	21.3	21.6	22.7	22.8	26.0	46.8	40.3
Others	39.4	34.7	29.8	38.6	37.7	52.1	51.0	49.5	48.4	48.5	48.8	51.1	48.2	42.2
Food and beverages	41.9	37.6	32.7	38.3	39.1	52.8	52.3	50.0	48.9	49.1	49.5	51.3	48.8	42.8
Textiles and clothing	38.8	33.1	28.1	38.0	35.6	51.4	50.4	48.8	47.1	46.8	48.0	50.2	47.2	41.3
Wood and furniture	40.2	33.7	28.7	38.1	37.5	52.1	50.8	50.0	48.3	48.4	48.7	52.0	49.0	42.9
Paper and printing	41.7	36.8	33.5	40.0	38.5	53.0	51.6	49.3	48.6	49.3	49.1	51.4	48.4	42.4
Nonmetallic minerals	41.6	38.0	31.7	38.9	37.4	52.0	50.8	50.5	49.7	49.3	48.7	51.0	48.1	42.1
Miscellaneous industries	32.3	29.2	24.1	38.1	37.8	51.3	49.9	48.6	47.6	48.2	49.0	50.6	47.9	41.9

Source: Taewon Kwack, *Depreciation and Taxation of Income from Capital* (Seoul: Korea Development Institute, 1985), reproduced with permission.

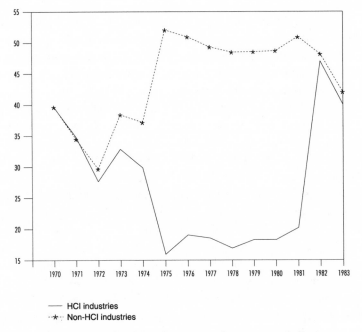

Figure 4-1. *Effective Tax Rates on the Marginal Returns to Capital*

Trade policy was another tool used to assist the favored industries. During the 1970s imports that were thought to compete with the output of the favored industries were severely limited, in a reversal of the import-liberalizing trend that began in the mid-1960s. In 1967 the positive list system of import approval, under which only those items on the list could be imported, was changed to a more liberal negative list system, under which imports required no prior government approval unless listed. At the same time the number of items on the negative list was reduced. As the data in Table 4A-1 show, the import liberalization ratio for the manufacturing sector in 1966 stood at under 8 percent; by 1970 it had risen to 42 percent.[2] During the 1970s, the ratio for the manufacturing sector as a whole declined, albeit marginally, to 40 percent in 1978. Note also that the decline was primarily due to the large drop in the liberalization ratios for the policy-favored industries. As part of the industrial policy, protection for the favored industries was increased by putting some products back on the negative list so that such imports once again required prior government approval. It became virtually impossible for anyone, with the exception of exporters, to import foreign products if domestic firms produced similar or substitute goods in the designated key industries.[3]

The most powerful tool the government used to implement its industrial policy was the allocation of investment funds. Through the National Investment Fund, established in 1974, the government directly allocated investment funds among various manufacturing industries and even among individual investment projects. The commercial banks, largely owned by the government at the time, were also directed to make loans to these investment projects. The loans to heavy and chemical industries and others—so-called policy loans—were offered at preferentially low interest rates. During the HCI period, the policy loans expanded to take on an increasingly large share of the domestic credit.

Table 4-2 shows the shares in total domestic credit to the private sector of three different kinds of policy loans for the 1970–1985 period. One is for foreign trade, which was available primarily for the purpose of financing exports. The other may be called "earmarked," and it includes the loans for the agricultural sector, small- and medium-sized firms, home construction, and some others. These two kinds of loans were available only for specified purposes and were not directly related to the HCI policy. The third is simply the remainder of the policy loans, and it is labeled "unearmarked" in Table 4-2. This was the source of investment funds available to the HCI projects. In 1971 various policy loans accounted for half of all domestic credit to the private sector. By the late 1970s and early 1980s, this share rose to 60 percent, and by 1985 its share fell back to about one-half. This rise and fall in the share of all policy loans is almost entirely due to the change in the share of unearmarked loans. From the mid-1970s to the end of the decade, the share of such loans rose approximately six percentage points, from 27 percent to around 33 percent. Then it declined to around 25 percent by the mid-1980s. Thus, at one point, the government had 60 percent of all domestic credit under its control, and more than half of it went to the projects favored by the industrial policy.

The significance of the credit policy can be better appreciated by looking at the interest rates on the policy loans in Table 4-3. While the loans for foreign trade always enjoyed the lowest interest rate, the favor conferred on loans for HCI investments was substantial. This is clear from a comparison of the interest rate in column 3 charged by the Korea Development Bank on loans to finance the investments in capital equipment in the key industries and the discount rate charged by the commercial banks on commercial bills in column 1. The rates reported in column 3 were 5 to 10 percentage points lower in the first half of the 1970s and about three percentage points lower in the second half; except for one year, they were always lower than the inflation rate (column 4), so that in effect the key industries were charged a negative real interest rate.

Table 4-2. Share of Policy Loans in Domestic Credit (in percentage)

	Unearmarked (1)	Foreign Trade (2)	Earmarked (3)	All Policy Loans (4)
1970	29.67	5.56	12.18	47.41
1971	30.25	6.11	11.91	48.27
1972	26.74	6.71	20.33	53.79
1973	25.54	10.53	19.37	55.44
1974	23.87	11.32	17.48	52.66
1975	27.18	9.01	16.57	52.76
1976	26.29	9.99	16.15	52.43
1977	29.25	10.41	16.18	55.84
1978	32.32	10.81	17.52	60.66
1979	33.43	10.63	14.97	59.03
1980	34.05	11.50	14.23	59.78
1981	31.30	12.73	14.64	58.67
1982	29.61	12.27	12.50	54.38
1983	27.99	12.68	14.03	54.70
1984	26.47	12.72	14.81	54.00
1985	25.12	12.85	14.79	52.77

Notes: "Domestic credit" includes all loans and discounts to the private sector by deposit money banks (commercial banks and special banks), the Korea Development Bank, and the Korea Export-Import Bank.

"Unearmarked" includes loans funded by the National Investment Fund and government fund, loans in foreign currency, and all loans by the Korea Development Bank.

"Foreign trade" includes the loans for foreign trade by deposit money banks and all loans by the Korea Export-Import Bank.

"Earmarked" includes the loans for agricultural industries, small- and medium-sized firms, and home building.

Source: Economic Planning Board, *Korean Economic Indicators* (1986), and Bank of Korea, *Economic Statistics Yearbook* (various issues).

In early 1979, the government estimated that 74 percent and 82 percent of all fixed investments made in the manufacturing sector in 1976 and 1979, respectively, went to the heavy and chemical industries.[4] This was primarily the result of the government's intervention in the allocation of investment funds, but because the preferential loans carried negative real interest rates, strong incentives were also in place for the private sector to invest in the favored industries. Trade policy, by strengthening the bias of the incentive structure, played an important role in complementing other policy measures. By guaranteeing the market for domestic firms, which effectively reduced their risk and artificially raised their profitability, trade policy made the private sector a willing partner of the HCI policy.

Evolution of Korean Manufacturing Industries, 1966–1985

During the 1970s, Korea's manufacturing sector grew very rapidly, with widely varying rates across different industries. This section describes the salient features of this experience, especially those facets that relate to the

Table 4-3. Interest and Inflation Rates (in percent per annum)

	Commercial Banks' Discount on Bills (1)	Interest Rate for Loans for Foreign Trade (2)	Interest Rate on Loans for Equipment to Key Industry (3)	Consumer Price Index (4)
1970	24.30	6.00	12.00	16.01
1971	23.00	6.00	12.00	13.51
1972	17.79	6.00	11.17	11.51
1973	15.50	6.67	10.00	3.20
1974	15.50	8.83	10.00	24.48
1975	15.29	7.67	12.00	25.20
1976	16.33	7.42	12.42	15.27
1977	17.25	8.00	13.00	10.17
1978	18.02	8.58	14.17	14.46
1979	18.75	9.00	15.00	16.26
1980	23.33	12.00	20.50	28.70
1981	19.50	12.00	18.00	21.30
1982	12.38	10.75	12.75	7.25
1983	10.00	10.00	10.00	3.38
1984	10.27	10.00	10.31	2.30
1985	10.75	10.00	9.56	2.47

Notes: The interest rates are weighted averages, with weights equal to the number of months the interest rates were in use in a given year. When source data are given as a range, the midpoint is shown in this table.
Source: Bank of Korea, *Economic Statistics Yearbook* (various issues).

HCI policies of the 1966–1985 period.[5] Manufacturing industries have been aggregated into two groups. The first, referred to as the HC group, consists of industries favored by the HCI policy; the second, referred to as the Light group, covers those not favored by the HCI policy measures. (For a more detailed explanation of the industry groupings, see Appendix 4A.)

Growth of Value-Added

The most outstanding feature in the evolution of the manufacturing sector from the 1970s was its rapid growth, at times exceeding 20 percent per annum in real terms (Table 4-4). However, the pace of growth slowed considerably in the last few years of the 1970s, and output declined in 1980. During the 1980s, the sector's growth partly recouped its earlier speed.

Two other notable features were that the industries belonging to the HC group grew faster than those in the Light group and that for the manufacturing sector in general the double-digit growth rate plunged below 10 percent after 1978. In the 1970–1978 period, the average annual growth rate of the HC group was about 30 percent, twice that of the Light group. The HC group, comprising basic metals, various machineries, including transport equipment, and chemicals, doubled its real value-added every

Table 4-4. Growth in Value-Added and Employment (in percentage change)

	Total Manufacturing	Heavy and Chemical	Light	Electric Machinery	Clothing and Footwear
Value-added					
1966–1970	21.0	23.2	17.8	29.5	18.0
1970–1973	20.2	32.2	19.2	56.4	32.8
1973–1975	13.8	25.0	11.5	19.5	19.6
1975–1978	20.0	31.2	15.7	38.9	16.1
1978–1980	4.8	3.6	5.2	3.7	−5.2
1980–1983	8.0	12.8	6.4	13.8	8.0
1983–1985	9.2	13.5	6.6	12.3	4.0
1970–1978	18.5	30.0	15.9	39.9	23.0
1978–1985	7.4	10.3	6.1	10.4	2.9
Employment					
1966–1970	8.8	11.8	8.2	22.5	0.0
1970–1973	9.6	15.5	8.2	33.1	12.4
1973–1975	15.6	18.0	15.1	21.6	18.6
1975–1978	8.4	13.5	7.0	18.5	8.1
1978–1980	−1.0	2.5	−1.8	3.3	−6.7
1980–1983	2.7	8.3	0.6	3.7	−3.5
1983–1985	2.1	5.1	0.8	4.6	3.0
1970–1978	10.6	15.4	9.4	24.6	12.2
1978–1985	1.4	5.7	−0.1	3.9	−2.6

three years or less. During the 1978–1985 period, the growth rates dropped sharply. The HC group again grew at much faster rates than the Light group, except between 1978 and 1980. As a result, the relative size of these groups changed considerably. In real terms, the value-added of the HC group was only a third as large as the Light group in the early 1970s but became seven-tenths as large by 1985.

Employment Growth
The second half of the 1960s saw a rapid employment growth in the manufacturing sector. It accelerated further during the 1970–1978 period (Table 4-4), to reach an average annual rate of nearly 11 percent. But the rate fell to about 1.4 percent per annum for the period 1978–1985. Although this sharp drop in employment growth is observed for both HC and Light groups, it was more pronounced for the clothing and footwear industries, where employment had surged in the first part of the 1970s and declined in the 1978–1980 period.

Capital Accumulation
Capital accumulation in the manufacturing sector also showed a pattern of rapid growth followed by a sudden slowdown (Table 4-5). The slow- down began in the early 1980s, somewhat later than it did in employment growth. The table also shows that the HC and the Light groups had contrasting

Table 4-5. Rates of Capital Accumulation (in percentage change)

	Total Manufacturing	Heavy and Chemical	Light	Electric Machinery	Clothing and Footwear
1966–1970	11.6	11.0	11.8	22.1	14.4
1970–1973	21.7	23.6	20.2	35.1	23.8
1973–1975	18.9	32.0	14.3	71.8	27.8
1975–1978	14.6	21.6	11.5	16.1	25.8
1978–1980	12.9	13.1	12.8	13.6	6.3
1980–1983	7.9	10.1	6.2	11.1	7.2
1983–1985	8.5	10.4	7.2	24.5	7.5
1970–1978	18.3	24.9	15.4	35.5	25.5
1978–1985	9.5	11.0	8.3	15.5	7.1

experiences in terms of capital accumulation in the mid-1970s. Until the early 1970s, capital accumulation proceeded at roughly the same rate in the two groups, but then capital accumulation accelerated in the HC group while decelerating in the Light group. During the 1973–1978 period, the average annual rate of capital accumulation was more than twice as high in the HC group as in the Light group. This could be the consequence of a response by the private sector to the different rates of return to investment in the two groups, a phenomenon little influenced by the HCI policy. But given that the HCI policy greatly favored the HC group and that the 1973–1978 period almost exactly coincided with the duration of the policy, it is highly likely that the contrasting capital accumulations in the two groups reflect the effect of HCI policy.

Changes in Capital Intensity

The capital intensity of production, measured as a ratio of capital stock to the number of workers employed, is bound to change as employment grows and capital accumulates. As we shall see, the change in capital intensity seems to reflect the effect of the HCI policy more closely than capital accumulation did. Table 4-6 shows that the capital intensity of the manufacturing sector as a whole increased sharply in two different periods. The first was in 1970–1973, when capital intensity increased at an average annual rate of 11 percent. With capital accumulating at about 22 percent per annum, capital intensity jumped even while employment increased by 9.6 percent per annum. The second sharp rise took place in 1978–1980. In contrast to the first episode, capital accumulation was much slower, increasing only by 13 percent, but capital intensity rose faster mainly because the associated levels of employment declined.

Underneath these changes for the manufacturing sector as a whole lay quite distinct movements of capital intensity for the Light and HC groups. A close look at Table 4-6 reveals that the capital intensities of the two groups twice moved in opposite directions, in the 1966–1970 period and again in 1973–1975. This could not have happened if they faced the same wage-rental ratio, because the capital intensity, an increasing function of the wage-rental ratio, must rise or fall in response to a rise or fall in the wage-rental ratio.

Of the two episodes, the 1966–1970 one, when the capital intensity rose for the Light group and declined for the HC group, was more apparent than real. Of twenty-three individual manufacturing industries, seven experienced a decline in capital intensity (see Tables 4A-2 and 4A-3). Of these seven, five were in the Light group and two in the HC group. Thus, the decline in the capital intensity was more widespread among the Light industries than among the HC industries, and a common feature of these industries was that their outputs were rising faster than the manufacturing average (see Table 4A-10). In response to the rapid increase in demand, firms must have temporarily been increasing labor inputs faster than their capital inputs.

On the other hand, in the 1973–1975 episode, where the capital intensity of the Light group declined at an annual rate of 0.7 percent while that of HC group was rising at 12 percent per annum, the contrast was highly unusual. Excluding the group "other manufactures" (see Table 4A-2), which had an inexplicably rapid rise in capital intensity, the capital intensity of the Light group declined by 2.3 percent annually between 1973 and 1975. Textiles, the largest industry in the Light group in terms of value-added and employment, experienced a decline in capital intensity of 18 percent a year. Unlike the 1966–1970 period, in none of the HC industries did capital intensity decline.

Two immediate causes can be posited for the contrasting experience of the two groups over the period 1973–1975. First, the HC group's capital accumulation, at an annual rate of 32 percent, was more than twice as fast as that observed for the Light group, at 14 percent per annum. The second was the employment surge, already noted, in the Light industries. Employment grew at an annual rate of 15 percent for the Light group, a near doubling of the growth rate over the previous period. (The growth rate of employment also rose for the HC group, from 15.5 percent over 1970–1973 to 18 percent over 1973–1975, but this acceleration was relatively modest compared to what happened in the Light group.)

Thus, during the 1973–1978 period, capital intensity rose faster in the HC group than in the Light group. From the late 1970s, as the HCI policy came to an end, this relative speed between the two groups was reversed: the capital intensity rose faster for the Light than for the HC group. For

Table 4-6. Capital Intensity

	Total Manufacturing	Heavy and Chemical	Light	Electric Machinery	Clothing and Footwear
Capital-labor ratio (in million 1980 won/worker)					
1966	3.9	6.9	3.1	2.3	0.3
1970	4.3	6.7	3.5	2.3	0.6
1973	5.9	8.2	4.8	2.4	0.8
1975	6.2	10.2	4.7	4.8	0.9
1978	7.4	12.5	5.3	4.5	1.4
1980	9.6	15.3	7.0	5.5	1.9
1983	11.1	16.0	8.3	6.7	2.6
1985	12.6	17.7	9.4	9.5	2.8
Percentage change in K/L ratio					
1966–1970	2.5	–0.7	3.3	–0.3	14.4
1970–1973	11.1	7.0	11.1	1.5	10.2
1973–1975	2.8	11.9	–0.7	41.2	7.7
1975–1978	5.7	7.1	4.2	–2.1	16.4
1978–1980	14.1	10.3	14.9	10.0	14.0
1980–1983	5.1	1.7	5.6	7.1	11.1
1983–1985	6.3	5.1	6.4	19.0	4.4
1970–1978	7.0	8.2	5.4	8.8	11.8
1978–1985	7.9	5.0	8.4	11.2	10.0

example, in the 1978–1980 subperiod, the capital intensity for the Light group rose much faster, at an average annual rate of 15 percent, as compared to the annual increase of 10 percent observed for the HC group. This more rapid rise in capital intensity continued well into the mid-1980s.

Factor Market Distortion

One can safely infer from the contrasting changes in capital intensity between the HC and Light groups that the two groups faced wildly different wage-rental ratios. During the 1973–1978 period, the wage-rental ratio must have been rising for the HC group but falling or rising very slowly for the Light group. For the 1978–1985 period, almost the opposite must have been the case: the wage-rental ratio was rising for both groups, but the rise must have been faster for the Light than for the HC group.

The wage-rental ratio for the HC and the Light groups would diverge if the rental rates the two groups faced diverged. Since there was no government attempt to fix wages at different rates for the two groups, it seems safe to assume that both faced the same labor market. The key to the explanation must be the effect of HCI policy measures on rental rates, which strongly favored investments in the industries in the HCI group during the 1970s. Various incentives and direct government involvement in credit allocation lowered the capital cost for the HC group but raised it for the Light group. The high cost of capital for the entrepreneurs in the latter group could have simply taken the form of unavailable investment funds from the banks at the government-controlled interest rates or high interest rates in the curb market. Thus, in the 1973–1978 period, the HCI policy must have lowered the wage-rental ratio for the Light group while raising that for the HC group. The decline in the Light group's capital intensity over the period 1973–1975, especially for textiles, suggests a high probability of an absolute fall in the wage-rental ratio for the group.

For the 1978–1985 period, however, the capital intensity of the Light group rose faster than that of the HC group, indicating that the wage-rental ratio rose faster for the former group of industries than for the latter. This could have been brought about by the denominator of the wage-rental ratio's (the rental rate) falling faster for the Light group than for the HC group if the two groups are again assumed to face the same labor market. This was indeed what happened. As one can see in Table 4-3, the interest rates on ordinary commercial loans (column 1) were three to four percentage points higher than the rates for the key industries (column 3), in the late 1970s and early 1980s, that is, toward the end of the HCI policy period and immediately after. By the mid-1980s, the difference almost disappeared. Thus, for the 1978–1985 period, the wage-rental ratio must have risen faster for the Light group than for the HC group.

The Effect of Resource Allocation: Capital Efficiency

This section assesses the effect of the HCI policy on resource allocation by estimating capital efficiency of the manufacturing industries and comparing the estimates. Capital efficiency, that is, the rate of return to capital employed in individual industries, was estimated under the assumption that there were only two factors of production—capital and labor—and that the wage rate was competitively determined.

If diminishing returns prevail, a capital efficiency estimate of the HC group higher than or equal to that of the Light group may be regarded as evidence that the HCI policy improved resource allocation. Since the policy had directed and encouraged investments to the HC group, the capital efficiency of the group would have been still higher than the estimates even without the policy. It must have been that the policy allocated the resources to the industries with higher rates of returns—an improvement in resource allocation and increase in output. Higher capital efficiencies in the HC group than in the Light group could also result if the investments under the HCI policy had the effect of shifting the technology of the HC group to a new, higher level. If this were the case, still greater incentives should have been given to the HC group so that still more capital may have been allocated to the group. On the other hand, if the capital efficiency in the HC group is estimated to be lower than in the Light group, it would indicate that the HCI policy induced excessive investment in the HC group, an evidence of resource misallocation.

This approach is motivated by the simple optimization rule that output is maximized when a resource is allocated so that its marginal product is equalized among different uses. It is also based on the recognition that the HCI policy affected primarily the allocation of capital among the manufacturing industries. Although the approach is clearly founded in comparative static, the estimates of capital efficiencies over the period 1966 to 1985 will shed light on the dynamic effects on resource allocation of the HCI policy.

Estimation Method of the Capital Efficiency

Although the concept of capital efficiency is fairly straightforward, its estimation here encountered a number of statistical problems. The first problem was the availability of value-added data. In order to estimate an industry's capital efficiency, it was necessary to have the constant-price value-added broken out into the components (for example, compensation to labor and indirect taxes). The constant-price value-added originating from individual manufacturing industries was available as part of the national income estimates by the Bank of Korea. However, this source did not break it down into its components. The breakdown was available only in current prices in the input-output (I-O) tables, also estimated by the Bank of Korea. Thus, the proportions of the labor compensation and indirect taxes in constant-price value-added were assumed to be the same as those in current-price value-added obtainable from the I-O tables.

Second, the reported value-added of an industry, in both current and constant prices, included indirect taxes, some of which may have been shifted to the buyers of a firm's output or to the suppliers of intermediate inputs. Hence, not all of the indirect taxes may represent value-added by the factors. Furthermore, how the burden of tax that was not shifted was shared between capital and labor is not known. No attempt was made to estimate the parameters needed in order to clarify these unknowns. Instead, two kinds of capital efficiency estimates were made: one under the assumption that all indirect taxes were shifted, that is, no part of the indirect taxes was value-added created by the factors, and the other under the assumption that half of the indirect taxes were not shifted but borne by capital. Thus, under the latter assumption, half of the indirect taxes were counted as the value-added created by capital.

Third, the compensation to labor reported in the I-O tables was that made to paid workers. Since there are unpaid workers—self-employed and family workers—the reported labor compensation understates the value-added created by labor. The value-added created by all workers in an industry was estimated by using the numbers of paid and unpaid workers that I-O tables provided. The reported compensation was first divided by the number of paid employees, and the quotient was multiplied by the total number employed. The result is taken to be the compensation that would have been made to all workers, had the unpaid workers gotten on average the same wage as the paid employees. This imputed compensation is assumed equal to the value-added created by the labor.[6]

Fourth, there was a valuation problem. Value-added in constant price, denoted as VA, as estimated by the Bank of Korea, consists of three elements, as follows:

(4.1)

$$VA = VA_e^* + VA_d + T,$$

where VA_e^* and VA_d are the parts due to export sales and due to domestic sales, respectively, and T represents indirect taxes. The valuation problem arises because prices need not be the same in the domestic and international markets when the former is protected. In Korea, value-added in producing exports can be taken as being reflective of international prices, since imported inputs for exports faced few nontariff barriers and were available at international prices, thanks to the tariff rebate system. On the other hand, protection of an industry tends to raise the domestic prices of the industry's outputs and value-added. Hence, the sum in equation 4.1 represents a sum of two items valued in different prices.[7]

Initially ignoring this valuation problem, two kinds of capital efficiency are estimated. The first, denoted as $q1$, was estimated under the assumption that all indirect taxes were shifted forward or backward and were not borne by the capital, as follows:

(4.2)

$$q1_i = \frac{VA_i \, (1 - t_i - s1_i)}{K_i},$$

where the subscript i denotes the ith industry, K stands for capital stock, and $s1$ and t are, respectively, the proportions of imputed labor compensation and indirect taxes in the current-price value-added.

Second, capital efficiency was estimated under the assumption that half of the indirect taxes were borne by the capital. The resulting measure of capital efficiency, $q2$, is defined as:

(4.3)

$$q2_i = \frac{VA_i\,(1-0.5t_i - s1_i)}{K_i}.$$

These two measures of capital efficiency, $q1$ and $q2$, do not yet take into account the fact that domestic sales and exports are valued under two different price regimes. Thus, a third measure, taking this into account, was estimated under the assumption that all indirect taxes were shifted away, the same assumption used in the estimation of $q1$. First, an industry's constant-price value-added less indirect taxes was divided into the proportion due to exports and that due to domestic sales, VA^*_e and VA_d, as follows:

(4.4)

$$VA^*_e = VA\,(1-t)\,sx$$

(4.5)

$$VA_d = VA\,(1-t)\,(1-sx)$$

where sx is the proportion of exports in an industry's current-price gross output less indirect tax, and the subscripts are suppressed. (See Table 4A-7 for sx.)

Then VA_d was deflated by the effective rate of protection and summed with the VA^*_e to yield a measure of value-added in international prices. From this sum, labor's imputed incomes were subtracted, and the result was divided by the industry's capital stock to obtain the third measure of capital efficiency:

(4.6)

$$q3 = \left[VA^*_e + \frac{VA_d}{(1+z)} \right]\left(1 - \frac{s1}{1-t}\right),$$

where z is the effective rate of protection, and $s1/(1-t)$ is the share of labor income in the current prices value-added after subtracting indirect taxes. Because indirect taxes are subtracted from the value-added, labor's share expands by a factor of $1/(1-t)$. This measure of capital efficiency was estimated for the years 1970, 1975, 1978, and 1983, when effective protection estimates were readily available.[8] (See Table 4A-8 for z.)

Estimation Results

The estimated capital efficiency, $q1$, of individual industries is shown in Table 4A-4; Figure 4-2 shows the results for the HC and Light. We also report estimates for a new industry group, which consists of the HC group but excludes the electric machinery sector, while estimates for $q2$ are shown in Table 4A-5 and Figure 4-3. Finally, Figure 4-4 shows the estimates for $q3$ for industry groups. (The full details are set out for individual industries in Table 4A-6.)

As expected, $q2$ was greater than $q1$, since the former regarded half of indirect taxes as created by capital. In addition, notice that in Figures 4-2 and 4-3 the difference in capital efficiency between the HC and Light groups as measured by $q2$ is wider than that measured by $q1$. The reason was that indirect taxes made up for a greater proportion of the value-added in the light industries than in the heavy and chemical industries. Hence, the margin by which $q2$ is greater than $q1$ is greater for the Light group than for the HC group. Leaving this difference aside, the two estimates show similar trends.

There were two salient features in the estimated capital efficiency. One was common to Light and HC groups, and the other revealed a difference between the two groups. The common feature was the general trend revealed by the estimates of $q1$ and $q2$ for the entire period under study. In the 1966–1973 period, the capital efficiency rose steeply; for the remainder of the 1970s, the rise stopped or decelerated; and in the 1980s the efficiency fell below the level observed in the 1970s. Estimates of $q3$, though available only for four years, tend to confirm this trend.

The rapid increase in the capital efficiency in the 1966–1973 period was, of course, the result of the returns to capital increasing faster than the capital stocks. The manufacturing sector value-added, including returns to capital, increased at an average annual rate in excess of 20 percent during the period. On the other hand, the average annual rates of growth for employment and capital accumulation were 8.8 percent and 11.6 percent, respectively, in the 1966–1970 period, accelerating to 9.6 and 21.7 in the 1970–1973 period. It appears that until the early 1970s, industry was in a transition, with employment of labor and capital stock at lower levels than those considered to be desirable by firms, and the factor inputs to growth accelerated to catch up with output growth. The rapid increase in capital efficiency in the 1966–1973 period appears to be a reflection of this stock adjustment process, which could not continue indefinitely.

The second feature that the estimates reveal is that capital efficiency was estimated to be higher in the Light group than in the HC group from

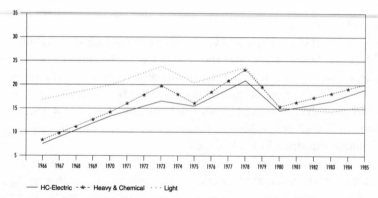

Figure 4-2. Capital Efficiency, q1

the mid-1960s until the end of the 1970s. This efficiency difference between the two groups is of interest because it tells us if the HCI policy improved resource allocation. According to the estimates of $q1$ and $q2$, the difference remained unchanged in the 1966–1973 period, but it seems to have narrowed for the rest of the 1970s, and in the 1980s the efficiency in the HC exceeded that in the Light.

Resource Misallocation

What do these estimation results imply regarding the effect of the HCI policy on resource allocation? Consider first the estimates for the second half of the 1960s. The capital efficiency was much higher in the Light group than in the HC group, and the efficiency was rising in both groups. This could not have much to do with the HCI policy, although industries belonging to the HC group were somewhat favored during the 1960s by the many promotional laws in place even then. The incentives to invest in heavy and chemical industries could not have been as strong in the second half of the 1960s and 1970s. As we have seen, the difference in the effective corporate tax rates between the HC and the Light groups began to widen after 1973. Similarly, direct government intervention in credit allocation in favor of the heavy and chemical industries did not begin in earnest until the mid-1970s. Thus, the HCI policy cannot explain the higher capital efficiency of the Light group compared to the HC.

The rising capital efficiency must have been a phenomenon in a transitory period. An industry's capital efficiency rises only if the value-added rises faster than capital input. The second half of the 1960s was likely such a period. The explosive export expansion that accelerated the

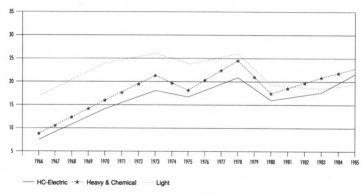

Figure 4-3. Capital Efficiency, q2

growth of Korea's manufacturing sector began in the early 1960s. By 1966, the first year when the capital efficiencies were estimated, only several years had passed. At the time firms must have been increasing employment of factors as fast as they could but still not fast enough to keep up with the rapid rise in value-added, causing the capital efficiency to rise.

Why, then, was the capital efficiency lower in the HC group than in the Light group while it was rising in both groups? The answer must have something to do with the fact that exports of the industries belonging to the Light group accounted for nearly all of Korea's export growth in the 1960s. Hence, the Light group's value-added and its capital efficiency must have begun to increase earlier than the HC group's. Thus, it is not surprising that the capital efficiency of the Light group was higher than that of the HC group while both were rapidly rising during the transitory period.

This transitory period would normally end as the capital efficiency of the Light group leveled off while that of the HC group kept rising so that the efficiency of the two groups became roughly equal. This indeed appears to have taken place (see Figures 4-2 and 4-3). Especially in Figure 4-2, by the late 1970s the capital efficiency of the HC group slightly exceeded that of the Light group.

Before accepting this conclusion, we note that it makes a considerable difference in the efficiency estimate whether electric machinery is counted as a part of the HC group. Excluding electric machinery from the HC group considerably lowers its efficiency, especially in 1978 (see Figures 4-2 and 4-3). Electric machinery was an industry favored by the HCI policy, and this is the reason that it is included in the HC group. However, its high capital efficiency in the 1970s may be as much a consequence of the changing pattern of Korea's comparative advantage

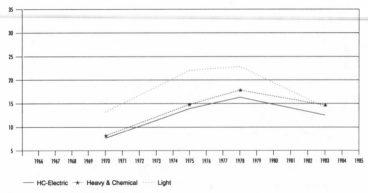

Figure 4-4. *Capital Efficiency, q3*

dictated by the industry's production characteristics as the effects of the favors of the HCI policy. As noted earlier, electric machinery is more capital intensive than clothing but less so than textiles (see Table 4A-2). As a rising wage rate shifts the comparative advantage away from labor-intensive industries such as clothing to more capital-intensive ones, electric machinery is likely to become competitive at an earlier point in time than other HC industries. Electric machinery, with its value-added nearly as large as clothing's, was already one of the most rapidly growing industries in the 1960s and 1970s. If electric machinery is excluded from the HC group (see Figures 4-2 and 4-3), the conclusion that the efficiency gap between the HC and Light groups narrowed during the 1970s is not very convincing.

In addition, it should be recognized that protection raises the prices of an industry's output and inputs above the free-trade levels. Hence, the part of an industry's value-added due to domestic sales often increases in value and does not reflect the true value to the society of the factor services rendered in producing it. This artificial increase in value due to protection under the HCI policy has to be deflated before true capital efficiency can be obtained.

The third measure of capital efficiency, $q3$, deflates value-added by the effective rates of protection, as shown in equation 4.6. According to this measure, the margin by which the capital efficiency of the Light group was greater than that of the HC group was five percentage points in the 1970s. This difference widened to seven percentage points in 1975, falling back to five percentage points in 1978 and virtually disappearing by 1983.

Consider the implication of the above on the effects of the HCI policy under the assumptions that the production functions of the manufacturing industries are linearly homogeneous and that the labor compensation equals its marginal product. Under these assumptions, the estimated capital efficiency may be taken as the marginal product of capital, expressed in percentage terms, since under a linearly homogeneous production function, output is exhausted by the products of factor inputs multiplied by their marginal products.

The discussion of the capital efficiency estimates indicates that the marginal product of capital was lower in the heavy and chemical industries favored by the HCI policy than in the light industries during the 1970s. Static optimum allocation of a scarce resource requires equalization of its marginal product among different uses at a given point in time. The marginal product of capital in the two industry groups could have been brought more in line with each other had capital accumulation been slower in the favored HC industries and faster in the Light industries under diminishing returns—that is, if there had not been the HCI policy.

In a dynamic sense, optimum allocation does not require the returns to capital of different industries to be equalized every year. In an industry, the return may be low at first if subsequently it becomes large enough to make up for the earlier low levels. However, it has to justify the low capital efficiency estimates in the 1970s for the HC group on this ground. While a big surge in capital efficiency is required later in time for the justification, instead the group's efficiency declined in the 1980s (see Figures 4-2 through 4-4). The surge may take place in the 1990s or even later. But the later it happens, the greater the efficiency surge has to be for the early low levels to be justified. Given that the capital efficiency or real rate of return to manufacturing capital was as high as 20 percent, which may be regarded as the discount rate to use in obtaining the present value of future returns, it seems hard to justify the excessive investments in the HC group.

Export Competitiveness

The previous section estimated the capital efficiency of the manufacturing industries in an attempt to assess the effect of the HCI policy on resource allocation. The estimation results of high capital efficiency for the Light group and low efficiency for the HC group, and the efficiency gaps between the two groups failing to narrow during the 1970s, suggest that the policy resulted in misallocation of resources. This section considers another effect of the HCI policy: the effect on export competitiveness, determined by examining Korea's share in world exports.

Table 4-7 shows two measures of Korea's market share in world exports: a percentage share in the total world exports (labeled "world exports") and total world exports less OPEC exports (labeled "adjusted world exports"). In this measure, OPEC exports are excluded from the world total to control the effects of the oil price rise, which reduces a nonoil exporter's market share. However measured, Korea's share in world exports, which was rising rapidly, peaked in 1978 and fell over the following two years before rising again. This unmistakable drop in Korea's market share indicates that there must have been other reasons for the drop besides the oil price rise.

It is possible that the drop in Korea's market share was caused by a shift in world demand away from Korea's export products. In order to see if this was indeed the case, Korea's share in world exports is compared with the sum of the shares of six countries whose export products composition was most similar to Korea's in the late 1970s.[9] In contrast to Korea's share, the combined share of these competitors continued to rise in the latter half of the 1970s (Table 4-7). Hence, a shift in world demand could not have been the reason for the decline in Korea's share in world exports. The reason must have been a deterioration of competitiveness, and the cause lay inside Korea.

Thus, Korea's market shares were examined in the world exports of both the HC and Light product groups (Table 4-8). Although these groups cover only the major export goods of the industries, they accounted for 80 percent or more of all exports of manufactures, as shown in the last column of the table. Korea's shares in these world exports show very distinct trends.

Korea's share in the world exports of HC products continued to rise throughout the 1970s and in the 1980s. The only exception to this trend was the drop in 1975, the year of the world recession. On the other hand, regarding Korea's share in Light products, the trend in the first half of the 1970s was a relatively smooth and rapid expansion in market share, while toward the end of the 1970s the market share virtually stood still or declined.

There are reasons to believe that the impact of the HCI policy explains the contrasting experience of the two export products groups. As we saw, there was a considerable slowdown in capital accumulation in the Light group, which produced the traditional major export goods. According to Yoo, a 1 percent increase in production capacity had the effect of reducing the export price of heavy and chemical industry products by 0.37 percent and the export price of light industry products (very close to the definition of Light group used here) by a full percentage point.[10] The estimation, based on quarterly data from the first quarter of 1972 to the third quarter of 1982, suggests that the export products of

Table 4-7. Market Shares in World Exports (in percentage)

	Korea's Share		Competitors' Share in World Exportsc
	World Exports[a]	Adjusted World Exports[b]	
1970	0.296	0.315	3.682
1971	0.337	0.364	3.970
1972	0.431	0.465	4.257
1973	0.615	0.669	4.327
1974	0.578	0.690	4.101
1975	0.639	0.745	3.935
1976	0.854	1.007	4.493
1977	0.965	1.129	4.435
1978	1.059	1.206	4.658
1979	0.988	1.153	4.898
1980	0.937	1.121	5.183
1981	1.157	1.367	5.474
1982	1.271	1.461	5.540
1983	1.462	1.637	5.776
1984	1.654	1.826	6.442
1985	1.697	1.854	6.625
1986	1.749	1.856	6.611

[a]Sum of exports from all countries.
[b]Sum of exports from all non-OPEC countries.
[c]Competitors are Hong Kong, Israel, Portugal, Spain, Taiwan, and Yugoslavia.
Sources: International Monetary Fund, *International Financial Statistics* (various issues); United Nations, *Yearbook of International Trade Statistics* (various issues).

light industries could have been more competitive had there been more fixed investment in the sector.

The difference in the behavior of the two groups of export products may also be related to the overvaluation of the won in the latter half of the 1970s. The exchange rate was kept constant at 484 won/US$ from 1974 to 1979, although the domestic inflation rate exceeded that of Korea's trading partners, resulting in overvaluation of the won. This period almost exactly overlaps with the period when Korea's share in world exports stopped expanding or even declined for the light industries. However, in order to explain the contrasting experience between the two groups regarding the market share with the fixed exchange rate, one has to believe that the overvaluation of the won does not affect the competitiveness of the HC products, while having a damaging effect on the competitiveness of the Light products. The more probable explanation would be that the effect of the won overvaluation reinforced the HCI policy on the competitiveness of the light industries' export products and, ultimately, of total exports in the late 1970s. Furthermore, a main reason that the fixed exchange rate was maintained during the HCI regime was to lighten, in local currency terms, the repayment burden of foreign debt that financed the policy-favored investments in the HC industries. In this

Table 4-8. Korea's Market Shares in World Exports of HC and Light Products (in percentage)

	HC Products[a]	Light Products[b]	Share of Manufactured Exports Accounted For
1968	0.03	1.35	83.18
1969	0.07	1.50	81.66
1970	0.07	1.83	87.24
1971	0.09	2.13	88.05
1972	0.20	2.45	87.83
1973	0.33	3.52	84.69
1974	0.42	3.44	84.46
1975	0.33	4.13	84.23
1976	0.48	5.51	84.38
1977	0.54	5.56	80.32
1978	0.70	5.92	83.93
1979	0.71	5.52	82.72
1980	0.80	5.27	82.67
1981	1.04	6.40	82.19
1982	1.25	6.10	83.36
1983	1.60	6.23	85.00

[a]Includes chemical elements and compounds (SITC 51); petroleum products (SITC 332); iron and steel (SITC 67); nonferrous metals (SITC 68); nonelectrical machinery (SITC 71); electrical machinery (SITC 72); and transport equipment (SITC 73).
[b]Includes rubber products (SITC 62); plywood (SITC 631); textiles (SITC 65); travel goods (SITC 83); clothing (SITC 84); footwear (SITC 85); and miscellaneous manufactures (SITC 89).
Sources: UN, *Yearbook of International Trade Statistics* (various issues), and authors' calculations.

sense the exchange rate policy was part of the HCI policy, and the effects on export performance should be regarded as part of the cost of that policy.

The 1979 Stabilization Program and the Policies in the 1980s

Thus far, our attention has focused on the HCI policy and its influence on the manufacturing sector. This section considers the overall performance of the economy and the background of the government decision in the spring of 1979 to discontinue the HCI policy. It also briefly discusses the direction of new industrial policy that emerged in the 1980s.

Data on the economy's performance over the period 1971 through the mid-1980s are presented in Table 4-9. Inflation, which had subsided after the first oil crisis, reemerged toward the end of the 1970s. The nominal wage, which had risen at an approximate annual rate of 30 percent from the mid-1970s, marginally decelerated in 1979. In foreign trade, real export growth sharply decelerated in 1977 and declined absolutely in 1979. Economic growth slackened, resulting in negative 4.8 percent growth in 1980.

The negative growth is often attributed to several unfavorable external developments. Above all, the second oil crisis in 1979, which adversely affected the world economy and international trade, is cited as a major reason. Others allude to the political uncertainty following the assassination of President Park in late 1979. In 1980, the unusually cool weather during the summer severely reduced the agricultural output in the fall. Although all of these factors influenced economic developments, they could not have been responsible for the worsening economic performances in the preceding years, 1978 and 1979, or for the rapid slowdown in real export growth that began as early as 1977.

In the late 1970s, it became apparent that the accumulated effects of the industrial policy were beginning to overwhelm the growth momentum generated and sustained since the early 1960s. Fortunately, the seriousness of the situation was recognized, and substantial changes began to be introduced in economic policy during the spring of 1979. In April 1979, the government announced the Comprehensive Stabilization Program, which attempted to redress the excesses of the HCI policy of the 1970s. The program was based on the recognition that the industrial policies had caused havoc in all aspects of the country's economic life: management of macroeconomic policies; management of small- and large-scale firms, in both the favored sectors and other industries; competitiveness in the export markets; and credit standing in the international financial market. Rather than set the general framework for industrial development, macroeconomic policies had become a hostage held by the industrial policies.

The stabilization program cited the following problems as being directly related to the excessive investment in the favored heavy and chemical industries: the increase in investment that outpaced the increase in the supply of skilled labor or the capacity to absorb the related technology, development of bottlenecks in the supply of light industry products, and low rates of capacity utilization. The extent of the capacity utilization problem is easily seen in Table 4-10, which was included in the announcement of the Comprehensive Stabilization Program. The major contents of the program included:

- Restrictive budget management with expenditure cuts and deferral of public investment projects.
- Restrictive monetary policy with particular attention given to improving the operation of preferential policy loans and interest rates.
- Plans to adjust investments in the heavy and chemical industries.
- Measures to facilitate the supply and stabilize the price of daily necessities.

Table 4-9. Selected Economic Indicators, 1971–1986 (in percentage change)

Year	Gross National Product	Wholesale Price Index	Consumer Price Index	Wages	Real Exports	Trade Balance ($ millions)
1971	9.1	8.6	13.5	16.2	29.45	– 1,045.9
1972	5.3	13.8	11.7	13.9	50.22	– 573.9
1973	14.0	6.9	3.1	18.0	57.20	– 566.0
1974	8.5	42.1	24.3	35.3	9.26	– 1,936.8
1975	6.8	26.5	25.3	27.0	22.76	– 1,671.4
1976	13.4	12.2	15.3	34.7	35.79	– 590.5
1977	10.7	9.0	10.1	33.8	19.06	– 476.6
1978	11.0	11.6	14.1	34.3	14.36	– 1,780.8
1979	7.0	18.8	18.3	28.6	–0.96	– 4,384.1
1980	4.8	38.9	28.7	22.7	11.39	– 4,384.1
1981	6.6	20.4	21.3	20.1	17.65	– 3,628.3
1982	5.4	4.7	7.2	14.7	6.43	– 2,594.4
1983	11.9	0.2	3.4	12.2	16.29	– 1,763.5
1984	8.4	0.7	2.3	8.1	15.66	– 1,035.9
1985	5.4	0.9	2.5	9.9	7.56	– 19.4
1986	11.7	1.5	2.8	9.2	12.98	+4,205.9

Source: Economic Planning Board, *Major Statistics of the Korean Economy, 1987* (Seoul: Economic Planning Board, 1987).

- Measures to prevent real estate speculation.
- Measures to support low-income groups.

The monetary and fiscal policies envisaged in the program were being implemented when, later in the year, the government switched to a reflationary policy package in response to the second oil crisis and the recession abroad. Nevertheless, the program was a turning point that set the economic policy off in a new direction, expressed at that time as the pursuit of a private-sector led economy as opposed to a government-led economy. The basic tenet that became more firmly established over the following years consisted of attaining price stability, establishing an unbiased incentive structure, and promoting competition within the domestic market and from abroad. The emphasis shifted from the promotion of particular industries to overall economic efficiency and from the intervention at the industry and firm level to greater reliance on the market.

Conservative management of fiscal and monetary policies succeeded in reducing the double-digit inflation rate to under 3 or 4 percent a year by 1983 (Table 4-9). The effort to bring inflation under control was helped by the decline in international crude oil prices and other raw materials, for which Korea heavily depended on imports. As inflation declined, the government reduced the subsidy elements in the preferential policy loans

Table 4-10. Capacity Utilization Rates of Selected Industries (in percentage)

Industry	1978	1979
Industrial machinery	62	60
Shipbuilding	28	29
Color television	54	26

Source: Economic Planning Board, *Comprehensive Stabilization Program* (April 1979).

by lowering the interest rates on nonpreferential policy loans faster than the rates on policy loans, with the result that the differential between the two types of loans largely disappeared in the early 1980s. Government-owned stocks of commercial banks were sold to the public as a measure to increase the banks' independence of government influence.

In order to counterbalance the increased concentration of economic power that had occurred under the HCI policy, the Anti-Monopoly and Fair Trade Act was enacted toward the end of 1980, and a Fair Trade Commission was created. The act also reduced the number of products whose prices had been under government control on the grounds that they were monopolistic or oligopolistic items. Establishment of small- and medium-sized firms was encouraged, and various support measures for them were devised in recognition of the reality that they could not compete with the giant conglomerates on an equal footing. Over the years there had been increasing dissatisfaction with the plethora of special laws purported to promote particular industries. These laws were either abolished altogether or replaced in 1986 by the Industrial Development Law, which was based on the principle that policy supports to specific industries should be abandoned in favor of functional supports.

Import liberalization measures were extended as an essential remedy against inflation and the distorted incentive structure. The government removed an increasing number of importables from the negative list (those that needed prior government approval to be imported) despite broad public opposition. The import liberalization ratio rose even during the late 1970s and early 1980s when the balance of payments was in severe deficit.

Conclusion: An Assessment of the Role of the Korean Government

Until recently the Korean government's intervention in the economy had been extensive, and at times pervasive. Although the two decades of the 1960s and the 1970s did not differ much in terms of the extent of government intervention, the content of the economic policies that were followed differed significantly. In the 1960s, the primary goal of nearly all economic policies was export expansion; in the 1970s, changes in the international economic and noneconomic scenes led the government to build a more advanced industrial structure, similar to those found in the advanced industrial countries. To pursue that goal, the government became directly and extensively involved in resource allocation at the sectoral, industry, and even firm levels. Thus, the decades of the 1960s and 1970s are fairly distinct in the content of government policies, while the 1980s are distinct from the two previous decades in that government intervention declined substantially.

The economic policies in the 1960s worked much better than the policies of the 1970s in terms of export development. Although protection of domestic industries was substantial, the main policy emphasis in the 1960s was to encourage the private sector's exports through a variety of incentives. This approach seems to have had two advantages over the industrial policy in the 1970s. First, the policy was results oriented. Under the policy in the 1960s, it was the private sector that made the efforts to achieve increased exports. In contrast, the policy in the 1970s was pro-cess oriented, which in no way abandoned the goal of export expansion but attempted to achieve the goal by promoting certain industries.[11] Under this approach, the government was deeply involved in picking the "right" industries and supplying them with the needed investment funds and complementary factors at the "right" price, time, and place. In effect, it was the government that tried to achieve the results.

The second advantage the export promotion policy of the 1960s had over the industrial policy in the 1970s is related to the effects the policy had on the incentive structure. In the 1960s, the government implemented export promotion policies on top of the protective measures of domestic production in the 1950s. The net effect was that numerous export incentives offset the bias against exports that had been engendered by the protection of domestic industries. One study concludes, after quantification of the effects of various policy measures at the time, that the incentives for firms to sell their products in the domestic market or to export were almost equal in the late 1960s.[12]

If this was, in fact, the case, the incentive system could not have remained neutral under the industrial policy of the 1970s, which had a strong import-substitution focus, with a bias in favor of domestic sales. Not surprisingly, exports expanded faster, and the economy performed better in the 1960s when the private sector faced a neutral incentive system than in the 1970s when the government attempted to substitute itself for the private sector and created a bias for domestic sales.

It is possible to disagree with this assessment of the effect of government intervention and call attention to the rapid export expansion and economic growth in the 1980s, arguing that the industrial policy in the 1970s laid the ground for the strong economic performance in the late 1980s. This argument sounds plausible in that the increases in Korea's exports in the 1980s were most visibly seen in such products as various kinds of consumer electronics, semiconductors, other computer-related products, telecommunications equipment, and passenger cars. These are the products of "heavy" industries that were promoted under the HCI policies. Should the economic policies of the 1970s, no matter how wrong they may appear now, be credited with the success of the 1980s? Is the rapid economic growth of the 1980s proof of the desirability of an industrial targeting policy? Before reaching any conclusion, it is necessary to consider the reasons for the rapid export expansion and economic growth and ask some counterfactual questions.

First, the increase in Korean exports was largely due to circumstances that could not have been anticipated in the 1970s when the industrial targeting policy was formulated or implemented. Most of the rapid increase in Korean exports in the 1980s was due to exports to the United States. From 1980 to 1987, Korean exports increased by $30 billion. Of this increment, nearly half went to the United States. The big increase in Korean exports to the United States was a part of the surge in U.S. imports, which resulted primarily from the failure of the U.S. government to close its fiscal deficit. Korean exports also benefited from the depreciation of the real effective exchange rate, due to an 8 percent depreciation of the won/dollar exchange rate in 1985 and the steep appreciation of the Japanese yen and German mark since that time.

Second, much of the rise in Korean exports was due to U.S. restrictions on imports from Japan, which created a market for Korean products at the cost of imports from Japan. These developments were especially favorable to the exports by the industries targeted by the industrial policy of the 1970s. These exogenous external developments contributed to the rapid increase in Korean exports to the United States and the rest of the world and were, of course, unforeseen by the policymakers who set forth the industrial development agenda of the 1970s.

One could argue that the industrial policies should get some credit, although their economic benefit may have been for unanticipated reasons. Two counterfactual questions seem important in this regard. First, what would have been the result if the government had persisted in its policy of promoting certain industries at the expense of others? There seems to be little doubt that the state of the economy would have worsened if the Comprehensive Stabilization Program of the 1979 had not corrected economic policy. This was exactly the reason that the same government that vigorously pursued the industrial targeting policy reversed its policy with the announcement of the program. If the industrial policy had been continued, the economy would have been seriously damaged, at least over the short term, and could not have benefited from the external developments that contributed so much to the export expansion in the 1980s. It is easier to create a heavy manufacturing capacity than it is to ensure that such capacity can compete internationally.

The second counterfactual question to ask is, What would have happened if the government had not promoted the heavy and chemical industries during the 1970s? If the current economic conditions in the 1980s are better than a plausible answer to the counterfactual question, then one could argue that government policy had desirable effects even though the effects were due to unanticipated reasons. To answer this question directly in a satisfactory fashion is very difficult. One possible solution is to look at the performance of Taiwan, an economy that was similarly situated in the mid-1970s but did not adopt the same kind of industrial policy. While any such comparison is fraught with statistical difficulties, it is clear that neither Taiwan's exports nor its income growth suffered as a result of following a different development strategy. To the contrary, Taiwan's exports expanded faster than Korea's. Although the composition of Taiwan's exports remains heavily concentrated on labor-intensive exports, Korea's exports have moved strongly to capital-intensive products.[13] The difference in the change in the commodity structure reflects the difference in the development strategy. Unlike Korea, Taiwan did not engage in a deliberate effort to change the structure of its industrial sector. Korea, like Taiwan and other newly industrialized economies, did not need an HCI policy to take advantage of the expanding export opportunities that had developed in the United States and other parts of the world. Only the product composition of Korean exports would have been different without the policy.

Finally, were the structural changes observed in Korea over the 1970s in any sense unusual, or were they the result of the transformation expected as income per capita rises? Comparing the changes in both industrial structure and export composition for six rapidly growing countries—Brazil,

Korea, Malaysia, Mexico, Philippines, Taiwan, and Thailand—provides little statistical evidence that the structural transformation in Korea was significantly different from those observed in other rapidly developing countries, once changes in per capita income are taken into account.[14] Although the HCI policies accelerated the changes in industrial structure and export composition and moved the economy away from labor-intensive production and exports, they did not dramatically alter the process of development.

The government's actual role in the experience of Korean economic growth was very different from the popular perception, inside and outside Korea, that the phenomenal increase in its exports and economic growth was due to industrial targeting. The government was not successful in the area of industrial policies, through which it attempted to create an advanced industrial structure in a short time period. When the economy performed well under extensive government intervention, as in the 1960s, the net effect of intervention was a neutral incentive system. The case in support of the Korean government's role in economic development seems stronger when its policies were not actively interventionist, such as policies that controlled inflation through conservative management of fiscal and monetary policies, maintained the trade regime that provided Korean exporters with access to foreign intermediate goods at international prices, liberalized imports, or corrected the overvaluation of the exchange rate. In many ways, the government's greatest contribution was its willingness to reconsider policies once they were found not to work. The ultimate criterion of policy decisions was economic performance, and the economic policy flexibly adapted to changing domestic and international circumstances. Ironically, the flexibility in economic policy was a product of an authoritarian government. Having come into power with questionable legitimacy, the Park Chung Hee and Chun Doo Hwan governments relied heavily on the performance of the economy to build and maintain their legitimacy, and the power elite left economic decision making largely in the hands of the technocrats. In general, Korean technocrats and bureaucrats have not had strong vested interests in the welfare of certain social classes, certain sectors, or certain industries of the economy. Their policy choices were more generally guided by a concern for overall economic performance. This is not to say that the political system or the bureaucracy was immune to the influence of interest groups or was corruption free. However, decisions on the details constituting the overall policy framework, especially those not materially affecting general economic performance, were more likely to have been influenced by pressures from interest groups.

Appendix 4A: Description of the Data

Value-Added

Value-added for the manufacturing industries is estimated as part of the national income estimates by the Bank of Korea. It was available in 1980 won at the three-digit Korean Standard Industrial Classification (KSIC) level.

Labor and Labor Share

The numbers of laborers employed in the manufacturing industries were obtained from employment tables, part of the input-output tables estimated by the Bank of Korea. The employment tables distinguish two groups of laborers: paid employees and unpaid workers, which includes the self-employed and family members. The number of laborers used in this study is the simple sum of the two groups.

Capital Stock

Pyo's estimates of capital stocks are used.[15] Included in these estimates are buildings and structures, machinery and equipment, and transportation equipment. Employing the polynomial-benchmark method, Pyo made use of investment data from two national wealth surveys for the years 1968 and 1977: the census and annual surveys of the mining and manufacturing sectors. He made two series of capital stock estimates: gross and net. The estimates were available at the three-digit KSIC level.

This study uses Pyo's estimates of gross capital stock in 1980 constant prices. Some adjustments on the estimates were made before using them. In a few instances, Pyo estimated the combined capital stock of two three-digit KSIC industries.[16] In these instances, the estimated capital stocks were split into two, one for each component industry, in the following way. First, Pyo's capital stock for 1973 was split into two by referring to the component industries' book values of capital stocks reported in the mining and manufacturing census for the same year. The splitting was done according to the component industry's share in the sum of the book values of the capital stocks. In the second step, annual increments in Pyo's capital stock were again split into two. This time, an increment was split according to the component industry's share in the sum of the acquisition of new capital stocks. In the last step, to obtain a new time series of capital stock for a component industry, the split increment of capital stock was added to the split capital stock for the years after 1973 or was subtracted from it for the earlier years.

Industry Grouping

The manufacturing sector consists of twenty-seven three-digit KSIC industries. At this level of aggregation KSIC is identical to the International Standard Industrial Classification (ISIC). Two industries—plastic products (KSIC 385) and industries not elsewhere classified (KSIC 356)—are omitted from the analysis for lack of data. These two activities accounted for about 1.5 percent of total manufacturing value-added in 1970 and less than 3 percent in 1985. In all the analysis the phrase "manufacturing total" is to be taken as excluding these two industries.

The analysis divides manufacturing into two groups: those that were favored by the HCI policy and those that were not. The favored group contains eight three-digit KSIC industries:

Industrial chemical (KSIC 351)
Oil refining (KSIC 353)
Iron and steel (KSIC 371)
Nonferrous metals (KSIC 372)
Metal products (KSIC 381)
Nonelectrical machinery (KSIC 382)
Electrical machinery (KSIC 383)
Transport equipment (KSIC 384)

The other seventeen industries are:

Food products (KSIC 311 and 312)
Tobacco (KSIC 314)
Textiles (KSIC 321)
Clothing (KSIC 322)
Leather and fur products (KSIC 323)
Footwear (KSIC 324)
Wood products (KSIC 331)
Furniture (KSIC 332)
Paper (KSIC 341)
Printing and publishing (KSIC 342)
Other chemicals (KSIC 352)
Petroleum and coal products (KSIC 354)
Rubber products (KSIC 355)
Pottery, china, and earthenware (KSIC 361)
Other nonmetallic mineral products (KSIC 369)
Other manufactures (KSIC 390)

In order to facilitate the analysis, the industries favored by the HCI policy, excluding oil refining, are aggregated and labeled the heavy and chemical industry group or (HC group). Oil refining was excluded because developments in this sector were strongly affected by the oil crisis in the late 1970s. In addition, because the industry is dominated by a few firms, it is more than likely that its value-added was exaggerated by monopoly profits. The seventeen industries not favored by the HCI policy were aggregated into the light industry group (Light group). This grouping excluded the tobacco sector, which was a government monopoly until March 1986 and a monopolistic public enterprise since then. The relevant data at the individual industry levels are shown in the following tables.

Table 4A-1. Import Liberalization Ratios by Manufacturing Industries
(in percentage)

Industry	1966	1970	1976	1980	1983	1985
1. Food	14.5	13.2	22.4	37.5	34.1	55.9
2. Beverages	0.0	0.0	0.0	0.0	13.0	19.6
3. Tobacco	0.0	0.0	0.0	0.0	9.1	9.1
4. Textiles	2.3	23.7	25.2	74.7	75.4	86.9
5. Clothing	0.0	16.7	16.7	70.6	44.8	95.7
6. Footwear	12.9	25.8	35.5	70.8	74.6	93.5
7. Wood	7.7	53.8	64.1	93.1	96.2	100.0
8. Furniture	0.0	14.3	14.3	0.0	60.5	95.6
9. Paper	2.9	40.0	20.0	63.2	88.5	88.0
10. Printing	0.0	27.3	54.5	90.9	100.0	100.0
11. Chemicals[a]	18.9	38.5	35.0	25.7	46.6	66.6
12. Other chemicals	8.3	43.3	51.7	54.9	59.6	66.4
13. Oil refining[a]	12.5	6.3	12.5	12.5	51.2	53.5
14. Petroleum products	27.3	100.0	100.0	100.0	100.0	100.0
15. Rubber	0.0	35.3	52.9	88.2	92.7	92.9
16. Nonmetallic minerals	5.7	71.4	65.7	77.3	80.1	83.6
17. Iron and steel[a]	4.9	64.6	67.1	84.2	93.3	95.6
18. Nonferrous metals[a]	4.9	64.6	67.1	84.2	93.3	95.6
19. Fabricated metals[a]	3.3	33.3	33.3	70.4	91.5	94.6
20. Nonelectrical machinery[a]	14.1	56.3	33.8	47.6	64.4	76.5
21. Electrical machinery[a]	0.0	23.5	17.6	31.0	46.9	64.5
22. Transport equipment[a]	0.0	65.0	13.8	44.4	58.8	69.2
23. Miscellaneous manufacturing	8.1	41.7	40.1	56.6	64.1	77.1

[a]Industries favored under the HCI policy regime.
Source: Kwang Suk Kim, *The Economic Effects of Import Liberalization and Industrial Adjustment Policy* (Seoul: Korea Development Institute, 1988), appendix table 1, reproduced with permission.

Table 4A-2. Capital Intensity (in million 1980 won/worker)

	1966	1970	1973	1975	1978	1980	1983	1985
Light industries								
Food	2.6	2.6	3.7	4.4	5.6	6.4	7.8	9.8
Beverages	7.9	5.8	6.9	7.3	8.2	12.5	12.5	19.3
Tobacco	15.3	13.8	14.1	13.9	11.0	29.7	42.5	49.1
Textiles	5.2	4.5	8.2	5.5	6.1	8.6	10.1	11.2
Clothing	0.3	0.5	0.6	0.7	1.1	1.4	1.9	2.0
Footwear, leather	1.2	1.4	2.3	1.7	3.3	4.1	5.0	6.9
Wood	8.1	5.5	4.9	6.7	5.9	9.2	11.5	11.7
Furniture	0.8	2.8	2.8	2.2	2.1	2.9	3.7	4.7
Pulp, paper	7.9	6.6	6.9	6.9	7.9	9.7	11.5	13.8
Printing	4.9	5.1	6.4	8.4	10.7	12.2	11.5	12.9
Other chemicals	2.2	2.8	2.7	3.0	3.7	4.5	5.0	6.0
Petroleum and coal products	2.1	3.8	5.3	6.0	6.1	7.5	9.2	11.8
Rubber products	2.6	3.9	4.9	5.1	5.8	6.3	6.5	6.0
Nonmetallic minerals	4.1	9.0	10.2	11.5	13.6	16.6	18.8	22.3
Other manufactures	1.1	1.0	1.5	4.2	3.9	5.2	6.3	7.2
Heavy and chemical industries								
Industrial chemicals	47.9	31.4	29.2	35.4	36.0	42.9	65.2	71.7
Oil refining	50.9	51.1	112.9	118.2	124.3	137.4	109.7	128.5
Iron and steel	5.3	6.8	14.8	22.8	34.6	37.6	37.7	38.0
Nonferrous metals	4.2	4.3	8.7	12.6	12.2	14.0	12.6	12.8
Fabricated metals	2.0	3.0	4.4	5.9	9.1	10.7	9.5	11.2
Nonelectrical machinery	3.0	4.9	6.6	7.9	13.2	14.7	14.3	14.2
Electrical machinery	2.3	2.3	2.4	4.8	4.5	5.5	6.7	9.5
Transport equipment	4.5	5.2	7.5	7.8	12.0	19.8	18.3	20.1

Table 4A-3. Changes in Capital Intensity (average annual percentage change)

	1966–1970	1970–1973	1973–1975	1975–1978	1978–1980	1980–1983	1983–1985	1970–1978	1978–1985
Light industries									
Food	0.2	12.1	9.2	8.7	6.2	7.0	10.3	10.1	7.7
Beverages	-7.4	6.3	2.3	4.0	23.6	0.0	24.1	4.4	13.0
Tobacco	-2.6	0.8	-1.0	-7.4	64.2	12.7	7.5	-2.8	23.8
Textiles	-3.4	21.8	-17.8	3.2	19.1	5.5	5.1	3.7	9.1
Clothing	18.0	7.7	8.6	12.8	14.1	11.6	1.8	9.8	9.4
Footwear/leather	3.7	18.6	-13.5	23.4	12.6	6.6	17.1	11.2	11.2
Wood	-9.2	-3.5	16.9	-4.4	25.2	7.9	0.8	0.9	10.4
Furniture	37.2	-0.4	-10.2	-2.0	16.9	8.6	12.8	-3.5	12.1
Pulp, paper	-4.1	1.4	-0.	4.5	10.6	6.0	9.3	2.2	8.2
Printing	0.7	8.1	14.2	8.6	6.3	-1.8	5.8	9.8	2.6
Other chemicals	7.2	-1.5	5.0	7.0	10.4	3.8	9.5	3.2	7.3
Petroleum and coal products	15.8	12.2	5.7	0.9	10.9	6.7	13.4	6.2	9.8
Rubber products	10.2	7.6	2.5	4.2	4.7	0.6	-3.4	5.0	0.6
Nonmetallic minerals	21.9	4.3	5.9	5.8	10.7	4.1	9.1	5.3	7.3
Other manufactures	-2.8	15.4	66.5	-2.6	15.2	6.3	7.5	18.7	9.1
Heavy and chemical industries									
Industrial chemicals	-9.8	-2.4	10.1	0.6	9.2	14.9	4.9	1.7	10.3
Oil refining	0.1	30.3	2.4	1.7	5.1	-7.3	8.3	11.8	0.5
Iron and steel	6.1	30.0	23.8	15.0	4.2	0.1	0.4	22.6	1.4
Nonferrous metals	0.9	26.3	20.0	-1.0	7.0	-3.4	0.7	13.8	0.7
Fabricated metals	9.7	14.5	15.5	15.2	8.6	-3.7	8.4	15.0	3.1
Nonelectrical machinery	12.8	10.7	9.3	18.4	5.4	-0.7	-0.3	13.2	1.1
Electrical machinery	-0.3	1.5	41.2	-2.1	10.0	7.1	19.0	8.8	11.2
Transport equipment	3.4	13.2	.3	15.3	28.5	-2.6	4.8	11.2	7.7

Table 4A-4. Capital Efficiency ($q1$) (in percentage)

	1966	1970	1973	1975	1978	1980	1983	1985
Light industries								
Food	26.9	34.3	26.1	22.1	22.2	14.5	13.9	15.3
Beverages	18.4	31.	44.5	42.1	41.0	19.8	17.8	19.1
Tobacco	13.7	39.2	55.5	35.5	33.1	14.9	8.2	5.6
Textiles	7.5	9.3	14.0	11.8	17.1	11.5	10.8	11.7
Clothing	68.5	65.4	119.2	80.7	43.7	22.1	12.3	24.4
Footwear, leather	41.1	44.5	68.7	74.4	62.0	27.3	9.1	19.4
Wood	7.7	8.1	13.1	10.3	17.2	−2.8	7.4	6.7
Furniture	6.2	21.7	− 2.3	21.1	28.1	−1.7	21.0	14.4
Pulp, paper	11.1	14.0	19.5	17.9	21.8	15.3	16.2	15.3
Printing	10.9	11.0	9.0	11.3	10.3	9.0	8.8	7.8
Other chemicals	39.9	36.7	77.9	69.0	78.3	57.7	54.5	52.3
Petroleum, coal products	74.4	56.6	62.3	51.1	53.5	65.1	44.6	44.3
Rubber products	5.7	12.1	17.4	14.7	19.6	18.2	12.9	15.4
Nonmetallic minerals	17.5	16.0	22.8	18.8	20.0	14.6	15.7	15.5
Other manufactures	17.7	44.7	31.3	22.7	20.4	12.2	10.4	8.6
Heavy and chemical industries								
Industrial chemicals	2.5	12.6	18.7	15.9	30.1	26.3	27.3	27.6
Oil refining	32.1	41.3	28.5	23.2	48.3	28.6	30.1	32.6
Iron and steel	16.6	13.3	18.5	13.2	14.8	15.8	16.6	19.4
Nonferrous metals	20.9	21.5	21.0	16.4	25.9	13.6	31.2	38.7
Fabricated metals	14.6	11.3	15.9	15.2	21.0	8.9	10.6	13.8
Nonelectrical machinery	16.1	11.7	15.5	23.0	26.9	14.0	14.6	18.2
Electrical machinery	26.5	26.4	50.8	21.1	38.8	22.7	29.4	25.2
Transport equipment	11.3	16.2	10.3	13.7	15.7	6.3	10.8	13.6
Industry groups								
All manufacturing	14.9	20.0	23.7	19.7	24.5	15.8	16.6	18.1
Heavy and chemical	8.5	14.3	19.8	16.3	23.4	15.7	18.4	20.2
Light	16.9	19.9	23.8	20.7	23.5	15.2	14.5	15.6
Clothing and footwear	60.2	60.9	105.7	78.7	50.6	24.1	11.0	22.4
HC-Electric machinery	7.6	13.4	16.5	15.4	20.9	14.5	16.5	19.0

Note: Assumption: No indirect taxes borne by capital.

Table 4A-5. Capital Efficiency ($q2$) (in percentage)

	1966	1970	1973	1975	1978	1980	1983	1985
Light industries								
Food	30.0	39.5	29.1	26.0	24.5	21.2	20.3	21.4
Beverages	33.9	62.4	77.1	84.0	86.2	62.1	63.0	63.9
Tobacco	34.5	82.3	93.4	86.5	96.4	80.6	70.2	69.3
Textiles	8.7	10.9	14.7	13.4	17.4	12.4	11.7	12.5
Clothing	69.4	66.7	121.1	84.6	43.7	28.5	19.4	29.9
Footwear, leather	42.2	48.7	72.8	77.3	62.0	29.8	10.3	21.0
Wood	8.2	8.9	13.8	11.8	17.2	-1.1	9.0	7.6
Furniture	6.9	26.3	4.5	24.7	32.5	6.0	29.8	19.6
Pulp, paper	11.7	15.4	20.5	19.9	22.0	16.8	18.0	16.5
Printing	11.2	11.2	9.2	11.7	10.5	9.9	9.5	8.4
Other chemicals	43.4	42.4	80.4	74.0	81.3	63.3	61.1	57.8
Petroleum, coal products	76.5	59.8	63.5	55.5	54.6	65.5	45.4	45.1
Rubber products	16.1	12.5	17.9	15.9	19.7	19.6	14.6	16.6
Nonmetallic minerals	18.5	17.2	23.8	20.2	20.2	15.7	16.9	16.1
Other manufactures	18.4	46.1	32.3	24.3	20.8	13.8	11.9	9.8
Heavy and chemical industries								
Industrial chemicals	2.6	12.8	19.4	17.5	30.1	28.5	30.0	29.4
Oil refining	49.5	82.9	46.3	40.9	68.6	56.4	44.2	46.3
Iron and steel	17.1	13.8	18.9	14.5	15.0	16.3	17.1	19.7
Nonferrous metals	22.4	23.5	22.7	17.8	26.1	14.6	32.9	39.6
Fabricated metals	15.1	12.9	16.1	24.2	27.2	15.3	16.0	20.0
Nonelectrical machinery	28.1	32.8	57.2	27.5	47.3	28.6	36.5	29.7
Electrical machinery	28.1	32.8	57.2	27.5	47.3	28.6	36.5	29.7
Transport equipment	12.1	20.9	12.8	16.0	17.2	8.6	13.0	16.7
Industry groups								
All manufacturing	18.3	26.1	27.9	24.6	28.1	20.9	21.3	22.4
Heavy and chemical	8.9	16.0	21.2	18.7	24.9	17.7	20.7	22.3
Light	19.7	23.9	26.4	24.4	25.9	19.2	18.6	19.4
Clothing and footwear	61.2	62.8	108.2	82.3	50.6	29.0	15.8	26.4
HC-Electric machinery	7.9	14.7	17.5	17.0	21.3	15.9	18.1	20.7

Note: Assumption: One-half of indirect taxes borne by capital.

Table 4A-6. Capital Efficiency ($q3$) (in percentage)

	1970	1975	1978	1983
Light industries				
Food	13.2	13.1	30.3	20.3
Beverages	36.5	52.8	39.1	18.3
Tobacco	41.2	51.5	19.1	5.5
Textiles	7.6	13.3	17.1	10.5
Clothing	63.6	124.7	23.8	10.5
Footwear, leather	34.1	60.3	63.9	9.4
Wood	4.3	7.8	18.0	6.9
Furniture	9.3	14.8	23.3	22.8
Pulp, paper	12.6	18.2	16.3	13.4
Printing	14.9	16.2	10.7	9.9
Other chemicals	12.7	43.0	54.2	40.7
Petroleum, coal products	29.5	149.3	24.6	44.7
Rubber products	6.6	13.7	20.6	12.8
Nonmetallic minerals	11.6	19.7	18.0	12.7
Other manufactures	14.0	18.3	20.0	10.7
Heavy and chemical industries				
Industrial chemicals	10.6	20.5	22.6	17.9
Oil refining	81.7	− 1.4	38.9	6.0
Iron and steel	5.0	4.8	12.3	13.5
Nonferrous metals	16.7	10.3	20.4	26.0
Fabricated metals	6.6	18.0	19.6	10.6
Nonelectrical machinery	6.4	26.5	19.5	12.1
Electrical machinery	12.4	18.3	25.9	24.0
Transport equipment	4.9	10.8	13.4	10.2
Industry groups				
All manufacturing	15.7	19.1	21.3	14.1
Heavy and chemical	8.3	14.9	17.9	14.8
Light	13.3	22.0	22.9	14.3
Clothing and footwear	57.2	104.3	45.3	10.1
HC-Electric machinery	8.0	14.2	16.6	13.3

Note: Assumption: Based on international price of value-added.

Table 4A-7. Export Shares in Gross Output (*sx*) (in percentage)

	1966	1970	1973	1975	1978	1980	1983	1985
Light industries								
Food	7.3	5.8	8.6	13.3	8.3	4.1	3.2	3.4
Beverages	1.7	0.8	3.4	3.7	2.4	0.5	1.0	1.9
Tobacco	10.2	0.2	0.4	0.2	0.1	0.7	2.7	2.0
Textiles	12.9	24.9	37.0	34.0	33.4	31.5	35.9	33.0
Clothing	18.5	31.3	66.4	48.5	61.6	55.8	70.4	82.4
Footwear, leather	4.6	6.6	26.3	44.6	52.8	53.0	58.3	33.1
Wood	35.7	39.4	67.4	42.6	36.5	33.9	13.4	9.5
Furniture	3.6	11.9	52.9	23.7	31.4	10.3	11.0	11.6
Pulp, paper	1.0	1.3	13.8	6.4	3.4	1.6	1.3	1.3
Printing	1.0	1.3	13.8	6.4	3.4	1.6	1.3	1.3
Other chemicals	0.2	2.5	4.5	3.6	3.3	5.8	5.6	6.8
Petroleum, coal products	0.0	0.0	0.1	0.2	1.6	0.4	1.4	1.0
Rubber products	17.5	23.3	48.4	54.2	49.3	58.5	67.1	64.0
Nonmetallic minerals	5.9	4.0	4.0	4.5	4.0	7.9	21.8	11.8
Other manufactures	24.7	54.9	54.3	59.9	66.0	55.2	55.6	64.6
Heavy and chemical industries								
Industrial chemicals	1.9	4.1	7.9	4.3	13.6	17.0	13.2	13.9
Oil refining	11.5	12.1	7.5	7.3	5.7	1.6	8.1	13.1
Iron and steel	9.2	4.6	24.8	15.8	14.7	22.3	21.3	18.1
Nonferrous metals	12.2	11.9	10.7	6.4	11.9	11.9	12.7	11.0
Fabricated metals	10.2	13.4	38.6	29.7	41.6	46.3	40.3	44.5
Nonelectrical machinery	8.9	3.2	24.9	10.0	10.0	11.0	9.1	7.6
Electrical machinery	10.6	23.3	50.2	41.4	35.4	38.9	40.2	46.1
Transport equipment	1.6	2.0	7.2	20.5	35.9	31.2	48.9	41.6
Industry groups								
Heavy and chemical	6.9	7.3	25.3	18.8	24.2	26.6	28.2	29.3
Light	8.3	14.0	26.0	24.8	26.1	23.9	28.0	26.4

Note: *sx* = [exports/(output – indirect taxes)]. Computed from the relevant input-output tables estimated by the Bank of Korea.

Table 4A-8. Effective Rate of Protection (z) (in percentage)

	1970	1975	1978	1983[a]
Light industries				
Food	190.5	86.5	−28.8	−32.6
Beverages	− 13.9	− 20.8	4.8	−4.1
Tobacco	− 4.8	− 31.1	73.7	50.0
Textiles	29.4	− 15.1	0.2	5.3
Clothing	4.1	− 51.5	142.7	93.8
Footwear, leather	33.5	51.8	−6.1	−2.4
Wood	323.9	67.9	−9.4	9.1
Furniture	182.6	65.5	36.1	−8.8
Pulp, paper	11.5	− 1.3	36.2	22.9
Printing	−26.4	− 31.7	− 3.6	−11.7
Other chemicals	202.7	64.0	46.4	36.5
Petroleum, coal products	91.8	− 65.8	121.6	−0.2
Rubber products	145.6	16.5	−9.6	2.0
Nonmetallic minerals	38.6	− 5.0	12.2	32.3
Other manufactures	−290.9	95.4	5.9	−5.9
Heavy and chemical industries				
Industrial chemicals	19.5	− 23.2	40.7	65.8
Oil refining	− 52.7	−798.8	26.1	681.9
Iron and steel	190.9	303.2	24.7	31.5
Nonferrous metals	32.5	65.7	31.6	23.6
Fabricated metals	90.4	− 20.7	12.8	0.0
Nonelectrical machinery	88.9	− 14.9	44.2	23.6
Electrical machinery	223.6	29.4	105.4	44.8
Transport equipment	248.2	36.3	30.4	12.4
Industry groups				
Heavy and chemical	94.4	9.5	43.2	32.7
Light	56.1	−8.2	3.6	−0.3

[a]ERP estimates for 1982.
Sources: Data for 1970 and 1975 are from K. S. Kim and S. D. Hong, *The Long-term Changes in the Structure of Nominal and Effective Rate of Protection* (Seoul: Korea Development Institute, 1982). Data for 1978 and 1982 are from Yoo Jung-hoo, *The Basic Task of Industrial Policy and the Reform Proposals of Industrial Assistance* (Seoul: Korea Development Institute Press, 1982). Reproduced with permission.

Table 4A-9. Proportion of Paid Workers among All Workers (in percentage)

	1966	1970	1973	1975	1978	1980	1983	1985
Light industries								
Food	86.5	88.6	87.5	90.3	89.7	90.6	87.9	86.5
Beverages	89.0	92.7	93.5	95.1	95.7	95.9	94.9	94.0
Tobacco	100.0	100.0	100.0	100.0	100.0	100.0	100.0	100.0
Textiles	94.5	96.7	96.9	98.0	97.7	97.4	97.1	97.2
Clothing	88.0	93.1	93.1	93.1	92.9	92.1	92.1	93.1
Footwear, leather	90.5	92.4	92.6	99.2	94.6	96.0	92.5	98.0
Wood	93.5	95.7	95.9	98.7	97.0	97.6	97.7	97.9
Furniture	60.7	87.1	87.0	93.0	92.7	93.8	92.5	94.1
Pulp, paper	94.1	95.7	95.9	98.7	97.0	97.6	97.7	97.9
Printing	95.2	96.9	96.8	96.9	96.9	96.5	96.6	96.0
Other chemicals	96.4	98.0	98.5	98.7	99.0	98.8	98.5	98.8
Petroleum, coal products	92.1	94.1	95.5	95.8	96.1	97.8	98.3	98.1
Rubber products	98.7	99.2	99.7	99.8	99.9	99.4	99.5	99.5
Nonmetallic minerals	91.7	94.2	95.2	96.2	96.9	97.7	97.1	97.1
Other manufactures	94.1	92.0	92.1	90.8	91.6	91.3	91.5	96.7
Heavy and chemical industries								
Industrial chemicals	97.5	98.9	99.5	99.6	99.7	99.5	98.5	98.7
Oil refining	100.0	100.0	100.0	100.0	100.0	99.7	99.6	99.5
Iron and steel	98.9	99.3	99.6	99.6	99.5	99.5	99.6	99.6
Nonferrous metals	96.7	98.2	98.7	99.0	98.3	98.4	98.5	96.7
Fabricated metals	87.0	88.0	89.1	97.6	90.3	93.0	94.2	95.8
Nonelectrical machinery	82.0	93.9	96.6	97.2	95.6	96.7	97.8	97.5
Electrical machinery	97.3	98.6	99.4	99.7	99.6	99.5	99.3	98.9
Transport equipment	96.6	97.3	97.7	97.8	97.6	98.1	99.2	99.1
Industry groups								
Heavy and chemical	92.3	96.0	97.3	98.7	97.6	98.1	98.3	98.3
Light	90.1	93.3	93.4	95.3	94.9	94.9	94.4	95.0

Table 4A-10. Rate of Growth of Manufacturing Value-Added (in average annual percentage changes)

	1966–1970	1970–1973	1973–1975	1975–1978	1978–1980	1980–1983	1983–1985	1970–1978	1978–1985
Light industries									
Food	15.8	9.9	5.3	11.6	10.6	7.1	10.9	9.4	9.2
Beverages	17.1	14.3	12.8	10.8	7.7	4.5	6.0	12.6	5.8
Tobacco	22.8	12.1	13.7	8.8	7.0	7.2	2.9	11.3	5.9
Textiles	22.2	29.3	13.3	14.2	7.0	5.0	3.1	19.4	5.0
Clothing	20.0	30.3	16.9	11.6	-1.7	9.1	5.8	19.7	5.0
Footwear, leather	10.1	43.7	28.5	27.4	-12.3	5.1	-1.2	33.5	-1.9
Wood	21.0	18.2	5.4	19.5	-12.8	-1.7	-2.6	15.3	-5.3
Furniture	20.9	-6.0	16.1	27.5	4.0	15.7	1.1	11.1	8.0
Pulp, paper	15.1	18.0	9.3	19.4	7.8	7.7	5.0	16.3	6.9
Printing	5.5	11.0	9.7	15.3	7.8	4.1	5.3	12.3	5.5
Other chemicals	24.2	24.4	16.3	23.5	4.2	9.2	10.3	22.0	8.1
Petroleum, coal products	4.8	10.6	2.3	7.2	9.8	3.2	10.1	7.2	7.0
Rubber products	9.7	34.4	17.1	28.6	16.4	7.1	13.1	27.7	11.4
Nonmetallic minerals	24.6	20.0	6.7	18.6	6.7	9.2	5.3	16.0	7.4
Other manufactures	38.9	11.6	11.5	21.7	-2.2	2.6	8.7	15.3	2.9
Heavy and chemical industries									
Industrial chemicals	47.9	28.5	27.5	22.5	9.8	4.9	6.8	26.0	6.8
Oil refining	43.6	11.7	0.6	19.5	5.9	-4.4	8.5	11.6	2.1
Iron and steel	25.6	41.5	22.4	22.3	19.9	10.8	5.4	29.2	11.7
Nonferrous metals	7.0	24.7	29.5	28.3	10.9	27.9	7.2	27.2	16.8
Fabricated metals	12.1	18.8	24.2	41.8	-0.6	10.0	10.0	28.3	6.9
Nonelectrical machinery	7.1	38.4	19.2	41.5	-7.1	15.6	15.8	34.4	8.6
Electrical machinery	29.5	56.4	19.5	38.9	3.7	13.8	12.3	39.9	10.4
Transport equipment	21.8	11.5	37.7	26.9	-8.2	20.3	31.7	23.4	14.3

NOTES

1. Taewon Kwack. *Depreciation and Taxation of Income from Capital* (Seoul: Korea Development Institute, 1985). The estimates take into account statutory tax rates and various tax incentives, as well as inflation.
2. The measure of import liberalization used here is defined as the ratio of import items that require no prior government approval, except for imports restricted on the grounds of health or safety standards, to the total number of import items used by the industry.
3. Exporters continued to have access to foreign goods at international prices through the tariff rebate system.
4. Economic Planning Board, *Comprehensive Stabilization Program* (Seoul: Economic Planning Board, April 17, 1979).
5. Data are shown only for years when the Bank of Korea prepared interindustry tables. The availability of such tables restricts the number of observations.
6. It is assumed that unpaid workers created the same amount of value-added as paid workers. However, it is likely that in the manufacturing sector, a self-employed or family worker creates, on average, less value-added than a paid employee. If so, the estimated returns to capital and the capital efficiencies are likely to be underestimated. The extent of this underestimation would be greater, the greater the proportion of unpaid workers. As shown in Table 4A-9, the proportion of unpaid workers was higher in the Light group than in the HC group by three to four percentage points during the period under review. On this ground, the capital efficiency of the Light group is likely to have been underestimated by more than that of the HC group.
7. Although the value-added used in this section is in constant prices, the difference in their valuation is a problem, given the Bank of Korea's method of estimating the value-added in constant prices. It first obtained the ratio of value-added to output in current prices and multiplied the constant-price output by the ratio to obtain the value-added in constant price. The value of an industry's output was a simple sum of exports and domestic sales that did not take into account the difference between domestic and international prices. Likewise, the value-added was a sum that did not recognize the price differences.
8. For the 1983 $q3$, the 1982 effective rates of protection were used. The effective rates for 1970 and 1975 were available in Kwang Suk Kim and Sung Duk Hong, *The Long-term Changes in the Structure of Nominal and Effective Rate of Protection* (Seoul: Korea Development Institute, 1982). Those for 1978 and 1982 are Jung-ho Yoo's estimates reported in *The*

Basic Task of Industrial Policy and the Reform Proposals of Industrial Assistance (Seoul: Korea Development Institute Press, 1982). These effective rates are reported in Table 4A-8.

9. The countries were Hong Kong, Israel, Portugal, Spain, Taiwan, and Yugoslavia. After excluding natural resource–based products, the product composition of the forty-seven largest trading countries' manufacturing exports of the late 1970s were compared with exports from Korea at the two-digit level. Austria, Italy, and India had compositions more similar to Korea's than to Yugoslavia's, Portugal's, or Spain's, designated here as competitors. However, they were not included as competitors on the ground that their per capita incomes were very different from Korea's.

10. Jung-ho Yoo, "Estimation of Some Disaggregate Export and Import Functions," *Korea Development Review* (Fall 1984).

11. See Chapter 5 for a discussion of the relationship between export development and the success of selected HCI projects.

12. L. E. Westphal and Kwang Suk Kim, "Korea," in B. Balassa et al., eds., *Development Strategies in Semi-industrial Countries* (Baltimore: Johns Hopkins University Press, 1982). For a more general discussion of export promotion and import substitution policies, see A. O. Krueger, "Trade Policy as an Input to Development," *American Economic Review* 70, no. 2 (May 1980).

13. See J. J. Stern, "Korea's Industrial Policy and Changing Industrial Structure," *Development Discussion Paper 352* (Cambridge: Harvard Institute for International Development, July 1990).

14. Ibid.

15. Hak-kil Pyo, "Estimates of Capital Stock and Capital/Output Coefficients by Industries for the Republic of Korea (1953–1986)," *Korea Development Institute Working Paper 8810* (Seoul: Korea Development Institute, 1988).

16. The pairs of industries for which capital stock was combined were apparel (KSIC 322) and footwear (KSIC 324); industrial chemicals (KSIC 351) and other chemical products (KSIC 352); petroleum refining (KSIC 353) and petroleum and coal products (KSIC 354); and iron and steel (KSIC 371) and nonferrous metals (KSIC 372). These industries were either individually interesting or, as in the case of petroleum refining and industrial chemicals, an industry favored by the HCI policy (industrial chemicals) lumped with one nonfavored (petroleum refining).

5

Evaluation: A Project-Specific Approach _____

When a government pursues an economic goal and seems to achieve its objective, it is tempting to conclude that the policy was correct and that its implementation was effective. Such a view is too simple. A policy may succeed at one level but, by introducing other economic distortions, may undermine developments elsewhere. Or the seeming success of the policy may have come about through exogenous factors, leading to the erroneous observation that the policy created the apparent economic success. And finally, a policy may appear to have been implemented when, in fact, the implementation was neither effective in practice nor so dramatically different from what might have occurred if the policy had not been enunciated. Disentangling all these elements is difficult.

Such is the case in any evaluation of the heavy and chemical industrialization (HCI) policy under which the Korean government mobilized tax, trade, and financial measures to promote the industries it designated as "important." Indeed, as noted in Chapter 4, the HCI policy represented a sharp break with earlier development policies, which had provided strong incentives to any activity able to export but had not provided special incentives favoring one activity over another. The HCI regime involved a switch to sector-, and in some instances project-, specific policy interventions. The experience from many countries would suggest that such a policy regime would lead to serious macroeconomic imbalances. While the HCI drive also contributed to a slowdown in growth, the shift to the promotion of specific projects and sectors apparently had less serious consequences in Korea than, for example, the experience with import substitution policies elsewhere. In fact Korea managed very rapid growth in both the pre-HCI period and the subsequent one.[1] As Table 5-1 shows, Korea has outperformed most other Asian developing countries. Moreover, this growth has been accompanied by a rapid structural transformation toward more skill- and

Table 5-1. Performance of Selected Asian Economies

	GNP/Capita Growth Rates (percent per annum)		
Country	1966–1975[a]	1976–1990[b]	1990 GNP/Capita (1987 $)
1. **Korea**	**7.3**	**7.2**	**$3,940**
2. Indonesia	5.4	4.3	498
3. Malaysia	4.5	3.8	1,698
4. Philippines	3.0	0.4	630
5. Taiwan	7.5	6.9[c]	6,017
6. Thailand	4.3	5.5	1,198

a Calculated from 1980 local currency GNP data.
b Calculated from 1987 local currency GNP data.
c For 1976 to 1988.
Sources: Council for Economic Planning and Development, Republic of China (Taiwan), *Taiwan Statistical Data Book: 1989;* and World Bank, Washington, D.C., *World Tables 1987* and *World Tables 1994.*

technology-intensive production and exports, with a concomitant decrease in the share of labor-intensive exports. For example, textile products, which accounted for 40.8 percent of total exports in 1970, constituted only 30 percent in 1981, falling to 25.2 percent in 1986. Electronic products, which formed less than 4 percent of total exports in 1970, were the second largest export category in 1986, when they formed some 20 percent of total exports. Similarly, the share of exports from the steel and machinery sectors increased significantly, and automobile exports, which were nil in 1970, formed nearly 5 percent of total exports in 1986.

Although there is a general presumption among neoclassical econo- mists that "Government cannot . . . identify in advance the particular lines and products in which [a] country will be successful," the continued rapid growth in GNP and exports, together with the accompanying structural changes, might suggest that Korea was different—that the HCI drive was, if not an unalloyed success, certainly not a failure.[2] Such an assumption of a causal relationship between a particular policy framework and some measure of macroeconomic success should not be accepted without further examination. Indeed, as has been suggested in Chapter 4, the interven- tionist policies of the 1970s did retard economic growth and introduced potentially economic and political destabilizing factors.

This chapter carries the analysis of the HCI drive one step further. Since the HCI policy targeted specific projects, any evaluation of that policy should focus on the projects promoted. Two questions need to be addressed. First, did the HCI policy promote activities that did not merit government support (in the sense that if one had applied the standard economic criterion justifying government interventions, the projects would have come up short)? And second, if the government did indeed promote economically unsound activities, did these eventually become viable?

If the HCI policy made it possible for government to promote projects that were economically sound but whose financial rates of return were too low to attract private investors, then government did no more than play its accepted role, albeit under the rubric of promoting a special set of deserving activities. By contrast, if government promoted unsound projects, in the mistaken belief that they would eventually become successful, then scarce resources were wasted, and growth was inevitably retarded. That is the all-too-familiar outcome of many special targeting efforts. There is a third possibility: government may have been successful in creating sound economic activities from projects that had such low economic rates of return that they should not have been implemented. If this was the outcome of the HCI program, then Korea's industrial policy achieved a success that would not have been attained under the more traditional role assigned to government.[3] This is the clearest measure of the success of industrial targeting.[4] The question to be addressed in the analysis of the specific projects is the degree to which they fall into this last category.

The Evaluation of Specific Projects

To see the role that industrial targeting may have played in Korea's industrial development, the financial and economic rates of return have been calculated for a sample of industrial projects. The rates of return are first calculated using data for the year the project was to be undertaken. They are then compared with the rates of return using current project data and prices, that is, data for around 1990. Projects that had an unacceptably low economic rate of return in the base year, but reasonable economic returns in the current period, are classified as instances of successful industrial targeting: activities that standard economic rationale would have rejected as being unsound and unworthy of government support but that have confounded their critics and become successful.

The data required for such ex-ante and ex-post project evaluations are considerable. Not only are project-specific data needed, but macroeconomic data are also required to construct the necessary economic prices for some early period. In the event, it was impossible to obtain all the needed project-specific data with the result that some missing data were crudely estimated. By contrast, it proved somewhat easier to construct the economy-wide variables needed for the project evaluation exercise. Even so, the results can be taken as only a rough indicator of the economic value of each of the projects studied.

Economic project evaluation requires estimates of the opportunity cost of the various factors of production. Table 5-2 summarizes the opportunity costs for foreign exchange, labor, and capital that are used in the project evaluations.[5] The procedure used to estimate the shadow prices, together with the results, are described in Appendix 5A. The calculation of shadow prices is never a simple matter, and the problem is compounded by alternative suggestions on the appropriate methodology to use under different policy regimes. Whatever the theoretical merits of the different methodologies, the strength of the procedure used here lies in the consistency of the results and their uniqueness for the time period under review.

Data to carry out the required cost-benefit analysis, using both pre- and postproject implementation information, are difficult to obtain, so the cost-benefit analysis is limited to the six projects listed in Table 5-3. Because of the small number of projects studied and because they were selected primarily on the basis of data availability, the projects obviously do not represent a random sample of HCI projects promoted. Although data availability restricted the number of projects for which a full cost-benefit analysis was carried out, two additional projects—POSCO steel and Hyundai automobiles—are reviewed in Chapter 6, together with an analysis of the developments of four sectors: aluminum, steel, automobiles, and shipbuilding. Although limited in number, the projects analyzed here do have the virtue of covering the major HCI sectors and

Table 5-2. Shadow Prices, Korea

Item	1975–1977	1978–1980	1981–1983	1984
Foreign exchange				
Official rate (won/US$)	484.00	525.13	729.13	
Shadow price (won/US$)	543.20	611.40	766.30	
Capital (percent)	10.18	8.10	9.39	
Labor[a]				
Unskilled (thousand won/yr)	374[b]	1,071[c]	1,651[d]	2,112
Semiskilled (thousand won/yr)	707	1,462	2,294	2,761
Technical/managerial (thousand won/yr)	1,890	3,819	5,383	6,330

[a]These data refer to the national average annual wage. Separate labor opportunity costs were calculated for the regions where the specific projects evaluated were located.
[b]For 1976.
[c]For 1979.
[d]For 1982.
Source: L. Sabin and H. Kato, "Shadow Price Calculation and Application: A Case Study of Korea," *Harvard Institute for International Development Discussion Paper* 313 (Cambridge: Harvard Institute for International Development, 1989).

Table 5-3. Projects Evaluated

Name of Project	Major Products	Sector
Korea Heavy Machinery	Power generation machinery; petrochemical plants	Nonelectrical
Boo-Kook Steel and Wire Company, Ltd.	Steel wire, steel rope; aircraft wire	Metal Products
Hyundai Pipe Company	Steel pipes	Metal products
Korea Steel Chemical	Chemical products; phthalic anhydride	Chemicals
Dong Yang Steel	Aluminum extrusions; steel furniture	Metal products
Samsung Electronics	Color TV; microwaves	Electrical

include one of the largest HCI projects, the Changwon machinery complex. A more thorough postproject appraisal should be based on data reflecting actual costs and should compare those to actual revenues. Such a formal postproject evaluation was carried out only for the Korea Heavy Machinery project at Changwon. For the other five projects studied, the ex-post analysis applies "current" market prices (market prices for a later period) together with an estimate of the appropriate opportunity cost of various factors, to the original project parameters. This procedure assumes that the projected structure, and technology, were actually put in place, a procedure akin to holding interindustry coefficients constant in an input-output model. This procedure obviously fails to account for the adoption of new technologies or changes in the production process that have occurred in response to relative price changes. This caveat needs to be kept in mind.

Of the six projects subject to cost-benefit analysis, all had internal rates of return that exceeded the opportunity cost of capital. But most had low, or even negative, internal rates of return at market prices. In fact, each was a legitimate candidate for government support, although this does not imply that such support was set at an appropriate level or efficiently administered.[6] Nor does it argue that these were the optimal sets of activities to support.

A review of the ex-post rates of return leads to the conclusion that only three projects—Hyundai Pipe, Dong Yang Steel, and Samsung Electronics—can be classified as successful in the sense that after the passage of some time they exhibited internal rates of return that exceeded the current opportunity cost of capital.[7] In terms of the classification scheme proposed in Chapter 1 (see Figure 1-1) none of the six cases would fall into quadrant IV—projects having a low internal rate of return at base-year economic prices and a rate of return exceeding the opportunity cost of capital at current prices. Put differently, in none of the cases studied here do we find instances in which the activity would have been rejected had the government actually screened projects using a cost-benefit test but which, in an ex-post sense, were in fact projects that raised national income. Using the definition put forward for successful industrial targeting, none of these projects supports the hypothesis that Korean planners were particularly adept at picking winners, since in no instance did government planners support a project that had a low economic rate of return only to have it become an economically successful project after a period of time.

Unsuccessful Projects

Korea Heavy Machinery. The Changwon integrated machinery plant was promoted as a heavy machinery project that would contribute to two objectives of the HCI drive: it would create an industry with considerable linkages to downstream users and energize a relatively poor region. The failure of this project provides a fascinating illustration of the government's attempt to promote specific activities and of the pitfalls such an effort faces.

The heavy machinery project called for the establishment of an integrated heavy machinery complex at Changwon of a magnitude and scope well beyond that of any other comparable installation in the developing world and with a product diversification and degree of integration rarely matched even in the developed world. The plant was to produce, under license from major U.S., German, Japanese, and French manufacturers (including General Electric, Westinghouse Electric Corporation, Hitachi Plant Engineering, and Harnischfeger International) a wide range of heavy specialized equipment for other activities to be promoted under the HCI drive. When completed, it was designed to supply as much as 40 percent of Korea's total anticipated needs for thermal power generating equipment, as well as machinery for the steel, petrochemical, and cement manufacturing subsectors, where it was expected that numerous new investments would occur in response to the incentives offered by the HCI policy.

Construction of the Changwon integrated machinery plant was to begin in November 1976, production was scheduled to start in 1978, and full, steady-state output was to be achieved by 1983. The project was to be implemented by Hyundai International Incorporated (HII), a private sector firm, with limited experience in producing industrial equipment but with close ties to one of the largest *chaebol* in Korea.[8] At full production the plant's annual output was forecast to reach

100,000 tons of machinery, valued at approximately US$400 million at 1976 prices. As with all other HCI projects, a major objective was import substitution, although the project was to have some potential for exports.[9]

Evaluated at 1975 market prices, the project had an after-tax internal rate of return of 5.8 percent and a negative net present value (discounted at the financial cost of capital) of –11.09 billion won. Evaluated using the opportunity costs for various inputs, the project had a marginally respectable economic rate of return of 17.5 percent. Had the government carried out an economic cost-benefit analysis, officials might have concluded that the project was an acceptable one, even without recourse to the industrial targeting rhetoric.[10]

Leaving the technical coefficients unchanged but using prevailing 1986 prices for costs and the actual prices received for outputs, the ex-post evaluation of the Korea Heavy Machinery project shows it to have a negative financial discounted cash flow (–63.24 billion won) and an after-tax internal rate of return of –14.6 percent. The results are no more encouraging when the evaluation is done using the opportunity costs of various factors. In economic terms, the project earns a negative internal rate of return (–2.0 percent).

As with any other project, many factors influenced the actual outcome as compared to the project proposal. But given the scale of the project and its importance to the HCI drive, it is surprising to find that at least some of the causes for the poor outturn on the project were the results of conflicting and poorly thought-out policy decisions.

In retrospect, it appears that the project was conceived in a period of excessive optimism about Korea's long-term growth and the develop-ment of downstream user industries for the project's output, an optimism that not only dominated the thinking of government officials but was widely shared by economists outside the government.[11] The promoters of the project felt they had the firm support of the government, not only because of the importance attached to the product mix but also because of the strategic location of the plant. The heavy machinery project was seen as a major anchor for the development of the Changwon industrial area, whose development had been assigned high priority in the national development program.[12]

Few of the assumptions used to justify the investment proved correct. Despite strong government backing, some basic aspects of the overall investment policy were changed, and these actions served to undermine the assumptions on which the project was based. For example, the Korea electric company modified its investment program to emphasize nuclear-based, rather than thermal-based, power generation plants, forcing the

Changwon project to redesign part of its facilities to meet the expected increase in the demand for nuclear power plants. This move not only substantially increased the project's costs but, in retrospect, proved to be a misguided response. Subsequently the government authorized three other firms to provide similar power-generating equipment, and Korea's electric company awarded contracts for thermal units to competing manufacturers. When Korea experienced a sharp reduction in growth in the late 1970s and early 1980s, the investment programs for some key industrial subsectors, including power generation, were sharply curtailed, further eroding domestic demand for machinery from the Changwon project.

Many of these events occurred at the beginning of the implementation of the project. In response, HII instituted major changes in the project design in the hope that the revised project would be better positioned to take advantage of the changing market and policy environment. But without commensurate reductions in other components of the project, these new plans served primarily to increase investment costs, extend the construction period, and increase the plant's complexity. In only two areas was the project scaled back. Because Hyundai Heavy Industries, a sister company of the project sponsor, was already producing marine diesel engines for export, this part of the heavy machinery complex was eliminated. And a proposal to include a steel rolling mill as an adjunct to the project's foundry and forge operations was eliminated, partly to reduce capital costs but also because similar capacity was being created by POSCO steel, another HCI-promoted activity. Both of these moves may in fact have weakened the profitability of the machinery complex. At the same time, HII insisted that the large forge and foundry units remain part of the project because it was felt that the complex could not rely on external suppliers for the critical machinery parts to be produced in these units. In actuality, the forge and foundry units have operated, until quite recently, at less than 50 percent of rated capacity. Finally, the project had to build its own harbor facilities since the Changwon harbor, built for the Changwon industrial complex, failed to provide loading and unloading facilities for heavy parts and components, particularly of the size required for the large-scale nuclear power plants that the complex expected to manufacture. The harbor was not completed until October 1983.

The project also experienced considerable delays in its implementation. Work on the project was essentially stopped in July 1979, when the implementation of the project was transferred from HII to Hyundai Heavy Industries. Work resumed again in January 1980 and continued at a low level under Hyundai's supervision until October 1980, when the government decided to take over ownership of HII and restructure it. A new enterprise, the Korea Heavy Industries and Construction (KHIC) Company, was formed, and the Korean Electric Power Company, as well as two state-owned banks, took over the existing shares of HII, providing additional equity for the financial restructuring of the company. Further attempts at restructuring the company continued throughout the 1980s.[13]

In addition to the problems created by changes in the project design and delays in implementation, the project was also affected by a sharp decline in its product prices, domestic as well as foreign, a decline that overwhelmed the increased earnings from exports following the rapid depreciation of the won. And although the project did supply components for seven nuclear power plants constructed for the Korea Electric Power Company, it never supplied components for nuclear power plants outside Korea. Moreover, domestic demand for nuclear plant components decreased with the worldwide decline in new nuclear power projects.[14] Given the various shortfalls, it is not surprising that the project never generated the forecast employment levels. Originally the heavy machinery complex was expected to generate some 8,000 jobs, a projection that increased to 10,000 jobs after the project was changed and enlarged. These employment levels were never reached. Current employment is around 5,000 persons.

There is little doubt that this was an unsuccessful project, and one of the two major project failures associated with the HCI policy.[15] Although the project never did exhibit a particularly high economic rate of return, the rate of return was sufficiently high to justify government support for the project. In retrospect, however, it is clear that the cost and demand projections were unrealistic. The forecasts were predicated on an excessive degree of optimism on the part of the project sponsors, an optimism that mirrored the hubris pervading much of the thinking behind the HCI drive. Whether a more sophisticated analysis, one that tested for sensitivity of the rate of return to different assumptions regarding prices, capital costs, completion time, and production performance, would have persuaded the government to forego this investment is, of course, unknowable. Nor is it clear that such an analysis was possible because many of the changes that did occur—for example, the decline in oil prices and the subsequent reduction in demand for nuclear generating plants—probably could not have been foreseen by any analyst, no matter how objective.[16]

Of equal interest, a review of the project's history suggests that the implementation of the HCI drive was far from coherent or smooth.

Conflicts between the heavy machinery project and other HCI projects were apparently resolved with little consideration of their impact on the heavy machinery project. Conflicts between HII and Hyundai Heavy Industries, two companies controlled by the same *chaebol*, were settled in favor of Hyundai Heavy Industries, to the detriment of the heavy machinery project, despite the fact that the Changwon project had received strong support from government planners. In the final analysis, the private view prevailed over the perceived public interest, suggesting that at least in this instance, the government was not particularly successful at imposing its vision on private entrepreneurs.

Korea Steel Chemical Company. The Korea Steel Chemical Company was established in 1974 to produce a wide range of chemical products, including coal tar and insecticides. Although the plant was in operation before the HCI program began, an expansion of the existing plant, supported by HCI measures, was begun in 1981 and completed in mid-1983. The expanded plant, which was to have an annual capacity of 15,000 metric tons and to generate foreign exchange savings of $10.6 million, would make it possible for the company to produce phthalic anhydride, an essential raw material for polyvinyl chloride products such as dyestuffs and paints. The plant, but especially the proposed expansion, had a classic import-substituting focus.

Analysis of the project's cash flow shows it to have a negative internal rate of return (−5.3 percent). Adjusting the cash flow to account for the differences between private and economic costs and benefits yields an internal rate of return of 10.8 percent, slightly above the estimated opportunity cost of capital for the relevant period. From an economic point of view, the project was marginally acceptable at best. The ex-post evaluation suggests that little has changed. The project has a financial rate of return of 6.6 percent and an economic rate of return of 7.3 percent, well below the estimated opportunity cost of capital. Although the project was supported under the HCI drive, and thus was meant to be internationally competitive, in fact it was little more than a standard import-substituting activity, and one that performed no better than most other such projects. This was in fact a marginal activity that should not have been promoted.

Boo-Kook Steel. The Boo-Kook Steel and Wire Company was established in 1956 with a capacity of 3,600 tons per year in wire and wire rope products. Capacity was gradually expanded to 58,000 tons per year. The expectation that the demand for wire and wire rope would increase with development as well as with increasing worldwide oil and coal exploration activities led to the decision to construct a second manufacturing facility in the Changwon industrial complex. The investment, promoted as part of the HCI drive, would add 22,800 tons per year to Boo-Kook's capacity, increasing total annual production capacity to 81,600 tons.

Production from the new facility was to begin in October 1982, with full capacity to be achieved by 1984. The expansion would increase the annual production of steel wire rope by 7,200 metric tons (nearly 19 percent) and of steel wire by 14,400 metric tons (nearly 71 percent), while adding 1,200 metric tons of stainless steel wire production capacity, for which Sumitomo Electrical Industries of Japan would provide technical collaboration. Seventy-five percent of the steel wire rope, nearly 70 percent of the steel wire, and all of the stainless wire rope were to be exported.

Evaluated at market prices, the project has an internal rate of return of only 2.1 percent and a negative net present value when costs and benefits are discounted at the market cost of capital. The economic evaluation indicates a more sanguine outcome, reflecting the presumed export orientation of the activity. It yields an economic internal rate of return of slightly over 16 percent.

Viewed from the current perspective, the project performs poorly in both financial and economic terms. The financial net present value is negative, and the internal rate of return is below 2 percent. This result reflects a declining price for exports, offset in part by rising prices for domestic sales, but accompanied by rising domestic and foreign input prices. Using economic values for purchases and for sales, the economic rate of return is 4 percent, well below the opportunity cost of capital. In part this reflects the decline in the expected economic benefits from both import-substituting and export-promoting activities as the premium on foreign exchange declined. But even if the project had sold to the domestic and foreign markets as forecast, it would not be financially profitable or add to national welfare. Although this result is perhaps less a failure of industrial policy than a result of unforeseen changes in prices, domestic and external, much the same argument can be applied to projects that are successful.

Successful Projects

Three projects—Hyundai Pipe Co. Ltd., Samsung Electronics Company Ltd., and Dong Yang Steel Industry Company, Ltd.—had high economic rates of return when evaluated at the prices prevailing when the projects were proposed and are successful in financial and economic terms, at current prices. Although their success may be ascribed to HCI policies, all three cases represent instances of activities that passed the neoclassical definition of acceptable activities and projects that did not, in fact, require any government support. Their success may well be due in part to the successful macroeconomic policies that characterize the Korean economy, but their success cannot be taken as an indicator of any unusual ability on the part of Korea policymakers to pick winners.

Hyundai Pipe Company. The Hyundai Pipe Co. Ltd. was established in March 1979 to produce steel pipe. A second plant was to be built in the Ulsan industrial complex, with an annual capacity of 304,000 metric tons. Although production from the first plant had served the domestic market, the new Ulsan plant would export nearly all of its output. The project had a negative financial internal rate of return of −1.2 percent but an economic rate of return in excess of 80 percent, a rate well above the opportunity cost of capital. Given these results, there is little doubt that the government was justified in implementing this project, and given the low financial rate of return, government support was clearly justified. When evaluated at current prices, the project appears to be successful, earning an estimated financial rate of return of over 23 percent, while its economic rate of return apparently exceeds 100 percent. This result seems robust enough to suggest that a more sophisticated analysis would not yield a different conclusion.

Dong Yang Steel. A similar picture emerges for the Dong Yang Steel Industries, established in 1956, in collaboration with ALCOA (USA), as a manufacturer of aluminum extrusions and steel furniture.[17] The proposed expansion of the plant would not allow or accommodate increased production but would allow for the introduction of new product lines. Thirty percent of the output was to be for the export market. Plant construction began early in 1979, with production scheduled to start about eighteen months later. Both the ex-ante financial and economic rates of return are above 20 percent. Although this project is one that raised national welfare, government support for this project raises a different problem. A major difficulty that any policy of targeting specific activities faces is not only the strong possibility that it will support projects that are economically unsound, even in the long run, but that resources will be used to support projects that do not require such support. Indeed the high financial rate of return calculated for this project suggests that none of the special incentives available to HCI industries were needed to ensure its success. To the extent that Dong Yang Steel Industries received subsidized credits and other subventions regularly available to HCI activities, resources were unnecessarily squandered. The ex-post evaluation suggests that, from the financial perspective, the project was even more successful than expected, an outcome that primarily reflects the difference in the movement of domestic and international output prices.

The current priced economic internal rate of return, at just below 20 percent, indicates that the project remains internationally competitive.

Samsung Electronic Company. The Samsung Group, a *chaebol* that had gained a reputation in more traditional manufacturing activities such as textiles, set up Samsung Electronic Co., Ltd. (SEC) in 1969 to produce simple electronics and electrical products such as black-and-white television sets, electric fans, stoves, and refrigerators. A joint venture agreement was signed with SANYO, to produce television and radio sets, and with NEC, to produce vacuum tubes. Government of Korea policy required that all joint ventures export part of their output as a means of recouping the joint venture costs. In 1969, when the Samsung Group wanted to set up Samsung Electronics, a number of other domestic firms were already producing electrical appliances, and the government was skeptical about the potential for another entrant. To win government approval for its new venture, Samsung committed itself to producing primarily for the export market, although the domestic market was, in fact, far from saturated.[18] On the strength of that commitment, permission was granted for the joint ventures with SANYO and NEC.

Production began in 1971, followed one year later by exports. When Japan stopped production of black-and-white television sets, Samsung became SANYO's sole supplier of these sets, with some of the production exported to the United States under SANYO's name.[19]

The project analyzed here is one that allowed the company to expand production of color television sets and begin production of microwave ovens.[20] The entire production was meant for exports, in part because forecasts indicated that domestic consumers would not have the necessary income for some time to buy these more advanced products.[21] An analysis of the project data reveals that it had a low financial rate of return, 5.8 percent, but a high economic rate of return, over 50 percent, suggesting that if the forecast cost, production, and export levels were achieved, the project would make a substantial contribution to national income. In all respects this was a classic export-oriented project, whose success depended on a capacity to meet international prices and quality standards.

There is little doubt that this was a successful undertaking. In early 1979, Samsung had produced exactly one crude prototype microwave oven; by 1987 it produced 3.5 million ovens in 250 models that were sold in over twenty countries. The project evaluation, from the current perspective, bears this out. The financial rate of return is now high (55 percent), with an even higher economic rate of return. In part, this outturn reflects the fact that while the real prices for microwaves and color televisions have fallen dramatically, input prices have fallen even more, resulting in a reduction of the ratio of material cost to output prices. Although all output was initially exported, currently only about one-third is exported. The remainder is sold domestically.[22] With the increasing saturation of the consumer electronics market, Samsung has moved into the production of VCRs and computers.

Successful as the project has been, the success cannot be entirely ascribed to Korea's industrial policy or Samsung's marketing and production skills. To some extent, Samsung was aided by the U.S.-imposed "orderly marketing agreement" on Japanese imports of televisions and other electronic products. Although it is uncertain to what extent the marketing agreement against Japanese electronic imports contributed to Samsung's ability to penetrate the American market, its importance is readily admitted by Samsung officials.

A Preliminary Summing-Up

Although Chapter 6 considers other sectors as well as projects sup-ported under the HCI drive, a review of the evidence from the six projects studied here allows us to draw two conclusions. First, the projects analyzed provide no evidence that Korea's industrial policy was particularly astute at identifying activities that would not have been accepted under the standard neoclassical acceptance-rejection criteria. Among the projects studied, all had at least marginally acceptable economic rates of return. Hence, the industrial planners did not promote economically unacceptable projects that eventually became economically viable. In that sense, the HCI policy is not an instance of successful industrial targeting. Second, although all the projects studied had economic rates of return that exceeded the opportunity cost of capital, a number had low financial rates of return. They were thus legitimate candidates for various incentives. Government support for such activities finds strong support in traditional economics without recourse to the political or military rationale that underlay the HCI drive as a whole.

These conclusions do not imply that the shift in resources from more traditional investments to the HCI activities was optimal, at least in the short run. Although all the projects studied had economic rates of return (ERR) that exceeded the opportunity cost of capital (P_k)—i.e., $ERR \geq P_k$ —few had very high rates of return. By targeting specific activities, there was, of course, no way of ensuring that resources were not denied to investment that had higher rates of return. As discussed in Chapter 4, the shift from a policy of promoting all export-oriented activities to the specific targeting carried out under the HCI regime contributed to Korea's poor performance in the late 1970s and early 1980s. In short, although there is no evidence to support the contention that Korean policymakers were able to pick winners, neither can we conclude that the shift to the HCI policy helped promote Korea's development. HCI policies may not have channeled money into bad projects, but neither is there strong evidence to suggest that it channeled resources into a set of outstanding projects.

Obviously, the issue of whether Korea's HCI drive was a successful strategy and, perhaps more importantly, whether Korea's industrialization process reflects a unique ability to pick winners is not going to be settled by an analysis of six projects. This analysis does, however, suggest the type of questions that should be asked in evaluating an industrial strategy, and it suggests a useful analytic framework as well.

Government support for industrial development, especially for what is often perceived to be the modern industrial sector, is not unusual in developing countries and is often justified on the grounds that government has a role to play in correcting market failures. However, the means through which such support is given, and the political and bureaucratic framework that guides an industrial program, will often determine its effectiveness. Proponents of industrial targeting contend that a more direct intervention is needed. They argue that some projects that would not normally be accepted should be promoted because such activities have special characteristics that make them uniquely important to the national development effort. One interpretation of this is that it should encourage the development of projects that, on initial evaluation, may appear to make only a marginal, or even a negative, contribution to national income but nevertheless should be implemented on the presumption that eventually such activities will become economically, as well as financially, profitable.

Korea's success in transforming its industrial sector from one dominated by labor-intensive manufacturing to one with substantial capacity in capital- and technology-intensive products, while maintaining rapid industrial growth and continuing to develop new export markets, has been ascribed to the success of industrial targeting. Yet the conclusion that the projects promoted under the HCI drive were activities that would not normally have been entitled to government support has never been tested. The limited sample of projects evaluated does not suggest that Korea's policymakers were any more astute at identifying successful industries than policymakers elsewhere.

Returning to the framework presented in Chapter 1, the projects studied are categorized in Figure 5-1. The three projects in quadrant I had internal rates of return that justified their implementation, even if some measures of government support were required to encourage entrepreneurs to undertake the project. That these projects became successful is not without interest. Undoubtedly, the generally sound macroeconomic policies played a role in this outcome, and the continued emphasis by the government on export development ensured that these activities did not become inefficient import substituters. By the same measure, the three unsuccessful projects indicate that even the best-laid policies involve errors. Although all three projects would have passed the standard cost-benefit test, in the end they did not contribute to national income for a variety of reasons. For Korea Heavy Machinery and Boo-Kook Steel, shifts in prices and demand eroded the forecast market and projected revenues. It could be argued that such shifts should have been foreseen; more realistically, they reflect the inherent risks in any industrial promotion activity. Moreover, a series of mistakes during the implementation phase, combined with shifts in policy, eroded any possibility the heavy machinery complex had of succeeding. No matter how good, some projects will fail, not because the industrial policy is flawed but because the analysis, no matter how carefully done, will be able to forecast future prices and demands only within certain limits. The third project, Korea Steel Chemical, was an import-substitution effort where the actual outcome did not reflect the optimistic forecast used to promote it.

For the six projects studied, Korea's industrial strategy was in fact largely market conforming, in the sense that it promoted activities with

Figure 5-1. Classification of Industrial Projects

		Current Prices	
B a s e Y e a r P r i c e s		$ERR > P_k$	$ERR < P_k$
	$ERR \geq P_k$	Quadrant I: Successful Dong Yang Steel Company Hyundai Pipe Samsung Electronics	Quadrant II: Unsuccessful Korea Heavy Machinery Korea Steel Chemical Boo-Kook Steel
	$ERR \leq P_k$	Quadrant IV: Successful	Quadrant III: Unsuccessful

reasonably high economic rates of return. All six projects passed the neoclassical acceptance test, although only three turned out to be successful. But even if this were true of a representative sample of all HCI projects, it in no way suggests that the HCI drive was an optimal development strategy. The measures used to shift resources to the favored sectors and projects may well have lowered the overall productivity of the economy, at least in the short run.

Although industrial targeting, in the narrow sense of promoting projects that did not have a reasonably high economic rate of return, does not seem to have been an important explanation of industrial development in Korea, the relative success of the HCI program, with its specific policy interventions, is remarkable. Why was Korea apparently different from other developing countries that also try to foster rapid industrial growth but too often promote inefficient projects? In part, the answer lies in Korea's continued effort to ensure that even the HCI industries were export oriented. This alone probably prevented the most flagrant abuses. Another factor may be that Korea looked to Japan for information on which sectors should be developed. Boltho, referring to Japan, suggests that "in the 1950s and 1960s [Japan] was sufficiently backward to be able to pick winning sectors by looking at the success stories in the United States."[23] In a similar vein, it can be argued that Korea in the 1970s was sufficiently backward that it was able to pick winning sectors by looking at the development of Japan, seeing which sectors had succeeded there and which ones were likely to lose their competitive edge, allowing a lower-cost producer to enter the market. If so, the choice of sectors and projects to be supported was made not on the basis of some nebulous idea of future comparative advantage or in response to the successful lobbying of pressure groups, but was the outcome of a review of developments in a more advanced society whose general policy framework was not so different as to make any comparisons unrealistic.

A related issue is that the distortions between economic and market prices were relatively small. There is increasing evidence that a relatively undistorted price regime is important in promoting efficient resource allocations. Policies matter significantly for the economic rate of return of projects. This too may explain why, despite the emphasis given to the HCI program, the projects selected were often sensible ones. Finally, when compared to the industrial policies of other developing countries, Korea's HCI program was pursued with considerable consistency and implemented by an able and relatively efficient bureaucracy. Whether it actually raised or lowered the growth rate above what it might otherwise have been is a question that may never be satisfactorily answered.

Appendix 5A: Estimating Shadow Prices for Korea

Market prices often do not reflect the economic values of goods and services because of divergences from the perfect competitive ideal. Monopolies, decreasing cost industries, institutional constraints, taxes, and externalities are just a few of the many distortions that exist in all economies. In addition, disequilibria such as foreign exchange and capital scarcities, unemployment, and underemployment may exist in developing countries, where it is common to find government regulation of foreign exchange and capital markets and where governments intervene in the setting of numerous prices and wages. In all such cases, imputed values— shadow prices—must be used in calculating the activity's true contribution to social welfare.

The calculation of shadow prices is never a simple matter and one that is further compounded by alternative suggestions on the appropriate methodology. There is an extensive literature dealing with the conceptual and methodological issues in project evaluation, such as differences between shadow and border prices, the appropriate choice of the discount rate, the estimating of shadow wages, and risk analysis.[24]

The most practical approach, and one that is rooted in classical economics, is the opportunity cost doctrine. Consider an economy where only two goods, X and Y, are produced. If the production of X is to be increased, the cost of producing the additional quantity of X is the value of the Y good that the community must give up. Analysis of the production and demand functions for the two commodities will provide the required data. The situation is, of course, more complicated when a multiplicity of goods is being produced, since this would require the impossible task of analyzing the production and demand functions for all goods produced. Fortunately, it is possible to estimate the opportunity cost using a less data-intensive methodology. In practice the estimation of a shadow price asks where the additional resources needed for the production of X come from. In general, there will be two sources for the additional factors needed to increase the output of X. Some of the additional resources will come from a reduction in the output of other commodities—good Y—and these are valued at the price current users place on those commodities. In addition, there will be an increase in the supply of the factors needed in the production of X—the increase brought about by the rise in the price for such inputs. The degree to which the factors needed for an expansion of X come from a reduction in other uses or from increases in supply will depend on the relevant elasticities of demand (for Y) and of supply (for inputs needed to produce X). This leads to the result that the shadow price for any factor of production is a weighted average of the value placed on the factor, or commodity, by current users and the price needed to compensate additional suppliers, each response weighted by the relevant elasticity of supply and demand.[25]

This, in a nutshell, is what the estimation of shadow prices entails. In reality the task is complicated. The project analyst must investigate whence the resources for a project will come and what their values are in those uses. And to complicate matters further, shadow prices should be calculated for every factor and input used, including such nontradables as electricity, water, government services, and insurance. Whether in any particular case additional insights are gained from calculating shadow prices for all inputs depends on the degree to which policies distort the general price structure in any economy and the degree to which any specific project makes use of the price-distorted input. If, for example, the price for telephone services is severely distorted but a project makes minimal use of such services, little is gained by estimating the real cost of such an input.

In the projects studied here, we restrict ourselves to estimating the shadow prices for three primary factors of production: foreign exchange (a measure used to correct the prices of all traded and potentially traded goods), labor, and capital. The last price is used as the appropriate discount rate to convert all future costs and benefits to their present value equivalence.

The Estimation of Economic Prices: Foreign Exchange

The shadow price for foreign exchange is derived from a foreign exchange model that assumes that the demand for imports is subject to both import tariffs and quantitative restrictions, while exports may receive subsidies, but where the local currency is allowed to fluctuate over time in line with market supply and demand conditions.[26] Such an economy, operating under a freely floating exchange rate, the shadow price, or the economic opportunity cost of foreign exchange (*EOCFX*), is given by:

$$EOCFX = \frac{E^m \times \left[\varepsilon^x \times (1 + K) - \eta^i \times (1 + T) \times \left(\frac{Q^i}{Q^x} \right) \right]}{\varepsilon^x - \eta^i \times \left(\frac{Q^i}{Q^x} \right)} \qquad (5A.1)$$

where E^m is the market exchange rate, K is the effective subsidy rate on exports, T is the effective import tariff rate, including the estimated tariff equivalent of any quantitative restrictions, ε^x and η^i are the elasticities of supply and demand for foreign exchange, respectively, with respect to changes in the exchange rate, while Q^i and Q^x are the quantities of foreign exchange demanded (imports valued at c.i.f. prices) and supplied (exports valued at f.o.b. prices).

This basic model can be readily modified to reflect alternative exchange rate regimes, as for example, the use of an adjustable-peg system where the nominal exchange rate is periodically devalued in an attempt to deal with a growing current account imbalance, or the rationing of foreign exchange.[27] Because the foreign exchange regimes that characterize Korea changed over time, different models were applied to derive the shadow exchange rate for the entire 1966–1986 period.

Korea's foreign exchange regimes can be roughly divided into three periods—1966–1974, 1975–1979, and 1980–1986 —each distinguished by the government's policy on exchange rate flexibility.[28] From the mid-1960s, when Korea embarked on its export drive, the nominal exchange rate was allowed to depreciate gradually to maintain Korea's competitiveness in the world markets, although quantitative controls were simultaneously used to control the current account deficit. In order to improve Korea's competitive position, the government devalued the won by 20 percent in 1974. From then until 1980, the exchange rate was held constant, even while Korea's inflation rate exceeded that of its major trading partners, so that the real effective exchange rate became overvalued. In part, government allowed the exchange rate to depreciate to spur investments in the heavy and chemical industries, a number of which were import substituting rather than export biased. In part because of the growing overvaluation of the exchange rate, export growth declined precipitously in the late 1970s.

As part of the overall liberalization of the economy and the move away from the HCI drive of the 1970s, the won was devalued by 17 percent in January 1980, and in February, the government introduced a controlled floating exchange rate system aimed at maintaining a relatively constant real effective exchange rate. By the mid-1980s foreign exchange rationing and controls were eliminated.

To account for these different trade regimes, alternative estimating equations, incorporating the essential elements of the trade policies in effect at the time, were used to calculate a time series for the economic opportunity cost of foreign exchange. For the period 1966–1974, when there was a combination of periodic devaluations and foreign currency rationing, the following hybrid model was used to estimate the opportunity cost of foreign exchange:

(5A.2)

$$EOCFX = \frac{\varepsilon^x \cdot E^m \cdot (1 + K) - \eta^i \cdot \left[E^b \cdot (1 + T) \cdot \dfrac{OER}{E^b} \right] \cdot \dfrac{Q^i}{Q^x}}{\varepsilon^x - \eta^d \cdot \left[\dfrac{Q^i}{Q^x} \right]}$$

where all the variables are as in equation 5A.1 except for E^b, which measures the black market exchange rate, and for the term (OER/E^b), which, by converting the tariff rate at the official exchange rate to a tariff rate at the black market exchange rate, makes the base consistent. This model is appropriate for the period 1966–1974, which was characterized by a combination of periodic devaluations and exchange rate rationing. For the period 1975–1979, when the government maintained an overvalued exchange rate and controlled imports through tariffs and quantitative restrictions, while continuing to ration foreign exchange, the following model is used:

(5A.3)

$$EOCFX = E^b \times \left[(1 + T) \times \left(\frac{OER}{E^b} \right) \right]$$

and the variables are all as defined before. Finally, for the period 1980 –1986 when the government allowed the won to depreciate to correct balance-of-payments deficits while simultaneously easing quantitative controls, the estimation procedure shown in equation 5A.1 was used.

The estimated opportunity cost of foreign exchange using these three alternative models is shown in Table 5A-1. The differences between the official exchange rate and its economic value trace out a general history of the foreign exchange regimes in Korea. The difference between the official exchange rate and its economic value was relatively high in 1965 (39 percent), when the current account deficit averaged over 8 percent of GNP, but the difference declined throughout the next decade, reaching a low of 10 percent in 1974. At that time, the nominal exchange rate was fixed at won 484/US$, with the result that there was again a growing discrepancy between the nominal value and the economic price of foreign exchange, which reached 25 percent in 1979. The current account, which showed a slight surplus in 1977, began to deteriorate, reaching nearly 9 percent of GNP by 1980. Subsequent adjustments in macroeconomic policies, combined with the introduction of a floating exchange rate, have served to keep the nominal exchange rate within 4

Table 5A-1. Opportunity Cost of Foreign Exchange (won/US$)

Year	Official Exchange Rate	Opportunity Cost of Foreign Exchange[a]	
		Annual data	Three-Year Average
1965	266.4	371.1	
1966	271.3	304.8	
1967	270.5	312.6	
1968	276.7	319.9	338.6
1969	288.2	336.1	330.0
1970	310.6	387.9	360.1
1971	347.2	425.6	413.3
1972	392.9	440.0	476.9
1973	398.3	436.9	477.3
1974	404.5	442.1	464.1
1975	484.0	531.8	534.0
1976	484.0	539.1	530.6
1977	484.0	558.8	533.3
1978	484.0	578.1	543.2
1979	484.0	607.3	558.7
1980	607.4	648.8	729.7
1981	681.0	716.5	798.5
1982	731.1	769.4	822.5
1983	775.8	813.1	820.4
1984	806.0	840.8	847.0
1985	870.0	902.6	911.7
1986	881.5	914.2	919.3

[a]The annual opportunity cost of foreign exchange is used in the ex-post evaluation where the best year-to-year estimate of the economic cost of foreign exchange is required; the three-year average is used in the ex-ante evaluations, which would use only the information available at the time the project was appraised.
Source: Sabin and Kato, "Shadow Price Calculation and Application."

or 5 percent of the real price of foreign exchange. The current account deficits were eliminated by 1986 and replaced by a substantial and growing surplus.

The Estimation of Economic Prices: Labor

The foregone marginal product of workers absorbed in a project is sometimes taken as their economic opportunity cost. It can, however, be argued that such an approach understates the true opportunity cost of labor by not adequately taking into account labor's locational preferences for which workers will demand compensation before moving. This criticism of the foregone marginal product approach has led to an estimation procedure, not unlike that used in the estimation of the economic value of foreign exchange, which uses a

Table 5A-2. Economic Opportunity Cost of Labor in the Manufacturing
Sector: Gyongsang Nam Do (thousand won/annum)

Category	1976	1979	1982	1984
Operatives				
Gross of tax wage	820.0	1,890.0	3,200.0	3,880.0
Economic cost	450.9	1,230.9	2,158.4	2,607.5
Conversion factor	0.55	0.65	0.67	0.67
Semiskilled				
Gross of tax wage	1,324.1	2,374.2	4,114.4	4,823.9
Economic cost	77.8	1,656.9	2,666.7	3,274.3
Conversion factor	0.59	0.70	0.65	0.68
Technical and managerial				
Gross of tax wage	2,930.0	6,780.0	11,460.0	13,900.0
Economic cost	2,097.5	4,347.9	6,321.3	7,594.9
Conversion factor	0.72	0.64	0.55	0.55
Expatriate labor				
Gross of tax wage	19,200.0	23,920.0	30,440.0	32,900.0
Economic cost	16,627.2	22,980.5	24,592.9	27,950.1
Conversion factor	0.87	0.96	0.81	0.85

weighted average of the private supply price, or wage, necessary to induce laborers to join the labor force in a particular area or region, and the demand price, measured by the marginal product of labor, to derive the value of labor used by the project.[29] As before, the weights are determined by the relative elasticities of supply of and demand for labor.[30]

This approach recognizes that the economic price of labor must take account not only of different qualities of labor but that different economic costs of labor must be calculated reflecting the different locations for various economic activities. In addition to a price for un- skilled labor, estimates were also made for semiskilled and technical and managerial labor, as well as for the use of expatriate personnel. In making these estimates, it was assumed that unskilled labor, or operatives, would be drawn from the relatively unprotected (small- and medium-scale) manufacturing sector in Korea. The small- and medium-scale individually owned firms were taken as representative of the unprotected sector, defined as the sector where compliance with labor regulations is likely to be weak or nonexistent.[31] Table 5A-2 summarizes the data by skill levels for the Gyongsang Nam Do region, where a number of industrial projects were located.

The results confirm the general story about labor supply in Korea. Beginning with a surplus of unskilled labor in the late 1960s and early 1970s, reflected in the large difference between the gross of tax wage and the economic cost of unskilled labor, the supply of such labor tightened considerably, as a result of the rapid growth in the labor-intensive export industries and subsequently in the heavy and chemical industries. These developments are reflected in the substantial rise in the conversion factor by 1979. The same dynamics explain the narrowing of the gap between the wage and economic cost of semiskilled labor, although the gap between the market wage and the economic cost of labor was never as large as it was for unskilled workers.

The gap between the wage and the economic cost of hiring technical and managerial labor has moved differently, widening over time. One possible explanation is that, while rapid industrialization increased the demand for such labor, the expansion of the educational system increased the supply of such labor at an even faster pace, reducing the economic cost of recruiting such workers.[32] Finally, the difference between the market wage and economic cost for expatriate labor reflects both the scarcity premium on foreign exchange and the fact that part of the wages paid to foreign labor is recovered as income tax (estimated at 20 percent), which, being a transfer payment, reduces the economic cost of using such labor. By the 1980s, when the distortions in the foreign exchange market were essentially eliminated, the difference between the economic cost and market wage of expatriate labor was nearly entirely due to such income taxes.

The Estimation of Economic Prices: Capital

No other issue in the literature on shadow pricing has generated as much discussion as the appropriate discount rate to use. It is agreed by all that under conditions of perfect competition, the market interest rate equates individuals' marginal time preference with the marginal rate of return on investments. In the real world, however, capital markets have numerous imperfections, which drive a wedge between the time productivity of capital, the rate of return, and lenders' preference rates, the marginal time preference. Various proposals have been put forward for determining the appropriate discount rate to be used in project evaluation. Some have argued that the opportunity cost of capital is determined by a consumer's time preference, while others argue that the correct discount rate is given by the rate of return on private investments.[33] Others, notably Dasgupta, Marglin, and Sen, have argued that the stream of net benefits should be discounted using the social time preference rate after adjusting the market cost of investment by an adjustment factor that reflects the economic cost of capital, a proposal meant to account for the fact that the benefits of a project should be measured in terms of the consumption generated while the costs should be measured in terms of the consumption foregone. One difficulty with this approach is that it requires fairly complex calculations.[34]

An alternative approach, suggested by Harberger, relies on both the estimated marginal productivity of capital and the rate of time preference by consumers.[35] In line with the procedure used to estimate the economic opportunity cost of foreign exchange and labor, this approach uses a weighted average of the marginal productivity of capital and consumer rate of time preference. The economic opportunity cost of capital (*EOCK*) can be expressed as:

$$EOCK = \frac{(\varepsilon^s \times r) - \left[(\eta^d \times \pi) \times \frac{I_t}{S_t}\right]}{\varepsilon^s - \left[\eta^d \times \frac{I_t}{S_t}\right]} \tag{5A.4}$$

where *r* is the marginal rate of time preference for savers, π is the gross of tax return on the marginal investment, ε^s is the elasticity of the supply of savings with respect to changes in the interest rate, η^d is the elasticity of demand for capital with respect to changes in the interest rate, I_t is the quantity of capital demanded by the private sector, and S_t is total savings available to the economy. As written, the equation assumes that there is only one group of investors and one group of savers. However, by disaggregating the equation so as to allow for different elasticities, marginal rates of time preference for different groups of savers, and different gross of tax return on investments, the model can readily accommodate the actual situation represented by different groups of savers and different rates of return on investments.

During the 1970s Korea's financial system was subject to considerable government regulation.[36] Controlled nominal interest rates coupled with high rates of inflation produced negative real interest rates throughout this period, and credit rationing and preferential loans to particular industries created a highly segmented financial market. These distortions were amplified when the government gave priority to investments in the heavy and chemical industries. As investment funds were channeled to large enterprises, productive but small- and medium-scale investors were effectively squeezed out of the official credit market. Such firms increasingly turned to the already sizable informal financial sector for investment capital.

In line with the liberalization policies introduced in the 1980s, the government introduced a series of staged reforms of the financial system, liberalizing the level and structure of interest rates and encouraging competition among financial institutions. In part because of the liberalization measures and in part because of a series of crises in the informal sector, this source of finance capital shrank. As a result of these measures, the overall size of Korea's official financial market expanded in the 1980s at a rapid pace.

Estimates for the economic cost of capital were made for three periods for which the requisite data were available: 1975–1977, 1978–1980, and 1981–1983. The estimated opportunity cost of capital is shown in Table 5A-3. These estimates reveal that the social discount rate in Korea was considerably lower than the market interest rates would suggest and did not change appreciably over the period considered. One might have expected that the high rates of economic growth and the concomitant scarcity of capital would combine to produce high real marginal rates of return to investment and thus a fairly high social discount rate. One possible explanation for the counterintuitive outcome is that policy-induced distortions, such as credit subsidies, channeled resources into inefficient projects, lowering the real rates of return to capital at the margin.[37]

If so, one might then ask why the estimated social discount rate shows only a marginal increase in the 1981–1983 period, when many of the distortionary financial policies were removed. Two forces, one working to raise the discount rate and the other working to lower it, apparently offset each other. On the one hand, the data show that the relaxation of credit controls led to an increase in the real return to investment as well as a rise in the rate of time preference of savers in the official market.[38] At the same time, changes in the structure and responsiveness on the lending side of the financial market acted to reduce the overall return to saving. The mix of these factors helps explain the lack of any substantial rise in the opportunity cost of capital in the early 1980s.

Although sensitivity analysis shows the opportunity cost of capital as not very sensitive to alternative estimates of the various factors, including the elasticities of supply and demand, it is sensitive to estimates of the "expected" inflation rate. The opportunity cost of capital is based on the real return to investment, but the available data refer to nominal rates of return, which incorporate inflationary expectations. Estimating the "expected" rate of inflation that is incorporated in the nominal rates of return is inherently difficult because there is no strong theoretical basis on which to predict how different income groups and investors anticipate future price changes.[39] The estimates derived by Sabin and Kato use a model that combines an estimate of the "core inflation," essentially a seven-year moving average, and actual inflation as a proxy for forecasts

Table 5A-3. Economic Opportunity Cost of Capital, 1975–1983

Period	Economic Cost of Capital
1975–1977	10.18 %
1978–1980	8.10
1981–1983	9.39

Source: Sabin and Kato, "Shadow Price Calculation and Application."

of the immediate future.[40] The weights on the core inflation decrease over time, while those on the current inflation increase, reflecting an assumption that people become sensitized to changes in inflation over time and as a result become better predictors of actual inflation. Whether this model accurately captures how inflationary expectations were reflected in the nominal rates of return investors demanded is unanswerable. However, the sensitivity analysis shows that using an alternative model, which reduces the expected inflation rate from 17 percent to 10 percent, increases the opportunity cost of capital from 10 to 16 percent. This may be an extreme case, in that an expected inflation rate of 10 percent is undoubtedly too low, but it is clear that if the estimated inflation rate is too high, the estimated opportunity cost of capital is too low. Given this uncertainty it is probably best to consider the above estimates of the opportunity cost of capital as minimum estimates.

NOTES

1. As always, one can argue about the appropriate time frame for such a comparison. For example, if one had looked at the Korean data for a period ending in the early 1980s, the performance would have looked less sanguine. But a counterargument would point out that Korea suffered a severe drought in 1980 and that the second oil shock further reduced growth in the early 1980s, events that had little to do with the impact of the HCI drive.

2. Charles L. Schultze, "Industrial Policy: A Dissent," *The Brookings Review* 2 (Fall 1983): 8.

3. Even then it is necessary to show that the discounted benefits from the promoted industry are sufficient to outweigh the temporary economic costs of the subsidies given to it. That is, the projects must pass the Mills-Bastable test.

4. There is another outcome that would favor industrial targeting but is not captured in the suggested analytic framework. Consider project X, which has an ex-ante and ex-post economic rate of return below the opportunity cost of capital ($ERR < P_k$). If the spillover effects from project X cause other projects to be successful and such spillover effects are not captured by the conventional cost-benefit analysis, then the promotion of project X would still enhance total national welfare, assuming that the discounted spillover effects are greater than the economic losses of the project.

5. In practice one would want to correct the market prices for any input or output where price does not equal marginal cost. It is quite common that the market prices for such items as railway transport, electricity, and water do not reflect marginal cost and need to be correct. However, in most cases these inputs form only a small part of total cost, and attempts to adjust their values probably have little impact on the overall analysis. Hence, we restrict the application of shadow prices to all tradable commodities, labor and capital.

6. The project data may have misrepresented expected benefits and costs. Since the project data were first used to obtain financial support from banks and government agencies, the investor presumably had an incentive to show that the project would be financially successful in order to convince potential lenders of the project's ability to repay the loan. There would seem to be little gain in skewing the data to show a low financial rate of return.

7. It is difficult to decide the length of time before an appropriate ex-post analysis can be undertaken, although presumably sufficient time should elapse to allow short-term start-up problems to be overcome.

8. The company was established under the name Hyundai International Incorporated in September 1962; the corporate name was changed to Korea Heavy Industries and Construction Co. Ltd. in October 1980.

9. It is doubtful whether the export projections for heavy machinery were realistic since this market is characterized by a number of special factors that make it difficult for new entrants to become established in fewer than ten to fifteen years. The reputation, and follow-up service, of machine tool producers is often a more critical factor than price comparisons, and it takes years for a new producer to attain a strong international reputation.

10. As is noted in the chapter appendix, the estimated cost of capital is highly sensitive to the model used to forecast inflationary expectations. If a lower estimate is used for the expected inflation rate, the opportunity cost of capital for the period 1975–1977 would rise from the 10.2 percent

shown in Table 5-2 to 16 percent, and the heavy machinery project, with an estimated internal rate of return of 17.5 percent, would be considered a marginal project.

11. Although with hindsight it is possible to find a number of economists and policymakers who now claim to have been skeptical of the heavy machinery project, a review of the literature of the period reveals little published opposition to the project. While this does not mean there was none, neither does it seem to confirm the argument that the government went ahead with this project against the advice of nongovernment economists.

12. The Changwon area, near the port of Pusan, was targeted for rapid growth in order to contribute to a better regional distribution of income and employment.

13. Some of the facilities were sold to Samsung Engineering.

14. The fact that KHIC's technical collaborator on nuclear power systems was Westinghouse Electric Corporation, whose nuclear generating system has been under attack as being less safe than systems used in France and the United Kingdom, obviously did not help the situation.

15. The other major failure is the Okpo shipbuilding complex, which the Daewoo group was forced to take over. By 1994, Daewoo had turned Okpo shipyard into one of the world's most efficient. Whether the current success of the Okpo facility would justify the economic cost of building the facility is less certain since the benefits are being received many years after the initial investment outlay. See "A Rescue at Sea in South Korea," *Economist*, November 26–December 2, 1994, pp. 81–82.

16. That conclusion can be challenged by those who would argue that policymakers should have discounted the forecast demand for the project's output and should have used more sophisticated cost-benefit analysis, including risk analysis, to evaluate such a large project. A more interesting question, to which we have no answer, is whether the initial projections were reasonable given the information available in 1975 or whether they were inflated. Probably like most other project forecasts, they were optimistic, but the extent to which the optimism should have been discounted is more difficult to fix.

17. The efforts to promote development of an aluminum sector failed, however. See the discussion in Chapter 6.

18. The situation was summed up by the executive vice president of SEC who noted that "when I started to work on TV production I did not even have a TV in my own home."

19. Interestingly, when Samsung tried to sell its sets directly to the United States, it had difficulties in meeting U.S. safety standards.

20. The story of Samsung's production capacity for microwaves, and its ability to develop export markets, is engagingly told in "Korea: Winning with Microwaves" in I. Magaziner and M. Patinkin, *The Silent War* (New York: Vintage Books, 1989).

21. Perhaps more to the point, when Samsung decided to begin production of color television sets, not a single television station in Korea broadcast in color.

22. In a conversation with senior management, it was suggested that the per unit profits were higher for domestic than for export sales but that Samsung continued to export because only with exports could it obtain the needed economies of scale.

23. A. Boltho, "Was Japan's Industrial Policy Successful?" *Cambridge Journal of Economics* 9 (1985): 187–201.

24. For a clear discussion of these issues see F. L. C. H. Helmers, *Project Planning and Income Distribution* (Boston: Martinus Nijhoff Publishing, 1979).

25. The literature on estimating shadow prices is extensive and not always easy to comprehend. For a clear discussion of the approach outlined above, see A. C. Harberger, *Project Evaluation: Collected Papers* (Chicago: Chicago University Press, 1976), and A. C. Harberger, "On the UNIDO Guidelines to Social Project Evaluation," in H. Schwartz and R. Berney, eds., *Social and Economic Dimensions of Project Evaluation* (Washington, D.C.: Inter-American Development Bank, 1977), and the much more extensive discussion in G. Jenkins and A. C. Harberger, "Cost-Benefit Analysis of Investment Decisions," unpublished manuscript (1988).

26. The discussion of the methodology used to derive the shadow prices for Korea draws heavily on L. Sabin and H. Kato, "Shadow Price Calculation and Application: A Case Study of Korea," *Harvard Institute for International Development Discussion Paper 313* (Cambridge: Harvard Institute for International Development, 1989).

27. For a detailed discussion see ibid.

28. See C. R. Frank, Kwang Suk Kim, and L. E. Westphal, *Foreign Trade Regimes and Economic Development: South Korea* (New York: National Bureau of Economic Research, 1975); P. Hasan, Korea: *Problems and Issues in a Rapidly Growing Economy* (Baltimore: Johns Hopkins University Press, 1976); Yung Whee Rhee, B. Ross-Larsen, and G. Pursell, *Korea's Competitive Edge: Managing the Entry into World Markets* (Baltimore: Johns Hopkins University Press, 1984); and D. M. Leipziger et al., *Korea: Managing the Industrial Transition* (Washington, D.C.: World Bank, 1987), vols. 1 and 2, for a discussion of the various trade regimes.

29. A. C. Harberger, *Project Evaluation: Collected Papers* (Chicago: Markham Publishing Company, 1976).

30. The main practical difference between the procedure for estimating the economic price of foreign exchange and of labor is that in the latter case we take account of labor's preferences regarding various working conditions and locales.

31. Note that this is not the sector economists generally think of as the informal market, where one would find shoeshine boys, newspaper vendors, and other unskilled laborers. We have assumed that in Korea, new entrants into factories would have already entered the manufacturing sphere, albeit at its lowest rung.

32. An alternative explanation may be that certain firms found it useful to pay a premium to skilled workers in return for extra productivity and loyalty. If so, this would be an additional factor explaining the observed differences between the market wage and the economic cost of technical and managerial labor.

33. Like capital theory, the estimation of the opportunity cost of capital is full of controversy. For a succinct summary of some of the alternative views, and for a discussion of how alternative discount rates would affect project selection, see F. L. Helmers, *Project Planning*, esp. chaps. 3, 8.

34. S. A. Marglin, *Public Investment Criteria* (Cambridge: MIT Press, 1967).

35. Harberger, *Project Evaluation*.

36. More complete information and analysis of Korea's financial sector can be found in D. C. Cole and Yung-chul Park, *Financial Development in Korea: 1945–1978* (Cambridge: Harvard University Press, 1983); D. Leipziger, *Korea*, vols. 1–2; and Yoon-je Cho and D. C. Cole, "The Role of the Financial Sector in Korea's Structural Adjustment," *Harvard Institute for International Development Discussion Paper 230* (Cambridge: Harvard Institute for International Development, 1986).

37. These estimates of the opportunity cost of capital are considerably lower than estimates of the rates of return on capital obtained by others. For example, G. T. Brown, *Korean Pricing Policies and Economic Development in the 1960s* (Baltimore: Johns Hopkins University Press, 1973), pp. 203–206, estimates that the rate of return on new investment in the period 1962–1967 was on the order of 20 percent, and under alternative assumptions considerably higher. It is, however, important to note that the opportunity cost estimated here is a weighted average of the return to capital and the consumer rate of time preference. The gross of tax returns on capital averages is well above 20 percent, the exact level varying by sector and time period. See Sabin and Kato, "Shadow Price Calculation," pp. 70–71.

38. See Sabin and Kato, "Shadow Price Calculation," pp. 70–73.

39. One way to estimate the expected inflation rate is to take the difference between the nominal interest rates for long-term loans and the real interest rate on short-term loans on the assumption that real interest rates remain roughly constant over time. This analysis breaks down in a highly regulated market such as prevailed in Korea during most of the period under review.

40. See Sabin and Kato, "Shadow Price Calculation."

6

Selected Case Histories

The case studies that form the core of this chapter deal with four industries: aluminum, shipbuilding, automobiles, and steel. Unlike the firm-specific analysis of Chapter 5, the focus here is on the industry as a whole, although in the case of steel, a single firm, POSCO, is coincidental with the modern portion of the industry. Although the analytic framework presented in Chapter 1 and applied in Chapter 5 is appropriate in the analysis of individual projects supported under the heavy and chemical industry (HCI) drive, data limitations make it desirable to supplement the project-focused approach with a broader review of the sectors that were the primary targets of the industrial policies of the 1970s.

In terms of the four sectors studied, the first, the aluminum industry, is a clear instance of a failure of industrial policy, although the total resources invested in this area were relatively small. The second, the shipbuilding sector, is an instance of industrial targeting gone awry, with policies that fostered a rapid expansion of the sector at considerable cost in terms of scarce resources expended and with decidedly mixed results. The third industry, automobiles, represents a case that can best be described as an instance of mixed success. Some firms, Hyundai being the best known, have become internationally competitive; others have failed to attain that standard. The fourth, the steel industry, is generally accepted as a case of successful industrial targeting. Because the government provided considerable capital for the development of the steel industry, the economic rate of return earned on the total investment is important to any firm conclusions as to the success of this venture.

In its broadest sense industrial policy encompasses all measures that affect production and trade. Industrial targeting—a set of decisions that are aimed at promoting specific projects in order to attain some specific development goal—is one possible focus of industrial policy. The outcome of industrial targeting is best analyzed using the ex-ante and ex-post cost-benefit framework described in Chapter 1 and applied in Chapter 5 to some of the specific project activities that were the focus of industrial targeting. The broader, industry-wide approach used in this chapter provides a useful adjunct to the project-specific focus, capturing the full impact of the industrial promotion efforts as they affect all firms in a specific industry.

Another way to characterize the link between the sector studies discussed here and the project analysis that formed the focus of the preceding chapter is to recognize that the sector studies are generally a blunter approach than the analysis of individual projects. Of necessity, sector studies deal with all the firms that make up an industry. Not all of the firms within an industry will produce the same product, have the same history, or be equally well managed. Thus, some firms established in a sector actively favored under the HCI drive were established before the HCI policy was introduced, while others emerged in response to the incentives offered. Similarly some firms might have succeeded even without the special policy measures that supported them; others thrived only because of them. In any sector, some firms survive and prosper while others fail, even in the same domestic and external environment. Focusing on individual firms allows us to deal with these issues in detail, but unless all firms within the sector are analyzed, the conclusions are necessarily limited. By contrast, industry studies describe events that affected the "average" firm that characterizes the sector, providing a different perspective on why some parts of the HCI drive succeeded while others failed. A review of the developments in certain industries thus complements the insights gained from project studies.

The Aluminum Industry

Products of the nonferrous metals sector, including aluminum, provide important inputs for the electrical, electronic, machinery, automotive, aviation, shipbuilding, chemical, and construction industries. Since the sector exhibits strong links to upstream and downstream user industries, it was a natural candidate for industrial promotion.

A second characteristic of the aluminum industry is its high energy intensity: smelting alumina requires a great deal of electrical power. Considering Korea's relatively high energy costs and the lack of any major raw material source, the promotion of the aluminum industry was a dubious proposition at best. In addition, the aluminum metals sector is also a highly capital-intensive activity, subject to considerable economies of scale, which call for long-term investments before returns to capital are realized. Given Korea's internal market, these scale economies could be realized only if domestic aluminum producers could effectively compete in the international market.[1] This they were never able to do.

Despite these factors, all of which should have argued against the development of an aluminum industry, the industry was considered important enough to warrant government support, not only because of its perceived downstream linkages but also because of its potential value in the development of construction materials. In the 1960s, the domestic demand for aluminum increased rapidly as the demand for aluminum products, especially in the construction sector, expanded rapidly. Prior to the establishment of a domestic aluminum industry, all aluminum products had been imported.

In 1969, in an effort to meet the rapidly growing demand for aluminum and to substitute imported aluminum, an alumina smelting plant with an annual capacity of 15,000 tons was established by the Korea Aluminum Company (KAC). The project was financed by $13.5 million in loans, obtained on commercial terms from Japan, together with some 2 billion won of domestic credit. The majority shares were owned by a state bank, the Korea Development Bank (KDB). Lacking a domestic bauxite source, KAC imported all of its alumina, which was smelted, using electric furnaces, into aluminum. In 1970, when KAC began full operation, it was able to meet nearly the entire domestic aluminum demand, but as domestic demand continued to increase and KAC reached its production capacity, aluminum imports again began to rise rapidly.

In 1973, KAC's name was changed to the Aluminum of Korea Company (AKC), and under a joint venture with a French firm, Pechiney, its annual capacity was expanded to 17,500 tons, a level that was never again increased, despite the continued growth in domestic demand. As a result, Korea's dependence on imports rose from about 21 percent in 1973 to over 90 percent in the 1980s.

To encourage domestic aluminum production, AKC received a 50 percent subsidy on its electric power costs. In part this subsidy recognized that Korea's electric power costs were considerably higher than those of other major aluminum-producing countries. For example, in 1989, the unit cost for electricity to industrial users in Korea was three times as high as it was in the United States and nearly five times as high as in Canada. Despite this subsidy, the company experienced deficits throughout its operating history. Even after the government allowed AKC to pass on the increased energy costs that Korea experienced during the 1970s and

1980s, the firm was unable to show a profit. Compounding the difficulty caused by rising energy costs, the company had to face increased pressure for imports as the international price for aluminum declined. Faced with these facts, the government decided that any further expansion of domestic production would only make AKC's operations even more unprofitable. In 1989, the government ceased subsidization of electricity costs, forcing AKC to stop operations.

As part of a privatization program, AKC was acquired by the Hyundai group, which changed the focus of its operation. About 70 percent of its turnover now comes from the processing of imported aluminum rather than from the production of aluminum itself.

A number of factors contributed to the failure of this venture. Although AKC was a monopoly producer of aluminum ingots, its production scale was well below the 100,000-ton level considered necessary to achieve reasonable economies of scale. Moreover, the smelting technology it used was outmoded. In 1973, when it signed a technical licensing agreement with Pechiney, it obtained the Söderberg smelting process, which became obsolete a few years later with the introduction of a new process that permitted considerable energy savings. Yet even if AKC had been able to shift to a less energy-intensive mode of production, the failure to achieve economically viable production levels meant that it would never be internationally competitive. Indeed, the domestic price for aluminum in Korea consistently has been one-third higher than the world price.

Because of AKC's inability to meet domestic demand and because of the high price of aluminum, a secondary aluminum ingot market, using scrap to manufacture ingots, has become important. The use of aluminum scrap saves on imported raw materials, and the reduction process used is less energy intensive. The main domestic uses of secondary aluminum ingots are for die castings and moldings, 80 percent of which are used by the automobile industry. The amount and rate of aluminum scrap retrieval in Korea is still low, and, lacking a modern processing technology, Korea's aluminum products remain relatively unsophisticated. Higher-grade products, such as aluminum coil used in making aluminum cans, continue to be imported.

Although the investment in the aluminum industry was never very large, it represents one of the clearest failures of the HCI drive. Despite the perceived strong linkages to other users, the lack of raw materials and the high energy costs that characterize the Korean economy dominated the outcome. Even with access to subsidized credits and energy, the industry never managed to become internationally competitive. The mounting losses the company experienced eventually forced the government to cease subsidizing electricity inputs and allow a private firm to rationalize the production process.

The Shipbuilding Industry

The Korean shipbuilding industry is a valuable case study of industrial targeting that at one time seemed to be successful but, in the light of more recent developments, apparently is another instance of unsuccessful industrial targeting. For many years, the failure of the Daewoo shipbuilding facilities at Okpo represented one of the two large failures of the HCI drive.[2] By 1994, the Okpo plant had become profitable, but given the long lag between the initial investment and the restructuring of the facility, it is doubtful that the discounted stream of benefits is sufficient to earn a reasonable return on the original investment.

In the early 1970s, the government targeted shipbuilding as a key industry and provided numerous incentives, including access to subsidized credits, tax incentives, and import protection, in its effort to stimulate shipbuilding. Although Korean shipbuilders have become a significant force in the international as well as domestic markets, the industry was severely affected by the world recession of the 1980s. This adverse climate, plus domestic labor unrest, combined with the appreciation of the won, led to the bankruptcy of one firm and major financial difficulties at the other three large shipbuilders.

Admittedly shipbuilding is an activity whose profitability is subject to substantial fluctuations reflecting changes in world trade levels and patterns. Successful shipyards weather these cycles by diversifying production, which allows them to build a variety of vessels as well as repair ships, and engage in the manufacture of large, heavy machines when demand for ships is slack. Unfortunately the diversification of Korea's shipyards into such other nonshipbuilding activities has not gone very far compared to the diversification found in more mature facilities, such as those of Japan.[3] This weakness accounts for much of the current difficulty faced by the industry, although it is far from clear whether these difficulties are short term and can be overcome or are structural in nature.

A number of characteristics of shipbuilding made it a particularly attractive industry to Korea's industrial planners. First, since shipbuilding is a labor-intensive activity, it was expected to create numerous jobs for the abundant labor supply that characterized Korea in the late 1950s and early 1960s. Second, the industry uses inputs from more than fifty other industries, including machinery, iron and steel, electronics, chemicals, and furniture, so it was seen as having strong linkages to many other industrial sectors. Third, Korea's long coastlines and its numerous ports are well suited for the development of shipyards. Indeed, Korea had a long history of shipbuilding and an active shipbuilding industry, focused largely on ship repair and the construction of small fishing vessels, well before the advent of the HCI drive. Fourth, Korea's continued security concerns were reflected in a desire by the navy to create a domestic shipbuilding and repair capacity. And finally, Korea's increasing supply of skilled labor available at relatively low wages was thought to provide a suitable labor force for the construction of modern, large vessels.

Well before the HCI drive of the 1970s, the government promoted the shipbuilding industry, providing it with considerable assistance. In 1962, the government enacted the Shipbuilding Industry Encouragement Act, which subsidized domestic shipbuilding in an effort to compensate for the price difference between locally manufactured and foreign-manufactured ships. The act provided for direct subsidies of up to 30 percent of production costs to local shipyards and duty-free imports of shipbuilding parts and materials, as well as special loans to companies replacing old ships. The government provided considerable capital to the Korean Engineering and Shipbuilding Corporation (KESC), founded in 1973 by the Mitsubishi group, which eventually became the largest shipyard in Korea, accounting for well over half of total production.[4] The subsequent enactment of the Shipbuilding Promotion Act (1967) and the Machinery Promotion Act (1969) extended financial support to shipbuilding and parts supplier industries by increasing the access for the industry to subsidized funds.

Partly in response to these various incentives, the industry experienced considerable growth. In 1962, the industry could produce ships up to a maximum size of 200 gross tons; by 1970, it was producing ships of up to 12,000 gross tons. Over the same period, total shipbuilding capacity rose from about 40,000 gross tons to nearly 190,000 gross tons. Nevertheless, the industry's technological capacity remained low, capable of producing primarily vessels for offshore and inland fishing, and was unable to compete in terms of price or financing with foreign shipyards.

In its effort to upgrade the quality of shipbuilding, the government fostered the development of a series of standard model ship designs. KESC, together with Seoul National University and Pusan National University, collaborated on a project that developed sixty standard designs as well as the block construction technology (which allowed the use of prefabricated and modular construction techniques in shipbuilding) that effectively contributed to the shortening of the construction period for ships while reducing construction costs. The government also encouraged an increase in the domestic content ratio by introducing such technologies as special welding and by encouraging the purchase of new, domestically produced communication equipment. In 1966, the KESC designs and technology received approval from the American Bureau of Shipping, opening the door for exports of steel vessels, which began a year later. Korea's shipbuilding industry became increasingly competitive in the world market, and by 1971, nearly $5.0 million of ships were exported.

Government support for the shipbuilding industry preceded the industrial promotion efforts of the HCI drive, and although there was a strong import-substitution bias in the policies pursued during the 1960s, the shipbuilding industry, like many other activities in Korea, attempted, with some success, to enter the export market. Although the designation of the shipbuilding industry as a key export industry under the HCI drive accelerated the developments that were already taking place, by no stretch of the imagination can the HCI policies be credited with having created a new activity from scratch.

Developments during the HCI Period

Encouraged by the developments in the preceding period, especially the potential for exporting ships, and believing that there would be a strong long-term tanker boom, especially for the VLCCs (very large cargo carriers), the government dramatically increased its financial support to the shipbuilding sector. In 1973, it enacted the long-term Shipbuilding Industry Promotion Act (SIPA), which aimed to increase the self-sufficiency ratio of Korean-built ships and promote shipbuilding as a leading export industry. SIPA called for the expansion of shipbuilding construction from 1 million gross tons in 1974 to 5.5 million gross tons by 1980 and to 9.2 million gross tons by 1985. During the 1973–1980 period, the government planned to invest some $570 million in the sector.[5] The target was for Korea to become one of the top ten shipbuilding nations by 1980, while substantially increasing the use of domestic parts and supplies. Both targets were achieved. By 1979, Korea produced over 6 percent of the world's total shipbuilding tonnage and established itself as the second-largest shipbuilding nation in terms of orders, while ranking seventh in terms of actual tonnage constructed. The domestic content of Korean-built ships rose from less than 30 percent in 1975 to over 80 percent by 1981.

Generous financing for ship exports was provided through Korea's Export-Import Bank. The loan ratios were often as high as 90 percent but averaged around 80 percent with a nominal interest rate of about 7 percent, at a time when Korea's inflation rate was running at 18 percent.[6] In response to the various incentives offered, KESC expanded its docks from 8,000 gross tons to 60,000 gross tons in 1973. Construction on the Hyundai shipyards began in February 1972, eventually adding 700,000 gross tons of capacity, and subsequent additions to the Hyundai shipyard added repair docks with an additional 700,000 gross tons of capacity. In October 1973, ground was broken for the Daewoo shipyard at Okpo. But the economic setback following the second oil shock delayed the construction period, and this facility was not completed until January 1981. Another large facility, the Samsung shipyard, was completed in 1980. Simultaneously, a number of medium-sized shipyards, such as Korea-Tacoma and Donghae, also came onstream. As a result of the rapid expansion of these modern facilities, construction capacity increased from 0.2 million gross tons in 1972 to 2.6 million gross tons in 1976. Table 6-1 summarizes the basic statistics for the four largest shipyards. Although some shipbuilders undertake repair work, two companies specialize in ship repair and conversions: Hyundai Mipo Dockyards Company and Pusan Dockyard Company. In addition, some of the main shipyards have associated facilities dedicated to repair works. Hyundai Mipo, located in Ulsan, is capable of handling vessels up to 400 deadweight tons (DWT), and Pusan, an affiliate of KESC in the city of Pusan, can handle ships up to 150 DWT.[7]

Table 6-1. Summary Statistics for the Four Major Shipyards

	Hyundai	Daewoo	KESC	Samsung
Location	Ulsan	Okpo	Pusan	Koje
Number of employees				
December 1985	30,184	22,996	4,085	5,807
December 1987	25,569	14,806	3,507	3,252
Sales (billion won)	1,251	703	301	437
Assets (billion won)	1,457	1,706	410	660
Capital (billion won)	496	217	33	− 12
Production capacity (gross tons)				
(1,000 tons)	3,015	1,362	216	315
Maximum vessel size				
(1,000 DWT)	1,000	1,000	150	250
Number of dry docks	7	3	3	2
Number of building berths	3	2	4	2
Ratio of exports/sales (%)	75	88	100	100

Source: *Industry Report, 1988* (Seoul: Korea Investor's Service, 1988).

The entire shipbuilding program had been predicated on the continued demand for VLCC. Unfortunately, the completion of the Hyundai shipyard coincided with the 1973 oil crisis, which caused a serious oversupply of tankers, a situation that was compounded by the reopening of the Suez Canal in 1975, which shifted the demand from giant tankers to small- and medium-sized ships. Korean shipyards, suited to the construction of large ships, saw their capacity utilization levels fall, although admittedly data on capacity and capacity utilization for facilities as complex as shipyards are often difficult to interpret. The government and the shipbuilders, more concerned with market share and capacity utilization rates than with profitability, continued to push exports, which increased from $5.5 million in 1974 to $137.8 million in 1975. During this period, the shipbuilding industry grew rapidly, and Korea became one of the world's leading shipbuilding nations (Table 6-2). Clearly the quality of Korean ships improved rapidly, but the technological level of shipbuilding remained rather low. Korean ships were very competitively priced, but in part because of their continued access to subsidized credits made available by the Korea Export-Import Bank, and because of the relatively low wage rates that continued to characterize the economy.

In order to close the technology gap, the shipyards were encouraged to seek access to technology. More than fifty technology agreements were secured for ship designs and hull construction during the 1970s. In the late 1970s, the Ministry of Trade and Industry designated twenty-eight subcontractors as parts manufacturers for vessels, providing them with further financial assistance. As a consequence, Korean shipbuilders rapidly gained the expertise needed to produce technologically sophisticated and high-valued ships, such as liquefied petroleum gas (LPG) and liquefied natural gas (LNG) tankers, and, beginning in 1976, complete-knockdown (CKD) marine engine plants.

Like other heavy and chemical industries, the initial stages of the development of the shipbuilding sector relied on the assembling of

Table 6-2. Indicators of Expansion of the Shipbuilding Industry

Item	1973	1974	1976	1978	1979
Capacity (thousand gross tons)	189	250	2,600	2,770	2,800
Construction (thousand gross tons)	43	562	684	776	556
Exports (thousand gross tons)	1	530	634	618	304
Operating ratio (%)	23	51	26	28	20
Export dependency (%)	–	94	93	80	55
World rank	46	14	9	8	7

Sources: Ministry of Trade and Industry, Government of the Republic of Korea, internal report (1980).

imported parts and components, supplied mainly by Japanese firms. In the 1980s, the government took various measures to achieve a more balanced growth between shipbuilding and the supporting parts and components industry. Programs to increase local content were started in the early 1980s and focused not only on developing local suppliers but also on ways to improve the quality of locally produced parts, as well as the promotion of the manufacture of such core items as diesel engines and propellers. One result was a rapid increase in the local content ratio, which rose to about 75 to 90 percent for domestic ships and 50 to 75 percent for foreign ships.

Despite the price competitiveness of Korean ships, much of the increased domestic demand for vessels caused by the expansion of coastal shipping was met by imported second-hand vessels from Japan, which were still cheaper than newly produced Korean vessels and were offered at favorable financing terms. In 1976, in an effort to bolster the substitution of domestically produced vessels for such imports, the government introduced its Planned Shipbuilding Program using the slogan, "Our own cargoes in our own ships." In order to ensure that Korean cargoes were transported in Korean-built ships, the movement of government cargoes was restricted to domestically built ships. Moreover, domestic ship purchases, financed through the National Investment Fund, were provided with credit at a 9 percent interest rate for half the ship's price. Imported raw materials used in the construction of ships destined for the domestic market were now exempt from all import duties. Not surprisingly, these incentives served to shift demand to domestically produced ships. By 1979 imports of ships totaled some $200 million, down from $392 million in 1974.

Encouraged by what had been achieved in the 1970s, the government in 1979 designated shipbuilding as one of ten strategic industries and formulated plans to make Korea the fifth largest shipbuilding nation by 1986, with a production capacity of 6.5 million gross tons and exports valued at $2.2 billion. Production capacity continued to increase with the opening of the Samsung and Daewoo yards in 1980 and 1981, bringing total production capacity to over 4.5 million tons. In retrospect, it is clear that Korea's shipbuilding industry expanded rapidly and contributed to labor absorption in response to the industrial promotion efforts of the 1970s. Although the incentive policies enjoyed by the industry allowed it to attain these industrial development goals, it is less clear that the HCI policies managed to create a viable and internationally competitive sector. Indeed, changing world conditions and the inherent weakness of the government's program soon began to be felt, causing major difficulties for the industry. Although the industry had grown rapidly, it rarely achieved any profits, in large part because of the interest payments on the debt incurred to finance the rapid expansion. In fact, the expansion was so rapid that the shipyards worked far below capacity throughout much of the 1970s and 1980s.

The Adjustment Period

No sooner had the Samsung and Daewoo yards been completed than the worldwide recession caused a severe slump in shipbuilding. Korea's shipbuilders, heavily dependent on export demand, suffered more than other shipyards that were more diversified in terms of product mix and markets.[8] Even worse, a number of buyers postponed delivery of new ships that had been ordered at earlier higher prices, aggravating the financial difficulties of the shipbuilders.

A structural defect of Korea's shipbuilding industry was the dependence by the four large shipyards—Hyundai Heavy Industries Company, Daewoo Shipbuilding Company, Samsung Shipbuilding and Heavy Industries Company, and KESC—on the production of large ships (those of 100,000 DWT and above). It was precisely this segment of the market that suffered the most severe decline in demand. These four companies accounted for over 90 percent of total production capacity; the remainder was spread among six (and, for a short time, seven) medium-sized and some 250 small-sized yards. Hyundai, the world's largest shipbuilder, has a nominal production capacity of 3 million gross tons, seven dry docks, and three building berths. Daewoo, the second largest shipbuilder in Korea, has a nominal production capacity of 1.4 million gross tons, three dry docks, and two building berths. Hyundai and Daewoo are both capable of producing ships of more than 1 million gross tons. Samsung shipyard, while much smaller, has a nominal production capacity of over 300,000 gross tons and two dry docks, while KESC, the oldest shipbuilder, has a smaller production capacity than Samsung, though it has three dry docks and four building berths.

As far back as 1977, the shipbuilding industry, in an effort to diversify its product mix and reduce its heavy reliance on the export of ships, began seeking out refit work and the construction of floating structures (rigs and special equipment). Refit work requires special training and skills, together with advanced technology and marketing arrangements. In 1983, Korea doubled its exports of refits to reach $1,543 million. The sales value of floating structures also increased from $109 million in 1981 to $365 million in 1983. In reducing the ratio of ship construction to nonship construction, Hyundai, Samsung, and KESC have reduced their dependence on what has generally been a highly volatile market and have gained the advantage of shifting to the building of higher value-added products. Until the 1990s, Daewoo had been less successful in pursuing this strategy so that shipbuilding still accounted for 90 percent of its production.[9]

As worldwide demand recovered in the late 1980s, the capacity utilization rates at Korea's yards rose to about 70 to 85 percent in 1986 and 1987. But maintaining price competitiveness in the face of the rapid appreciation of the won and increased labor costs, as well as continued dependence on Japan for technology and intermediate goods, were problems that continued to plague the industry. The most visible concern in the late 1980s was the controversy over the government's bailout efforts for two major shipbuilders, Daewoo and KESC, which suffered from huge debts and accumulated losses.

A number of other factors worsened the situation facing Korea's shipbuilders. First, since the 1981–1982 recession, Korea's shipyards faced excess capacity as prices for new ships dropped precipitously. Second, the demand pattern for ships changed. When worldwide trade in petrochemical products decreased and the trade in coal and feedstock increased, the demand for VLCC stagnated as the demand for container ships and specialized product ships (e.g., LPG) increased. Unfortunately, low value-added vessels, including tankers and bulk carriers, accounted for the majority of ships constructed by Korean shipbuilders. In 1987, the proportion of such vessels reached about 85 percent, while high value-added ships, such as container ships and chemical tankers, accounted for the remainder of total construction volume. The change in marine transportation patterns had negative repercussions for Korean shipbuilders whose docks were designed for the construction of very large tankers. Third, wage hikes accompanied by union strikes and the rapid appreciation of the won exerted a cost-push pressure, eroding the competitive edge the shipyards had enjoyed over Japan, a development compounded by the rising price of parts and components.

Labor disputes, which plagued the economy during the early 1990s, dealt a further blow to the Korean shipbuilding industry. These disputes resulted in unexpected large wage increases, and strikes delayed the delivery of ships. It was estimated that in 1987, about 20 percent of sales were lost as a result of shutdowns from labor disputes. In December 1988, a bitter strike began at Hyundai; in April 1989, three ships (worth $110 million) had been cancelled, and the negotiations on nine others (worth $400 million) were terminated. After receiving wage increases of 16 to 19 percent in April 1989, Samsung shipyard workers had the highest wages (an average of around 600,000 won monthly) of any other major shipbuilder. Nonetheless, in June they struck again, seeking 25 percent wage hikes (to narrow differentials with white-collar workers) and four-month bonuses. The strike lasted about two weeks, without labor's demands being met. But because the strike caused as much confrontation between groups within the union as between the workers and the company, labor unrest prevailed.

Adding to the unfavorable conditions at home and abroad, the Korean shipbuilding industry suffered from declining orders. Total shipbuilding orders for the first ten months of 1988 declined to 1.4 million gross tons, down about 50 percent from the same period a year earlier, while backlog orders declined to 5.1 million gross tons as of the end of October 1988, down 9.2 percent from the previous year. As a result the number of employees working at the twelve largest shipbuilding companies dropped from 75,643 in 1984 to 57,100 in 1987.

Korean shipbuilders are debt ridden from past expansions and losses. In the four years from 1985 to 1988, the four large shipyards lost some 765 billion won, including 342 billion won in 1988 on sales of 2,290 billion won. All but Hyundai Heavy Industry registered growing losses after the collapse of earnings began in 1985, and in 1988, even Hyundai lost money. Interest on debt is the major reason for overall losses; major firms actually had operating profits in 1987.

KESC, the smallest of the big four, has been fighting to survive since 1983. The company's financial position worsened when the delivery of six completed ships was not taken up.[10] In April 1987, a court placed KESC's finances under the control of the Bank of Seoul, its major creditor, and the Korea Export-Import Bank. It did not receive any new orders but continued to employ about 3,500 workers for finishing orders previously booked. KESC was "auctioned," although what was involved were more negotiations over how much capital a buyer and the government would each put up to save the firm. Hanjin, a major Korean shipping company that also controls Korean Air, tendered the best bid at the May 1989 sale. Hanjin expected to use KESC for the repair and building of its own ships. KESC was obliged to merge with its three subsidiaries under the command of Hanjin and to increase its capital by 50 billion won in three years. In return, Hanjin was exempted from the payment of corporate and other taxes.

Daewoo, the second-largest builder, recorded a loss of 213 billion won in 1988, and strikes in 1987 and 1988 were settled with wage increases averaging between 15 percent and 20 percent. In 1988, Daewoo asked the government for financial support, saying it could not function with its accumulated debts, now 1.3 trillion won, coupled with wage increases and reduced orders. The government responded with unexpected harshness, requiring the Daewoo Group chairman personally to contribute additional capital. The situation was seen as a major test of the Sixth Republic's willingness to control the *chaebol*. Although over 13,000 jobs and the economic well-being of the area around the shipyard were at stake, there seemed to be little public support for a government bail-out of what was perceived to be a badly managed *chaebol* subsidiary.

Daewoo proposed selling and merging four of its other subsidiaries into Daewoo Shipbuilding and Heavy Machinery (DSHM), as well as contributing an additional 850 billion won in new capital. In return, the government proposed a seven-year grace period covering the interest on some 250 billion won of outstanding loans while providing additional loans of 150 billion won, all with a seven-year grace period followed by repayments in ten equal installments. The government also provided a tax exemption on the sales of subsidiaries. The Daewoo Group chairman assumed personal direction of DSHM in 1987, a move seen as part of fulfilling a pledge to striking shipbuilding workers that the company would be revived.

Evaluation

In many ways, the development of the shipbuilding industry represents the best and worst outcomes of the HCI drive. Using numerous incentives, some of which predated the formal enunciation of the HCI drive, a modern industry was created, providing employment for thousands of workers and creating demand for suppliers of heavy machinery, steel, electrical equipment, and electronics. Yet the very tools used to create the industry have come back to haunt it. Although loans were provided at below-market rates, the large amounts of capital raised created an unsustainable debt burden. Moreover, the initial success of the shipbuilding industry in entering the export market, combined with a faulty forecast about the types and quantities of ships needed, led to a rapid expansion of capacity that proved to be unwarranted. And although all four major shipyards were members of *chaebol* that had diversified structures, none was able to weather the market downturns and other events of the late 1980s without encountering serious financial difficulties. Neither the reliance by government on *chaebol* to carry out its industrial development plans nor the reliance by the *chaebol* on a diversified corporate structure would seem to be a foolproof development strategy.

Automobiles and Parts

The development of the automobile industry shares a number of characteristics with the shipbuilding industry. Like the shipbuilding industry, the automobile industry was perceived to have numerous backward linkages to domestic suppliers, in particular to some of the industries to be promoted under the HCI drive of the 1970s. The development of the automobile industry was also expected to contribute to the development of the industrial sector as a whole. Automobile production, which is both technology and capital intensive, was to provide a ready market for related materials and components. The potentially stimulative effect on other sectors was presumed to be important in the overall industrialization drive.

Like the shipbuilding industry, the automobile industry was started and supported by the government well before the HCI drive. Unlike the shipbuilding industry, however, the automobile sector first developed entirely as an import-substitution industry, moving only slowly and cautiously into the export market in the late 1970s.

In the mid-1960s, Korea's policies toward the automotive industry aimed to shift it from parts production and repair to local assembly. To achieve that end, imports of fully assembled cars were effectively banned. To help promote the industry and to control its development, the government enunciated, in its first five-year development plan (1962–1967), a five-year plan for the automobile industry. At the same time, the government encouraged the formation of the Korean Automobile Manufacturers Association, a trade group charged with ensuring that government plans were followed and effectively implemented by the various manufacturers.

In 1972, the government decided to concentrate auto production in the hands of four major companies: Hyundai, Kia, Asia Motors, and a joint venture between General Motors (GM) and Daewoo.[11] A new set of guidelines, the Plan for Nurturing the Auto Industry, was set forth in 1973, followed a year later by another policy paper, Long-term Strategy for Promoting the Auto Industry. The goal of these policy initiatives was to develop domestically owned automotive production facilities, capable not only of assembling but also of designing and producing cars of international standard, using locally produced components. To a considerable extent the policy succeeded. In 1977, automobile exports were only 1,287 units; by 1981, they totaled 26,384 units, and from 1984 to 1987, vehicle exports increased at an annual rate of 117 percent. Automobile exports, in particular to the American market, now account for more than half of domestic production, although only Hyundai sells in the American market under its own name. By 1987 the Korean auto industry accounted for 2 percent of world automobile production and 4 percent of world automobile trade. In fact, Korea remains the only developing country to have achieved international status as an exporter of domestically built cars.

Development of the Automobile Industry, 1967-1972

Korea's automobile industry began in the early 1960s with the assembly of semi-knockdown (SKD) parts imported from Japan, moving up to become an assembler of CKD vehicles in the late 1960s with technical assistance and capital from Japan and the United States.

To assist the nascent industry, the government in 1962 banned imports of completed automobiles while allowing duty-free imports of parts for assembly plants. With the assistance of Nissan from Japan, the New-World Automobile Co. began assembling imported SKD components, but it quickly ran into serious difficulties, largely due to a lack of infrastructure and a persistent shortage of foreign exchange. In 1966, the company, renamed ShinJin Automobile Company and reorganized, turned to Toyota Motor Company as its parts supplier. Initial production capacity was only slightly more than 3,000 cars per year. With the development of a local parts industry, ShinJin eventually raised the domestic content of the cars produced to 21 percent, although the domestic content was concentrated on car bodies rather than on the more technologically advanced engine parts, drive trains, or axles.

In 1966, in an effort to increase the local content of domestically assembled vehicles, the government established a domestic content schedule and provided for preferential allocations of scarce foreign exchange to plants producing parts. As a result, the automobile parts manufacturing industry expanded rapidly, and the domestic content ratio increased to 60 percent in 1972. The rapid rate of localization, a development that took place in advance of the HCI drive, led to higher production costs and lower quality. The price of parts and components, which had been stable, rose fairly rapidly after 1970, and these increases were reflected in a rise in automobile prices. As long as the domestic market was well protected, the price increases could be passed on to consumers, but the effect was to make penetration of export markets more difficult, contrary to the government's intention.

Korea's first modern highway, built in the 1960s, combined with rapid economic growth to increase transport demand. Although a variety of high taxes served to discourage private car ownership, the government continued to encourage the formation of joint ventures in the automobile industry, and foreign capital and technology from advanced countries flowed in through a number of joint venture projects. In 1968, Hyundai Automobile Co. was formed as a joint venture with the British Ford Motor Company and quickly moved to produce cars from CKD parts with about a 30 percent domestic content. By 1969, with the advent of a third automobile assembler, Asia Motor Company, which received technical assistance from

Fiat of France, Korea's four auto assemblers had a combined capacity of 72,600 units per year.

The plants were equipped only to assemble cars, not to manufacture them; none possessed facilities to make engines, axles, frames, or bodies. Moreover, they concentrated only on the assembly of passenger cars, allowing the demand for buses and trucks to be met from imports. Most auto parts manufacturers were too small and too technically and financially weak, to invest in high-volume production. Because of the low level of domestic production, parts manufacturers were unable to achieve economies of scale, a problem compounded by frequent model changes as the assemblers switched licensing partners.

Developments during the HCI Period

As part of the HCI drive, the government encouraged auto assemblers to develop their own Korean car models and to increase the local content ratio. These efforts were supported by the Long-Term Promotional Plan for the Automobile Industry, which set the goal of developing a "general public car," with an 80 percent domestic content ratio, and an export target of 75,000 automobiles by 1981. The plan also called for the government to limit the number of assemblers of passenger cars, buses, and trucks to four: Daewoo, Hyundai, Asia Motors, and Kia.[12] Since these companies merely assembled models manufactured by such foreign automobile companies as GM, Toyota, and Isuzu, it was difficult for the domestic producers to achieve economies of scale. Nevertheless, the government encouraged these four producers to invest in large-scale production capacity and to develop their own models with higher domestic content, a radical departure from the previous policy of concentrating on the production of CKD vehicles.

In response, the four automobile assemblers not only increased investment in modern assembly and parts production facilities but also boosted efforts to develop their own car models. In 1974, Kia manufactured the first Korean car, the Brisa, and in the following year, Hyundai introduced the well-known, and much more successful, Pony, which became the first domestically produced car to be exported, largely to the Middle East and Asia. Daewoo launched its own domestic car, the Gemini, in 1977.

The government's policy, with its emphasis on joint ventures as a means of acquiring the necessary technology, encouraged the 1972 joint venture between GM and the Daewoo (ShinJin) Motor Company. By 1973, GM Korea, as the venture was known, became the nation's largest auto assembler, with an annual production capacity of 25,000 units, and in

1974, it established an engine foundry capable of casting 50,000 units per year. In 1975, Hyundai Motors increased its production capacity with the completion of a new passenger car production facility with an annual capacity of 48,200 units, increasing its capacity by more than sevenfold, from 7,800 units to over 56,000 units. Kia Industrial Company increased its passenger car production facility from 7,200 units in 1974 to 24,000 units in 1975. At the same time, expansion projects were carried out for trucks. Hyundai Motor Company increased its truck production capacity from 6,900 to 20,000 units per year, and Kia tripled its annual capacity to 24,000 units.

Although the rapid expansion of the sector allowed the manufacturers to gain expertise and laid the foundation for the eventual development of Korea's own models, these gains were not achieved without substantial cost. Domestic cars, continuously protected by a near-total ban on imports, sold for more than twice the world price of comparable cars even while the accumulated debts of many of the automobile companies sharply reduced their profitability.[13]

By 1975, the Korean automobile industry had completed four engine plants. GM Korea began producing gasoline engines in September 1974, and Hyundai Motor, Kia, and Han-Kuk Machine Industrial Company completed gasoline and diesel engine plants in 1975, starting commercial operations in early 1976. By then, a substantial portion of the raw materials could be supplied domestically, although not always at competitive prices.

Korea's economic growth barely faltered in the aftermath of the first oil shock, and the economy returned to high growth rates very quickly.[14] Although government policies to restrict fuel consumption shifted demand for passenger cars to subcompact cars of less than 1,500 cc, continued rapid economic growth, together with the incentives offered to the automobile sector under the HCI drive, engendered a climate that saw automobile production soar after 1976 (Table 6-3). Total automobile production increased at an annual rate of over 42 percent over the period from 1976 to 1979, although the economic downturn of the early 1980s hit the industry hard, causing automobile production to decline sharply.[15]

In line with its policies to promote an integrated automobile sector, the government initiated policies to develop automobile parts production. In 1975, the government changed the import procedures relating to auto parts, so that a recommendation from the Korean Auto Industries Cooperative Assocation (KAICA) was required to import any parts that were also produced domestically. KAICA represented the interests of assemblers and parts manufacturers and effectively limited imports to items not domestically produced. The government also set an annual

Table 6-3. Automobile Production, 1965–1987

Year	Cars	Buses	Trucks	Others	Total
1962	1,710	—	67	—	1,777
1970	14,487	3,803	10,529	—	28,819
1975	18,509	3,808	14,973	—	37,290
1976	26,701	3,468	19,219	340	49,728
1977	43,981	5,453	35,263	1,623	86,320
1978	86,823	7,279	63,446	2,678	160,226
1979	113,564	12,307	76,661	1,915	204,447
1980	57,225	12,053	51,660	2,197	123,135
1981	68,760	13,358	47,918	4,248	134,284
1982	94,460	20,931	43,705	3,494	162,590
1983	121,987	25,594	66,095	7,343	221,019
1984	158,503	26,554	73,042	7,262	265,361
1985	264,458	29,090	78,171	6,443	378,162
1986	457,383	36,386	107,777	N.A.	601,546
1987	799,125	58,431	128,183	N.A.	979,739

Source: Korean Auto Industries Cooperative Association, as quoted in Korea Exchange Bank, *Monthly Review* 10, no.11 (November 1986): 4, with permission.

domestic content schedule implemented through a variety of incentives such as import licenses, preferential access to foreign exchange, and "administrative guidance." These measures played a decisive role in promoting investment by parts manufacturers as well as increasing technology licensing.

Encouraged by the heavy investments in automobile production facilities and government support, the automobile parts and components industry expanded, raising the domestic content ratio to above 90 percent by the end of the 1970s. Initially, many of these downstream producers, promoted through HCI policies, produced inferior quality goods at prices substantially above world prices. Over time, as the quality of parts improved, they began to gain international acceptance, and parts exports, consisting primarily of such relatively unsophisticated items as piston rings, springs, and electric bulbs, reached $10 million in 1975. Exports of complete engines began on a small scale in 1976.

In 1978, the government adopted measures to develop the subcontracting system as an effective means of promoting the parts and components industry. Fifty items were selected for subcontracting, while the production of functional items such as engines, transmissions, axles, and bodies was left to assemblers. The government also designated firms to specialize in the production of particular items. These designated firms were given access to numerous supporting measures, including subsidized loans, in the belief that the development of an effective subcontracting system would contribute to the standardization of specialized parts and components. In addition, numerous technical licensing agreements and joint ventures, as well as the establishment of research centers by auto assemblers, assisted the progress of the auto parts industry. Beginning in the mid-1970s, product quality improvement enabled exports of component parts to increase, and in 1981, such exports amounted to $111 million.

Although it is true that the quality of automobile parts and components has risen substantially as a result of improvements in technology, as well as the introduction of foreign technology, quality levels remain low by international standards, except for a few items such as wheel discs and springs. At the same time, the prices of domestically produced parts and components are generally much higher than world prices. Small-scale inferior facilities continue to be major obstacles to achieving international competitiveness in the parts and components sector, restraining the overall progress of the nation's automobile industry.

Technology for the automobile and parts industry was acquired through licensing and joint ventures. During the 1950s and 1960s, production of parts and components was done mostly by traditional methods, which required simple technology, and relatively small investments and efforts were concentrated on the upgrading of the existing technology. Technological progress was of a capital-saving nature, fostering the development of smaller ancillary firms, which played a dominant role in employment and value-added until 1970. As a result, capital intensity in the parts and components industry remained virtually unchanged between 1966 and 1970, although total factor productivity increased rapidly.

With the introduction of the HCI policies, the capital-saving improvements in existing technology were increasingly of limited usefulness in meeting the demands of large-scale production, and access to more modern equipment became increasingly important for the parts and components industry. As a result, the parts and components industry relied more on foreign technology in expanding their production capacity in order to meet increasingly complex demands.

It was not until the early 1970s that Korea began to import foreign technology; the number of technology licensing agreements with foreign firms increased rapidly between 1975 and 1979. In 1975, when imports of parts were regulated, assemblers complained because the quality of domestically supplied parts was not as reliable and their prices exceeded import prices. Once the government protected the domestic parts industry by requiring import recommendations from KAICA before parts could be imported, foreign parts manufacturers had to transfer technology to Korean auto manufacturers or forgo a lucrative market.

Between 1962 and 1987, there were 183 technology-licensing contracts, 48 percent of them with Japanese companies. Most licenses were for manufacturing technology (Table 6-4), and not for design technology, because little effort was made by parts manufacturers to develop new designs during this period.

In the 1970s, licensing with foreign companies was the major source of obtaining technology, while research and development (R&D) expenditures were generally less than 1 percent of sales. When Korean auto companies started to export in the 1980s, it became more difficult to obtain access to foreign technologies, forcing Korean companies to increase their R&D investments to about 3 to 5 percent of sales.[16]

The Adjustment Period

Shortly after the automobile sector had put its expanded production facilities in place, the economy was hit by a severe recession. Real gross national product (GNP) declined in 1980, and export growth slumped in 1982. As part of a general stabilization program and a shift away from the HCI policies of the 1970s, which were partly blamed for the economic downturn, the government tightened its monetary policy and curtailed

Table 6-4. Sources of Technological Licensing (number of licensing agreements)

	Japan	United States	Germany	United Kingdom	Italy	All Others	Total
General manufacturing	29	9	5	—	64	53	160
Styling	1	—	—	3	4	2	10
Engine manufacturing	8	—	4	9	—	4	25
Engine design	1	1	—	3	—	—	5
Body design	1	—	—	—	—	—	1
Parts manufacturing	36	13	4	5	—	3	61
Productivity	2	2	1	—	—	—	5
Quality control	2	2	1	1	—	—	6
Model change	—	—	1	1	1	—	3
Others	7	3	—	3	—	1	14
Total	**87**	**30**	**16**	**25**	**11**	**14**	**183**
(Percent)	47.5	16.4	8.7	13.7	6.0	7.7	100.0

Source: Korean Auto Industries Cooperative Association, *20 Years of KAICA* (Seoul: KAICA, 1983), reproduced with permission.

credit. The resulting slowdown in economic activities, and particularly in construction, led to a severe decline in sales of commercial vehicles. The automobile sector was then hit by the long-overdue adjustment in domestic gasoline prices, which were increased by nearly 60 percent in July 1979 and increased again following the devaluation of the won six months later. As a result, sales of passenger cars and commercial vehicles declined sharply, adversely affecting the profitability and financial structure of automobile manufacturers.

Fearing for the health of some of the large *chaebol* involved in automobile production, the government decided that measures had to be taken to rationalize the automobile industry and to eliminate what it saw as duplicate and excessive investment. Indeed, capacity utilization rates for passenger cars, never higher than 61.6 percent of capacity, fell to 23.5 percent in 1980, with only a slightly better performance for truck and bus plants. Even parts manufacturers saw their capacity utilization ratio drop to 43 percent in 1980, well below the peaks of nearly 70 percent achieved during the 1970s.

The government designated the automobile industry as a strategic export industry, and steps were taken to increase specialization, develop mass production systems, and improve international competitiveness. The government decided that competition among automakers was to be curtailed in order to achieve greater scale economies. Under the Automobile Industry Rationalization Plan of 1980, Hyundai and Daewoo were to merge and to specialize in the production of passenger cars, while Kia and Asia were to cease production of passenger cars and concentrate only on trucks weighing less than 5 tons.

Shortly after they were announced, the merger plans had to be aborted. General Motors insisted on retaining a 50 percent share of the merged company, while Hyundai insisted that GM be limited to a minority position, with vehicle design and production managed entirely by Hyundai. In short, GM wanted Korea to be a production site for the GM "world car," while Hyundai was adamant on continuing to produce a "Korean car" for domestic and export markets. The rationalization plan had to be abandoned.

The Export Period

Although export markets had not been a major aim of the automobile industry, as early as 1975 Korea had made a modest entry into the world market when thirty-one trucks were sold to the Middle East. Eventually limited export markets were developed in Latin America and Africa, in addition to the Middle East. Major export items were Hyundai's Pony, the Pony pickup, the Stellar, and Asia Motors trucks.

Now faced with sluggish domestic demand, the auto manufacturers focused efforts on increasing exports as a means of raising capacity utilization. In 1982, the Hyundai Motor Company met the European Economic Community noise, safety, and emission standards, but it was not until 1985 that the company met the more stringent U.S. standards. In 1983, Hyundai shipped some 2,500 Ponies to Canada.[17] In the same year, auto exports totaled 16,405 passenger cars, 192 buses, and 7,852 trucks, earning $121 million. Hyundai knew that unless it could enter the U.S. market, the world's largest automobile market, it would have difficulty becoming an efficient producer. Exports to America began in 1986. The initial export target was 150,000 units, but nearly 170,000 units were sold the first year. The second year, 1987, saw sales of over 260,000 units, and in 1988, it sold 270,000 units.[18] The appreciation of the yen and the voluntary export restraints (VER) imposed by the United States against Japanese cars, which forced Japanese companies to move up to mid-sized cars, left the subcompact car market open, an export niche that Hyundai exploited with extreme success.

In late 1982, with an economic recovery underway and with reductions in the excise tax on gasoline as well as a decline in real energy prices, domestic sales increased sharply, growing at 60 percent per annum from 1983 to 1987. As a result of the expansion of domestic and export demand, motor vehicle production increased at an annual rate of 44 percent during the period 1983–1987. By 1987, Korea exported half a million cars, equal to 4 percent of world auto exports; Korea now ranked eighth among the world auto exporting countries.[19] Automobile parts exports jumped from $157 million to nearly $1.6 billion. With the successful export of cars to Canada and the United States, automobile production again expanded, from 162,590 in 1982 to 601,546 in 1986.

A number of factors contributed to what has been called the most successful introduction of a new car into the U.S. market. With an initial base price of $4,995 and styling drawn heavily from pricier Japanese competitors, the Hyundai Excel quickly became a hit among first-time buyers and others seeking an "affordable car that makes sense," as the advertising copy put it. Since potential dealers knew that Hyundai had successfully sold the Excel in Canada, the company was able to develop a strong distribution network in the United States, eventually establishing over 300 dealerships. But perhaps most important for Hyundai's success, the Japanese automakers upgraded their cars in the face of the U.S.-imposed VER, even while domestic U.S. producers were not ready to meet the now-unmet demand at the low end of the price range, a demand that Hyundai was well positioned to meet. And the depreciation of the won from 659 won/US$ in 1980 to its peak of 890 won/US$ in 1985 helped immensely. Hyundai, which had expected to lose about $1,000 per car on its initial efforts to break into the U.S. market, found itself instead in the enviable position of being able to lower prices and still earn a profit.[20] By 1989, when Korea's automobile market had been liberalized and Hyundai received no direct government assistance, it remained a viable and profitable company, although the expansion of car sales in the American market has slowed considerably. In 1988, export growth slowed, and 1989 exports declined 38 percent.

Several factors account for this result. First, following a string of balance-of-payment surpluses, the won appreciated, falling from 892 won/US$ in October 1985 to 684 won/US$ by the end of 1988, or about 30 percent in three years. This eroded international competitiveness and the profitability of investment. Second, like the shipbuilding sector, the automobile industry experienced sharp increases in real wages, which often followed bitter and disruptive labor disputes. The continued labor disputes delayed production and increased the defects ratio, damaging Hyundai's reputation. And finally, Hyundai failed to follow up its initial success with the Excel with another, somewhat more advanced model, because a variety of difficulties, including labor disputes, delayed the introduction of a newer model, the Sonata, until well into 1990.[21]

Evaluation

Although the automobile industry in Korea is now fairly well established, the pace of its initial success may be hard to maintain.[22] Like other sectors studied, the automobile industry was established, and indeed supported by, government, well before the HCI drive was put into effect. Whether the development of the industry would have occurred without the HCI incentives is difficult to answer, but it is undoubtedly true that exogenous factors, including the impact of the VERs on Japanese car exports to the United States, allowed Korea to exploit a marketing niche. This development clearly had little to do with Korea's industrial policy. Yet without the prior growth and maturation of the industry, in part fostered by the HCI drive, Hyundai and the automobile sector as a whole would not have been in a position to take advantage of the marketing opportunity when it arose. Whether the returns to Korea's heavy investment in the automobile sector have in fact paid off is difficult to judge. The fact that some of Korea's car manufacturers have entered the international market provides some evidence that the investment created an efficient industry, but it provides little information as to whether the rate of return on automobile investments was higher than the returns that could have been earned elsewhere. The conclusion about the successful promotion of the automobile sector must be tempered while recognizing that for a variety of reasons Korea avoided the pitfalls that beset many other countries pursuing technologically advanced industrial development; it did not create a series of inefficient producers that continue to impose costs on consumers and other users.

The Steel Industry and POSCO Steel

During the first five-year economic plan (1962–1966), with GNP growing at 7.8 percent per annum, steel demand increased by over 18 percent per annum, from 264,600 metric tons in 1962 to 520,400 metric tons in 1966. With the acceleration of economic growth to nearly 10 percent per annum during the second five-year plan, the rate of increase in steel demand rose to nearly 25 percent per year. Domestic steelmaking capacity was ill suited to meet this growing demand, and imports of steel and steel products rose dramatically in response (Table 6-5).

Korea had no experience with a modern, integrated steelmaking facility. Moreover, the existing steel industry was characterized by an imbalance among its iron- and steelmaking and rolling facilities, all of an inefficient scale and relying on fairly simple and outmoded technologies. A relatively high tariff protected this inefficient steelmaking sector, with the inevitable result that domestic prices were considerably above the world price for competing products.[23]

Well before the advent of the HCI drive of the 1970s, the government made several attempts to develop a large-scale integrated steel industry

Table 6-5. Growth in Steel Demand (thousand metric tons)

	First Plan Period		Second Plan Period	
	1962	1966	1967	1971
Domestic demand	262.0	488.4	743.7	1,569.5
Exports	2.6	32.0	11.6	201.3
Total demand	264.6	520.4	755.3	1,770.6
Domestic production	141.6	334.2	469.7	1,460.9
Imports	123.0	186.2	285.6	309.8
Import dependency[a]	46.5%	35.8%	37.8%	17.5%

[a]Defined as imports/total demand (domestic demand + exports).
Source: Ministry of Trade and Industry, *Internal Report 1980* (Seoul: Government of the Republic of Korea, 1980).

of sufficient capacity to meet domestic needs. These attempts came to naught, in large part because of Korea's inability to raise the needed capital, a difficulty compounded by the view of various experts who argued that the domestic market was too small to allow any plant to achieve needed economies of scale. At the end of 1966, the Korea International Steel Associates (KISA) was formed, and in November 1967, it established the Integrated Steel Works Construction Committee, charged with designing a long-term plan for the development of the steel industry. The committee eventually selected Pohang as the future site for an integrated steel mill and recommended that a plant be built with an annual production capacity of 600,000 tons.[24] On April 1, 1968, Pohang Iron and Steel Company, Ltd. (POSCO) was formally established. The KISA consortium that was to build the plant consisted of seven members from four countries: Koppers, Blaw Knox, and Westinghouse Electric International from the United States; DEMAG and Siemens from Germany; Societa Italiana Impianta from Italy; and Wellman Steel Works Engineering from England. Initially, Japan was to participate, but it dropped out of the consortium and was replaced by France. Although the contract between KISA and the government called for KISA to raise the needed financing by 1969 and to dedicate an integrated mill by 1972, the consortium was dissolved in 1969 because Koppers, the lead firm, could not raise the required capital and KISA, given its complicated management structure, was unable to act decisively.[25]

Korea next hoped that funding could be obtained from the World Bank, which had earlier indicated a willingness to finance a steel mill. However, the Bank abruptly reversed its position. In April 1968, at the aid consortium meeting held in Paris, the bank expressed doubts about the financial viability of a Korean steel mill, arguing that the construction of an integrated steel mill in Korea was premature, given the level of development and the availability of skilled labor, and it would be financially unfeasible. Shortly afterward, the Bank officially withdrew from the proposed steel project. Another cost-benefit study, undertaken by a British firm, reached the same conclusion, noting that the rate of return on the project did not justify the investment.[26] Faced with the loss of World Bank financing and confronted by a reluctance of other donors to fund a steel mill, the government was hesitant to proceed with the project. Given the opposition, the government decided that perhaps it should try to build a small plant that would cater primarily to domestic demand.

Despite the failure to obtain financial support, President Park continued to insist that a steel plant be constructed. The job of turning that vision into reality was then given to Park Tae Joon, a retired army general. He eventually approached a Japanese delegation to see whether any funding would be forthcoming from Japan and was told that "the Republic of Korea should improve its purchasing power first before building a steel mill." Chairman Park responded that Korea (at the end of the 1960s) was far ahead of Japan when it built its first steel plant, but in any event a steel mill did not have to be commercially viable since "it was needed as a backbone for development."[27] Not much progress was made in lining up financial support until, as part of a normalization of Japan-Korean relations, Japan established a wartime compensation fund. Although these funds were primarily intended for agricultural development, it was eventually decided that the reparations payments could be used to construct a steel mill.

The Japanese then suggested that they would be willing to finance a plant of sufficient scale to meet Korea's current needs. The Korean negotiators insisted that a larger plant be built because, as Chairman Park noted, the development plans put forward by the Park government called for substantial increases in infrastructure investments, which would require significant quantitites of steel and steel products.[28] Since the profitability of capital-intensive industries, like steel, is highly sensitive to full-capacity utilization, especially when loans dominate their capital structure, the financial success of POSCO depended on a rapid growth in demand for its products. The combination of sound macroeconomic management and large-scale investments in complementary downstream industries yielded the necessary rapid sustained growth in domestic steel demand. Chairman Park also informed the government that if the steel plant could export 30 percent of its output, it would cover the foreign exchange cost of the imported raw materials and its debt-servicing payments.[29] With the financial constraint eased and with technical assistance from Japan, the steel project was finally able to move ahead.

To assist POSCO, the government enacted the Steel Industry Promotion Law in 1970, providing for financial assistance for the construction of an integrated steel mill, for the expansion or replacement of existing facilities, and for the acquisition of modern technology; reducing fees and tariffs on utilities to be used by the plant; and giving subsidies and long-term, low-interest loans to suppliers of domestic iron ore and other raw materials to be used in steelmaking.

The Development of POSCO Steel

Construction on the Pohang facility started in April 1970, and the mill was completed on July 3, 1973, a record construction period of slightly more than three years. (See Appendix 6A for a chronology of POSCO's development.) The rapidity of the construction, as well as the implicit savings on finance and on the construction period interest, is one reason for POSCO's relatively low production cost.[30] The plant, with a production capacity of slightly over 1 million tons of crude steel a year, was constructed on an area of 1,000 acres with access to a good port location. When completed, the facility included a large-scale continuous production process for iron- and steelmaking, consisting of integrated facilities equipped with a blast furnace and two LD (Linz-Donawitz) oxygen converters, and rolling facilities. The blast furnace had an inner volume of 1,660 cubic meters and an initial production capacity of 949,000 tons, and the two LD converters had a steel production capacity of 1.032 million tons. In addition, there was a foundry pig iron furnace with a production capacity of 150,000 tons, a blooming and slabbing mill, a billet mill, a plate mill, and a hot rolling mill (Table 6-6).

Construction costs totaled $304 million: $168 million in foreign exchange plus 54,300 million won in domestic costs. Part of the financing was in the form of loans from the Japanese Export-Import Bank ($50 million), and part ($42 million) came from the Economic Cooperation Fund, together with a $30.8 million loan from the Property and Claims Fund. Since there was no knowledge of steelmaking technology in Korea, it all had to be imported. POSCO was able to obtain the most modern production

Table 6-6. Structure of the Iron and Steel Sector

| | May 1966 | | October 1973 | |
	Capacity (thousand tons)	Units (number)	Capacity (thousand tons)	Units (number)
Pig iron	78	2	1,153	2
Ferro alloys	6	2	22	3
Steel	529	15	2,183	14
Open hearth	123	3	140	1
Converters	190	8	222	5
LD oxygen converters	—	—	1,032	1[a]
Electric furnace	216	4	789	7
Continuous casting	—	—	440	2
Structural and wire rods	493	35	1,276	48
Strip mills	56	2	627	3
Hot strip mills	56	2	27	1
Cold strip mills	—	—	600	2[b]
Medium and heavy plate	—	—	583	3
Steel pipes	94	6	480	10

[a]POSCO.
[b]Union and Ilssin Steel.
Source: Ibid.

facilities and technologies from Japan, as provided for under an agreement between POSCO and the Japan Group, consisting of Nippon Kohan (NKK) and Nippon Steel Corporation (NSC). Ancillary technologies were obtained from the United States, Germany, and England. Except for some technical advice, the planning and construction of equipment, preparation for operations, and general factory operations were carried out entirely by Korean technicians.[31]

Even after completion of the project, Korea's demand for steel continued to outstrip the capacity of POSCO steel, especially in the ironmaking sector. In addition to POSCO, Korea had only two relatively large-scale facilities: a plant located at Pusan, operated by Dongkuk Steel Mill Co., and a plant at Inchon, operated by the Inchon Iron Works Co. Aside from these facilities, there were twelve plants with steelmaking and rolling capacities, while another forty-six had only rolling mills. The annual production capacity of the ironmaking sector totaled slightly more than 1.1 million tons, while steelmaking capacity was about 2.2 million tons and the rolling sector had a capacity of about 3 million tons.[32] The result was that steelmaking and ironmaking capacities remained at only 73 percent and 38 percent of rolling capacity, respectively. Aside from the POSCO facility, the scale of the iron and steel plants was small, and in particular, the rolling mills were of an uneconomical size, with most having an annual production capacity of 50,000 tons. Even the Pohang mill, the largest in Korea, was small by international standards.

To meet the rapidly increasing demand for steel, as well as the demand forecasts embedded in the HCI documents, and to ameliorate the imbalance in its production facilities, POSCO planned to expand its production capacity to 2.6 million tons of crude steel by 1976 and to construct another large, integrated, iron and steel mill, with an annual capacity of 7 to 10 million tons, by the end of the decade. The first expansion was started on December 1, 1973, and was again rapidly completed, with a construction period of only two and a half years. The expansion involved an investment of $600 million, about 60 percent of which was procured from foreign lenders. Downstream firms also enlarged and modernized their production facilities in response to the growing demand for steel and steel products.

With the expansion completed, POSCO now had a blast furnace with an inner volume of 2,254 cubic meters, an additional LD oxygen converter, as well as continuous casting facilities. More important, the expansion allowed POSCO to produce such new products as rails, I-beams, H-beams, channels, sheet piles, and cold sheets, products that had been almost entirely imported. Korea's ironmaking production capacity now totaled 2.6 million tons, while its steelmaking capacity was 4.6 million tons, and rolling capacity reached some 7.1 million tons.

As the demand for steel continued to increase, POSCO announced a third expansion to 5.5 million tons, planned for early 1979, as well as a fourth expansion, which would raise capacity to 8.5 million tons by 1981.[33] POSCO's third expansion was made over a period of two and a half years with an investment of 660.8 billion won, of which about 44 percent was domestically raised. With the dedication of the third expansion project in December 1978, POSCO now had a steel capacity of 5.5 million tons, 1.5 million tons of heavy plates, 200,000 tons of billet, and 1.9 million tons of hot-rolling capacities.[34] With steel demand still rising, POSCO planned a fourth expansion, to be completed in June 1981 (Table 6-7). In addition, specialty steel mill capacity was expanded. Existing companies expanded electric furnace capacity, and the rolling facilities for structural and cold-rolled strips were increased.

One outcome of the implementation of the HCI projects was that the demand pattern for steel changed. During the 1970s, the demand for rolled products grew faster than the demand for other products; by the end of the decade, rolled products accounted for over half of total output, a development that reflected the growth of such sectors as shipbuilding, automobile, and other heavy machinery. Between 1962 and 1971, the demand for bars increased by 7.6 times, for sheets and plates by a factor of 4.6, and for casting and forging products by 3.6 times; during the 1972–1980 period, the demand for sheets and plates increased nearly fourfold, exceeding that for bars, which increased about 3.6 times.

Table 6-7. Capacity Expansion of POSCO (thousand tons)

	Phase II	Phase III	Phase IV
Heavy plates	336	1,512	1,512
Hot-rolled coil	460	650	2,897
Hot-rolled sheets	200	146	500
Hot-rolled hoop	138	138	344
Cold-rolled coil	170	138	271
Cold-rolled sheets	175	200	200
Tin plates and sheets	60	67	135
Galvanized coil	28	28	28
Wire rods	52	52	52
Electric plates and sheets	—	446	446
Billets	141	200	200
Slab	186	566	566
Bloom	120	—	—
Cast iron	150	150	200

Note: Phase III: August 1976–December 1978; Phase IV: January 1979–June 1981.
Source: Korea Iron and Steel Association, *Annual Report* (various years).

With the completion of POSCO's fourth expansion phase in May 1983, the thirteen-year project came to an end, and the company's annual total integrated capacity reached 9 million tons. For the country as a whole, annual production capacity in 1983 for ironmaking was 8.8 million tons (a forty-four-fold increase over the 1972 level), for steelmaking 14 million tons (a fifteen-fold increase), and for steelrolling 14.6 million tons (a fivefold increase) (Table 6-8). Moreover, the increased capacity greatly improved the structure of production, which had formerly favored the rolling sector over steelmaking, as evidenced by the fact that ironmaking and steelmaking capacity improved from, respectively, 29 percent and 54 percent of rolling capacity in 1973, to 61 percent and 95 percent by 1983. With the completion of the fourth expansion of Pohang Steel Works in the early 1980s, Korea produced nearly 2 percent of the total world crude steel, and POSCO had become the tenth largest steel-producing company in the noncommunist world.

The rapid growth of the steel sector enabled Korea not only to meet domestic steel demand but to export substantial quantities as well. Beginning in 1971, when imports exceeded exports by 110,000 tons, Korea achieved a surplus of 3.9 million tons by 1983, and steel product exports reached $1.7 billion. The share of exports in total steel demand (domestic demand plus exports) increased from 1.5 percent in 1967 to 26.2 percent in 1973 and 31.9 percent in 1974, and increased again to 36.3 percent of total demand in 1983. Although domestic capacity increased rapidly, a substantial quantity of semi-processed products used in the production of finished products for export still had to be imported. Consequently, the import volume increased in proportion to the increase in export volume. In particular,

Table 6-8. Production Capacity of the Iron and Steel Sector (thousand metric tons)

Year	Ironmaking	Steelmaking	Rolling
1972	203	931	2,081
1973	1,153	2,183	4,023
1977	2,640	4,635	6,337
1978	2,515	5,040	8,472
1979	5,267	8,680	9,379
1980	5,267	9,335	12,634
1981	8,019	12,587	13,711
1982	8,069	13,115	14,468
1983	8,832	13,715	14,553

Source: Ibid.

materials for semifinished products had to be imported in order to meet the domestic and export demand. The main export items are heavy and medium plates, which account for 0.9 million tons, or some 19 percent of total steel exports, and steel pipes, which totaled 0.98 million tons and constituted some 21 percent of total steel exports.

The most important export markets were in East and South Asia, accounting for over 40 percent of all exports. The United States was also an important market, taking as much as half of the total iron and steel exports during 1977–1978, but the importance of the American export market declined sharply as various regulations, led by the trigger price mechanism aimed at restricting imports of iron and steel products, came into play.

The iron and steel industry is a large consumer of energy and raw materials, much of it imported. The production of 1 ton of crude steel requires approximately 3 tons of iron ore, coking coal, scrap iron, limestone, alloying metals, and refractory products. Of the major raw materials required, only limestone can be domestically supplied. Iron ore, coking coal, and scrap have to be imported. This import dependence has increased *pari passu* with the increase in crude steel production. Before the development of POSCO, domestic iron ore was exported mainly to Japan, in part because the technology then in use in Korea was unsuited to the processing of low-grade ore. Currently, virtually no iron ore is exported, and in 1983, 95 percent of the nation's total iron ore demand was imported, primarily from Australia, Peru, Brazil, New Zealand, and India. Similarly, imports of coking coal increased sharply from 30,000 tons in 1972 to 6.0 million tons in 1983, with supplies coming mainly from the United States, Australia, and Canada (Table 6-9). Although Korea has experienced no major problems in securing adequate supplies of iron ore and coking coal, which are relatively abundant and easily available through world trading channels, the situation with regard to scrap is less certain. As might be expected, the domestic supply of scrap has increased over time, so that in 1983, of the 6.5 million tons of scrap iron used by Korea's steel industry, slightly more than half was domestically generated, with the rest imported from the United States, Australia, and Japan.

Construction of Kwangyang Steel Works
The continued increase in domestic demand for steel in the 1970s caused by the swift economic growth and the rapid development of the heavy and chemical industries made necessary the construction of a second integrated steel mill. The depressed region of Kwangyang Bay on the

Table 6-9. Raw Material Supplies for Steel Production (thousand metric tons)

	1975	1977	1979	1981	1983
Scrap					
Demand	1,287	2,491	4,658	4,956	6,458
Domestic supply	321	855	2,714	3,296	3,557
Imported supply	966	1,636	1,944	1,661	2,901
Import share (%)	75.1	65.7	53.7	33.5	44.9
Iron ore					
Demand	1,858	3,887	7,339	11,627	12,050
Domestic supply	457	567	434	426	553
Imported supply	1,401	3,320	6,905	11,201	11,497
Import share (%)	75.4	85.4	94.5	96.3	95.4
Coking coal					
Demand	757	1,828	3,585	6,027	6,032
Domestic supply	3	7	—	—	—
Imported supply	754	1,821	3,585	6,027	6,032
Import share (%)	99.6	99.6	100.0	100.0	100.0

Source: Ibid.

southeastern coast was selected as the site for this mill, with the first phase of construction commencing on November 4, 1981.

The construction posed numerous engineering challenges. Up-to-date technology was required to reclaim the land from the sea and to harden the soft soil in order to prepare the site for plant construction. The foundation work itself took three years to complete. The first-phase construction of the Kwangyang Steel Works, with a capacity of 2.7 million tons, began on March 5, 1985, and was completed on May 7, 1987, fully six months ahead of schedule. Its blast furnace is designed to maximize production of pig iron while minimizing the use of iron ore and coking coal. The facility employs highly sophisticated techniques, such as an all-coke operation and a bell-less factory.

The most difficult problem confronting the Kwangyang first-stage project was purchasing the needed facilities. The Japanese steel companies had become reluctant to sell ever more modern facilities to Korea, now a major competitor in the international iron and steel markets. However, taking advantage of the keen competition among steel facility makers worldwide, POSCO was able to purchase the most up-to-date facilities and advanced technology, further strengthening its international competitive position. To make effective use of the integrated steelmaking facilities, the construction of the second-stage project with an annual capacity of 5.4 million tons was begun on September 30, 1986, and was completed on July 12, 1988, bringing POSCO's total capacity to 15 million tons (9.6 million tons at Pohang). As a result, POSCO had become the third biggest steelmaker in the world, making Korea the sixth-largest steel producer among noncommunist countries and the eighth largest in the entire world.[35]

With continued structural change, the demand pattern for steel products has shifted from hot rolled to cold rolled and toward specialty steels. In 1987, demand for sheets and plates represented well over half of total demand for steel products, while demand for steel bars ranked second, with about 42 percent, and the remainder was accounted for by steel foundry/forgings. The demand for specialty steel products increased at an annual rate of 17 percent over the period 1982–1986. Demand totaled 1.4 million tons in 1986, of which 47.2 percent was domestically supplied. Of total demand for crude steel products, specialty steel accounted for 9.4 percent in 1986, up from 5.4 percent in 1984. By 1988, domestic steel demand had grown to 16.9 million tons, up from 1.8 million tons in 1972, and exports had grown from 0.8 million tons in 1972 to 7.1 million tons in 1988 (Table 6-10). Korea had attained a self-sufficiency ratio of about 75 percent while producing steel at internationally competitive prices, a development that had been unforeseen by many.

Forecasting further demand increases, POSCO initiated a third expansion for the Kwangyang plant in October 1988. Construction of the third phase began in January 1989 and was completed in January 1991, when Kwangyang Steel Works would have a capacity of slightly over 8 million tons and the highest productivity based on the most up-to-date facilities and technologies.

Localization Efforts

In line with Korea's development policies under the HCI drive, POSCO made efforts to improve the localization ratio of machines and equipment. POSCO insisted that foreign contractors form a consortium with Korean

Table 6-10. Steel Production and Demand

Year	Demand (million tons)			Production (million tons)	Production-to-Total Demand (%)
	Domestic	Export	Total		
1972	1.80	0.88	2.68	0.61	22.7
1975	2.96	1.23	4.19	2.56	61.0
1980	6.08	5.23	11.31	8.56	75.5
1982	7.48	6.46	13.94	11.26	84.3
1985	11.31	6.31	17.62	13.54	76.8
1986	12.21	6.41	18.62	14.56	78.2
1987	15.19	6.47	21.66	16.77	77.4
1988 (est.)	16.86	7.14	24.00	18.05	75.2

Source: Public Information Department, Pohang Iron and Steel Corporation, *POSCO's Present and Future*, (April 1988).

suppliers in order to strengthen the capacity of local producers to absorb the new technology. This allowed local producers to gain access to up-to-date technologies, which were, in fact, under monopoly control by a small number of advanced steel-producing countries. In the first phase of the Pohang Steel Works, local suppliers were able to produce only 12.5 percent of total cost for machinery and equipment (Table 6-11). This ratio increased to nearly 50 percent for the first phase of Kwangyang Steel Works and rose to over 55 percent for the second phase.[36] Of the 2.579 trillion won investment in the total facility costs incurred until the second phase, 1.044 trillion won, or slightly over 40 percent, went to local manufacturers. This outcome not only reflects the deliberate policy efforts that were made to increase the local content ratio of investment but also suggests that machinery and equipment suppliers had become increasingly competitive and sophisticated.

An Evaluation of POSCO's Success

The successful establishment and subsequent rapid expansion of POSCO made it one of the success stories of Korea's industrialization period. There is little doubt that POSCO was financially successful, able to enter and successfully compete on the international market, while supplying reasonably high-quality products at low prices to domestic downstream consumers.

Table 6-11. Local Supply of Machinery and Equipment for POSCO Facilities

Construction Project	Costs of Machinery and Equipment (trillion won)		Domestic (%)
	Total Costs	Domestically Supplied	
Pohang phase			
1	752	94	12.5
2	1,614	250	15.5
3	4,469	1,008	22.6
4	4,464	1,567	35.1
Total	11,299	2,919	25.8
Kwangyang phase			
1	9,390	4,692	49.4
2	5,105	2,826	55.4
Total	14,495	7,518	51.8
Total for Pohang/Kwangyang	25,794	10,437	40.4

Source: Ibid.

In 1973, after POSCO's annual production capacity reached 1.03 million metric tons, a study carried out by PaineWebber, and quoted with pride by Chairman Park, established that POSCO's operations were profitable from the start.[37] While this may be correct, Auty reaches a less sanguine conclusion. He notes that POSCO's overall profitability has been disappointing, with pretax income to assets averaging around 4 percent since 1979.[38] Nevertheless, compared to steel industries elsewhere, POSCO's profitability, measured as the after-tax profits-to-revenue ratio, is relatively high. Enos and Park note that POSCO's accomplishments are substantial considering that "Korea had to create a steel industry out of nothing, that the creation involved a very rapid expansion of capacity and output, and that all this took place at a time when the steel industry in the rest of the world was in depression."[39]

Encouraging as this information is, it refers only to the financial rate of return. Information on the economic rate of return is more difficult to come by. Amsden suggests that even if the value of government support were subtracted, such as the interest rate subsidy and the discounted user charges levied for many government services, the project would still be profitable. A full economic evaluation would have to recognize that the government provided a considerable amount of additional support, including site preparation and infrastructure investments, which may have been equivalent to 14 percent of the total first-stage construction cost.[40] Even so, we are inclined to agree with Amsden's conclusion that "even after adding in subsidies to POSCO's cost, POSCO was operating with a cost structure that was neither less nor more favorable than that of Japan, the world's premier producer."[41]

Admittedly none of this allows for a definite assessment of POSCO's economic or financial feasibility. The initial project studies all agreed that the establishment of a steel mill would be neither financially profitable nor economically desirable. In the end, POSCO earned a profit, although its financial profitability was not exceptionally high, and it may not have been charged full cost for either the capital invested or the services provided. Hence, its economic success is even more questionable.

Like the automobile and shipbuilding industries, attempts to build an integrated steel mill began well before the HCI policies were in place. Nevertheless, the policies of the HCI period contributed to POSCO's success in two ways. First, they provided a strong rationale for the subsidies given to the sector, including the construction of the port facilities, as well as access to utilities and credits at below cost.[42] Second, and more important perhaps, the rapid development of the downstream industries, such as automobiles and shipbuilding, as well as the continued high level of construction activities during the 1970s, provided a strong and steady market for POSCO's output.[43] But none of that would have mattered if POSCO itself was unable to produce steel competitively. That, in the final analysis, is what guaranteed its success. From where did that competitive edge come?

In part, POSCO's success rests on the low construction cost of its two steel mills at Pohang and at Kwangyang. The average unit construction cost was well below the level for other countries. Low construction costs reflected the reduction in construction periods, the purchase of foreign facilities through competitive international bidding, and the securing of long-term, low-interest foreign loans, first through access to the Japanese reparations funds and eventually through POSCO's own high credit standing. Equally important, POSCO's management had realized the importance of prompt construction and at an early stage had sent its engineers to Japan for field training, where they participated in the construction and operation of local mills with their Japanese counterparts. The construction periods for the first- and second-stage projects were shortened by more than one month from the planned schedule, by five months for the third-stage project, and by four months for the fourth-stage project. Such reductions in the construction period implied substantial reductions in construction costs.

POSCO also realized the need to achieve a normal operating rate as quickly as possible. The Japan Group, based on its experience with Japanese mills, had forecast that POSCO would need at least one year to achieve normal operating levels. Despite the absence of any experience in the operating of an integrated steel mill, POSCO managed to put the blast furnace of the first phase of the Pohang Steel Works into normal operation within 107 days of its initial fire-up, a world record. The start-up period was reduced to 80 days for the second stage, to 70 days for the third, and to a remarkable 29 days for the fourth blast furnace.[44] The achievement was particularly impressive in the case of the third blast furnace, whose capacity was nearly double that of the second.[45] POSCO was also able to bring the steelmaking facilities on-line quickly, although since these involve both chemical and engineering processes, the speed was not nearly as great as with the blast furnaces. Nevertheless, the ability of Korean engineers to construct these complex projects swiftly and bring them on-line quickly did much to lower overall production costs.

The modern facilities, which POSCO has managed to operate at nearly 100 percent of their rated capacity, combined with the efficient siting of steel mills in coastal regions with good port facilities and access to the interior regions, have allowed Pohang Steel Works to attain the world's lowest unit production costs for steel for six consecutive years since 1982.[46] In 1987, for example, production costs at Pohang Steel per ton of hot-rolled steel were $259.50, or 80 percent of U.S. and 60 percent of Japanese costs.

Although Korean steel products continue to lag in terms of precision and uniformity of product when compared to Japanese products, Korean steel mills approximate those of Japan, in terms of operational technique. Crude steel production at 654 tons per worker in 1986 compares favorably with a figure of 516 tons per worker for Japan.

Finally, POSCO, in no small part because of its dynamic chairman, was able to maintain its independence from the government. Although started with 300 million won in paid-in capital provided by the Ministry of Finance, and with a further 100 million won from the Korea Tungsten Steel Company, POSCO quickly established its status as an independent corporation. Even though it is a semipublic enterprise, POSCO has firmly resisted outside pressures that might influence its decisions on the purchase of equipment, allowing it to buy needed equipment at competitive rates, often below world prices. POSCO has also asserted independence in personnel promotion, refusing to let the government appoint outside figures to top management posts, although this was often a contentious issue. As a result, all executive posts are now filled by those who have been promoted within the company, in sharp contrast to the experience of most other public enterprises.[47]

Like all other government entities, POSCO has at times been subject to political pressures. POSCO's selection of the site for its second steel plant led to a political battle, as did its decision to allow over-the-counter transactions of POSCO stocks. When the government in December 1987 announced a program aimed at allowing the general public to share the profits of public companies, POSCO, in view of its sound financial structure backed by high profitability and its ample potential for continued growth in the future, was chosen as the first public company to join the government's privatization program, and it sold 34.1 percent of its equity to the public in June 1988. At the same time, POSCO introduced an employee stock ownership plan, designed to allow all employees to participate in management as stockholders and share in the company's profits. On the whole, POSCO has operated like a well-run competitive firm, with most decisions made to ensure that prices remain low and profits high.

The overwhelming evidence suggests that Korea managed to create a successful, competitive steel industry out of nothing and that the creation involved a very rapid expansion of capacity and output.

More impressive yet, all this took place at a time when the steel industry in the rest of the world was in depression. Although numerous factors, including excellent management, help account for this success, it remains without doubt one of the more remarkable achievements of Korea's industrialization drive.

Appendix 6A: Chronology of POSCO's Development

Date	Event
April 1, 1968	Pohang Iron & Steel Co., Ltd. is incorporated.
April 1, 1970	Construction of the first-stage project of Pohang Steel Works commences.
July 3, 1973	The first-stage project is dedicated (1.03 million ton capacity).
October 10, 1973	International Iron and Steel Institute membership is obtained.
May 31, 1976	The second-stage project of Pohang Steel Works is dedicated (capacity increased to 2.6 million tons).
December 8, 1978	The third-stage project of Pohang Steel Works is dedicated (capacity increased to 5.5 million tons).
February 18, 1981	The fourth-stage project of Pohang Steel Works is dedicated (capacity increased to 8.5 million tons).
November 4, 1981	The site for the construction of Kwangyang Steel Works is selected.
May 25, 1983	The second phase of the fourth-stage project of Pohang Steel Works is dedicated (capacity increased to 9.1 million tons).
March 5, 1985	Construction of Kwangyang Steel Works commences.
April 1, 1986	USS-POSCO Industries, a joint venture with USX, is incorporated.
May 7, 1987	The first-stage project of Kwangyang Steel Works is dedicated (2.7 million tons capacity).
June 10, 1988	POSCO goes public (becoming the first company to offer "national stocks").
July 12, 1988	The second-stage project of Kwangyang Steel Works is dedicated (capacity increased to 5.4 million tons).
October 1988	Construction of the third-stage project of Kwangyang Steel Works commences.

NOTES

1. For example, data suggest that an aluminum refining plant with an annual capacity of 200,000 tons can produce aluminum for $2,900 per ton of capacity, while a plant with an annual capacity of 100,000 tons will produce output at a cost of $3,400 per ton of capacity.

2. The other substantial failure was the Korea Heavy Machinery complex at Changwon, discussed in Chapter 5.

3. See A. Amsden, *Asia's Next Giant* (New York: Oxford University Press, 1989).

4. As part of its effort to rationalize and further stimulate the shipbuilding sector, the government sold KESC to a private shipping magnate in 1968.

5. A further $360 million was invested during the subsequent five years.

6. As measured by the average annual increase in the wholesale price index. Economic Planning Board, *Major Statistics of Korean Economy* (Seoul: Economic Planning Board, various issues).

7. The six medium-sized companies are primarily engaged in the construction of ships for the domestic market; Korea-Tacoma Marine Industries, Ltd., specializes in the manufacture of yachts, military ships, and multipurpose vessels. The small-sized shipyards continue to construct wooden fishing boats used primarily for inland fishing.

8. Depending on the shipyard, the export dependence varied from 70 to 90 percent in the early 1980s.

9. In pursuing this diversification strategy, the Korean shipbuilders were following the lead of their Japanese counterparts. However, the proportion of nonship to total production volume is much lower in Japan than in Korea. For example, the ratio of shipbuilding to total sales in seven major Japanese shipbuilders was around 24 percent in 1985. This diversification allows the Japanese shipbuilders to weather the downturns of the world ship market more easily than the Korean firms.

10. It became increasingly common in the mid-1980s for buyers to walk away from an order even after the ships had been completed and certified for delivery. In September 1985, for example, twenty-two ships constructed in various Korean yards, worth $567 million, were not accepted because the buyers decided they no longer had need for them or could no longer pay for them.

11. Initially, the joint venture was between GM and ShinJin.

12. Not until 1989, after Korea's automobile manufacturers had attained considerable domestic and international success, did the government remove restrictions on the types of vehicles each automaker could build or allow new entrants into the market.

13. In fact, domestic and foreign cars were not comparable since the quality of the domestic cars was far below those produced elsewhere.

14. See the discussion in Chapter 4.

15. In fact, the 1979 output level for cars was not recaptured until 1983.

16. This compares favorably to the levels recorded in the United States at between 3.3 and 4.0 percent and in Japan at between 3.4 and 3.0 percent of sales.

17. Hyundai claims that it initially lost money on exports, a loss partly offset by government subsidies.

18. The 1989 outturn was considerably less sanguine. During the first nine months of 1989 Hyundai sales were off by 30 percent compared to the same period a year earlier. The price of the Excel had risen, reflecting the appreciation of the won and rising Korean labor costs, while Hyundai had delayed the introduction of a newer model, the Sonata.

19. The North American market accounted for 87 percent of total exports in 1987. Hyundai successfully built an overseas organization, distributing its cars through its own dealer network, while Daewoo and Kia distributed through GM's and Ford's dealers. The success in the North American markets, combined with the emergence of large trade surpluses, brought on trade friction between Korea and the United States. As pressure to open the Korean automobile market increased, the Ministry of Trade and Industry liberalized the market for imported automobiles over 2,000 cc in 1987, and for those under 2,000 cc in 1988.

20. As a vice president at HMC said: "We thought we would lose money but instead we made lots of money. This is a very lucky company." Interview. Please see Bibliography.

21. Determining the appropriate time to evaluate a project is critical. It may well be that Hyundai's success in breaking into the American market will be hard to sustain. If so, future reviews of car exports from Korea may reach a less sanguine conclusion.

22. About twenty-five developing countries produce automobiles, manufactured or assembled, but only a handful have achieved sizable output. With the exception of Korea, none has yet managed to achieve large-scale production or make substantial inroads into export markets, and only four—Korea, Brazil, Mexico, and Taiwan—have attained output levels exceeding 200,000 units, which is the traditionally accepted optimal size for a single manufacturing plant. See Yannis Karmokolias, "Automotive Industry Trends and Prospects for Investment in Developing Countries," *IFC Discussion Paper 7* (Washington, D.C.: World Bank, 1990).

23. As of January 1969, for example, the price of domestically produced bars was 15 percent higher than in Japan, wire rods 21 percent higher,

and heavy plates 28 percent higher. Similar price discrepancies prevailed against other major steel producers. All prices were converted at the then-prevailing exchange rates. Data as reported by the Iron and Steel Foundation of Japan.

24. An earlier plan had called for a smaller plant of 300,000 tons, but it too came to naught.

25. J. L. Enos and W. H. Park, *The Adoption and Diffusion of Imported Technology* (New York: Croom Helm, 1988), pp. 178–179.

26. After POSCO had been built and was well established, Chairman Park, president of POSCO steel, was awarded an honorary degree by a British university. During the award ceremony he was seated next to the author of the report that had recommended against British government aid for the construction of POSCO. Chairman Park asked whether the author still stood by his conclusions. "Yes," was the reply, "my analysis was correct, but you proved it wrong." Interview with Chairman Park, Seoul, 1989.

27. Interview with Chairman Park, Seoul, 1989.

28. Chairman Park noted the government's forecasts for infrastructure development, and he therefore felt confident that the domestic demand for steel would in fact increase quite rapidly. Thus, he was confident that only a larger-sized plant would suit Korea's development needs. Interview with Chairman Park, Seoul, 1989.

29. The 30 percent export target has been consistently met by POSCO despite the strong domestic demand for steel. It also provides an indication that the plant was capable of producing steel at world prices right from the start.

30. Taking $500 million as the average cost of a million-ton-per-year iron and steel plant (the POSCO facilities cost less), an extra year spent on construction would add something like $1 to $2 to each ton of steel. See Enos and Park, *Adoption and Diffusion of Imported Technology*, p. 186.

31. Operations reached their planned level within six months after the plant began operation, and the plant was able to produce at near full capacity in its first year. Both developments confounded experts and the other steelmaking facilities in developing countries, where typically plants have considerable teething troubles.

32. In addition, there were cast iron facilities with a capacity of about half a million tons.

33. POSCO, nearly from its inception, exported about one-third of its output, in part because it had calculated that exporting such an amount would approximately cover the cost of imported raw materials.

34. Korea now had an annual production capacity of 8.3 million tons of steel and 8.9 million tons of rolled steel. Cast iron facilities totaled 1 million tons, while forging capacity was 146,000 tons per year. Of the

total annual steelmaking capacity, 66 percent (5.5 million tons) was provided by LD converters, nearly 33 percent by electric furnaces, with the remainder coming from open hearth furnaces.

35. Korea, which had ranked eighteenth in terms of steelmaking capacity in 1980, ranked eighth in 1988, just below Italy and Brazil. International Iron and Steel Institute data.

36. It is expected that the third phase of Kwangyang Steel Works will see local producers supply more than 60 percent of the total machinery and equipment.

37. Enos and Park note that over the period 1973 to 1984, POSCO was consistently profitable, although not appreciably more so than Japanese firms. And by all accounts POSCO remains profitable today. See Enos and Park, *Adoption and Diffusion of Imported Technology*, pp. 212–215.

38. One reason that POSCO's financial returns may be relatively modest is that it sells steel on the domestic market at below the import competing price. See R. M. Auty, "The Financial Performance of South Korean HCI/RBI:Steel and Petrochemicals," *Working Paper 64b*, Lancaster University (1988).

39. See Enos and Park, *Adoption and Diffusion of Imported Technology*, p. 215.

40. Auty, "Financial Performance."

41. Amsden, *Asia's Next Giant*.

42. The interest rate on funds borrowed for the various Pohang facilities ranged from 2.0 to 8.5 percent, with a repayment period of 1.5 to 19 years; for Kwangyang, the interest rate ranged from 2.0 to 6.95 percent, with a repayment period from 7 to 19 years.

43. Real construction value-added grew at an annual rate of 11.8 percent during the period 1970–1979. See Economic Planning Board, *Major Statistics of the Korean Economy: 1988* (Seoul: Economic Planning Board, 1988).

44. The start-up period was reduced to eighteen days for the second blast furnace at Kwangyang, breaking POSCO's own record.

45. In part, as Enos and Park note, the speedy working in of the third blast furnace was due to the large number of foreign engineers on site at the time of the start-up, although the contribution of Korean engineers, and the skills they had acquired from the first two projects, must be admitted. See Enos and Park, *Adoption and Diffusion of Imported Technology*, p. 185.

46. Over the period from 1977 to 1984, POSCO operated at 101.8 percent of its rated steel production capacity, while the average for all noncommunist countries was 70.2 percent. See Enos and Park, *Adoption and Diffusion of Imported Technology*, p. 215.

47. Unlike most public enterprises, POSCO earns sufficient profits to pay taxes. It has been the country's largest taxpayer for five years since 1983, with cumulative tax payments since its founding amounting to 717.9 billion won.

7

Conclusion _____

Has the Republic of Korea's heavy and chemical industry (HCI) development been a success? And to the degree it was or was not a success, what lessons can others learn from the experience? What lessons have the Koreans themselves drawn from their efforts to accelerate the development of these industries?

Because the Korean economy has done so well overall, there is a tendency to assume that Korean economic policies were uniformly supportive of that overall performance. The issue then becomes one of determining which Korean policies were effective and attributing whatever success was achieved to those policies. How could policies that achieved an annual growth rate of gross national product of 9 or 10 percent per year have been anything but well conceived? Could any realistic set of policies actually have done better?

Although many foreign observers have approached Korea's (HCI) drive from the viewpoint of a disciple wanting to learn from the master, many Korean economists have been highly critical of the HCI program as it was originally conceived in the early 1970s. They attribute many of Korea's economic ills in the 1979–1981 period to that program. Who is right? There is no simple way to reach conclusions about the contribution of the HCI drive to the overall performance of the Korean economy. The approach in this study has been to examine this area from a number of different angles.

The Korean HCI program was implemented at a particular time in Korea's economic and political history and can be properly understood only in that historical context. But the historical context alone cannot answer the question of whether the program's net economic contribution was positive. To deal with this latter question, one must do a systematic analysis of the HCI drive at both the macro- and microlevels. That was the task undertaken in the preceding chapters of this study. What is it ·that was learned?

The Context

Any understanding of the Korean HCI program must recognize that it was carried out for political-military objectives as well as economic ones. Furthermore, most of the key decisions were made not by economists but by engineers and a president of the country who was a politician and a general, and at a time, the early 1970s, when Korea appeared to be increasingly vulnerable to external political-military pressures.

If the political-military context explained much of the support behind the HCI drive, there would be little point in analyzing that effort in primarily economic terms. But President Park and his engineer-advisers knew from the outset that Korea could not afford a program that was pursued at the expense of economic growth. The Korean economy by 1973, after only a decade of rapid growth, was still poor and vulnerable. An ambitious attempt to build an independent weapons industry capable of meeting most of Korea's military needs could have bankrupted the economy. President Park and his advisers therefore wanted an HCI program that would further strengthen the Korean economy, not weaken it.

In the 1960s, the Korean government had also wanted to build a strong economy capable of making Korea more independent of U.S. economic and military aid. But in the 1960s, there was a recognition of the need to give priority to the development of manufactured exports in order to earn foreign exchange. Heavy industries were desired, and laws were passed to encourage their development, but the focus of economic policy was on light manufactures, the only sector that could reasonably expect to become competitive internationally in a short period of time. And the policies adopted in order to encourage these light manufactures were of a general nature. A manufacturer that met certain general criteria was eligible for the various export subsidies that were then available. It did not matter whether the firm produced cloth, garments, or shoes; if exports grew at the required pace, the subsidies were paid out. To be sure, various sectors were expected to meet export targets, but the sectors themselves, not the government, set these targets. President Park and his government rewarded those who set and met ambitious targets, but the president did not select the industries or give them detailed instructions about what to produce.

As Korea geared up to promote heavy and chemical industries, however, the modus operandi of the government changed. In the HCI drive that began in January 1973 and ended in early 1979, it was the government that decided which industries would be promoted and which firms would be selected to carry out the government's wishes. In fact, President Park himself often made these decisions and did so after consulting with Oh Won Chol, the chief of the group brought into the Blue House to plan the HCI drive. From an approach in the 1960s that emphasized general incentives on a nondiscriminatory basis, the government by 1973 had converted to an industrial policy designed to pick winners. Korea's HCI drive therefore became a case study of an approach to industrial policy advocated by those who feel that government is often in a better position than private businesses to pick and promote new industries. The private sector in Korea in the 1970s had a peripheral role at best in deciding which sectors to develop. Its role was to implement the decisions of the Blue House, and these private firms could count on extensive government support if they did so.

The criteria the government used to target particular industries involved a combination of approaches. The relevance of the particular sectors to military strength, of course, played a role. Engineering feasibility was in many ways the key criterion. Oh Won Chol and his staff went to great lengths to attempt to discern whether Korea had the technical skills needed to carry out particular projects or could expect to acquire these skills quickly enough. Economic criteria also crept into these engineering studies. One issue, for example, was whether domestic demand was likely to be sufficient to support an efficient scale of production. Since the usual answer was that domestic demand was insufficient, the next step was to ask whether it was realistic for the industry being considered to become an exporter.

In answering these various questions, a common approach was to look at the experience of other nations at what the Blue House staff deemed to be a comparable stage in their development. Various European states were visited, but the model par excellence was Japan. Japan, in the eyes of these Korean planners, was perhaps fifteen years ahead of Korea in its technological capacities. By looking at the experience of Japan and other industrial countries, the Oh Won Chol staff was, in effect, applying a kind of Kuznets-Chenery pattern of growth analysis to their data. These Blue House engineers did not recognize the approach as such, but they basically looked at these other patterns of changing industrial structures and attempted to place Korea at the proper point along the regression line.

Conspicuously absent from this approach was any use of cost-benefit analysis or other similar project-appraisal techniques. Occasionally outside groups such as the World Bank applied these techniques to projects being considered for loans, but the Blue House did not. Nor were the macroeconomic implications of the HCI drive looked at in any systematic way. One of the purposes of this study has been to discern whether the approaches actually used were an adequate substitute for what, from an economic viewpoint, were the correct rigorous approaches to determining economic feasibility.

This effort at industrial targeting ended in 1979 and was never revived in the 1980s, except in the telecommunications sector. Economists opposed to the whole approach of the HCI program dominated economic policy when President Chun ruled, and the attitudes of the Chun Doo Hwan years carried over into the presidency of Roh Tae-Woo. Furthermore, there was no longer any doubt that heavy industry would keep on growing whether or not it received special help from the government. International pressures, mainly from the United States, reinforced the move away from industrial targeting.

Was Government's Role Necessary?

Would the heavy and chemical sectors in Korea have begun developing rapidly in the 1970s even in the absence of special help from the government? Even if the answer to this question is negative, it does not follow that government intervention was desirable from an economic point of view. Perhaps Korea would have been better off waiting until the 1980s to start the steel or heavy machinery sectors.

Although it is possible to make the case that HCI development in Korea should have waited a bit longer, the evidence in the preceding chapters makes it clear that the decision to go ahead on HCI promotion was, at most, a few years ahead of its time, if it was ahead at all. The question of whether heavy and chemical industries would have developed without government support therefore is a relevant one. If the private sector was chafing to go ahead on its own without government support, the case for an active government industrial policy would indeed be weak.

But was the Korean private sector in a position to press forward in 1973 on its own? Economists often assume the answer to this question is straightforward. If the incentives are right, private entrepreneurs will respond.

Korea certainly had a considerable number of able entrepreneurs by 1973. If they had access to the large capital loans required, if they could hire the engineers needed to start up the new plants, and if they could be assured that all of the necessary infrastructure would be in place, they no doubt would have responded. In the 1970s, when the government guaranteed their access to these critical inputs, they did respond. But could they have obtained these inputs on their own?

If Korea's economy had been run on free market principles over the 1960s, entrepreneurs may well have gotten started on the HCI program on their own. But as this study has made clear, the Korean economy in the early 1970s, like many other economies in the developing world, was a far cry from some free market ideal. The banks were government owned, and loans were made at subsidized rates at government direction. Much of the infrastructure—electric power, for example—was also provided by state-owned enterprises. Imports of critical inputs were subject to government quotas. The education system was part public, part private. By the 1980s, many of these government controls had been dismantled, and those that remained operated more in accordance with market principles, but that was not the case in the 1970s.

Thus, it is difficult to conceive how Korean firms could have built the Pohang Iron and Steel complex or several of the other large-scale plants on their own. The government had to be involved in their support. Without government guarantees, the hundreds of millions of dollars in credits required would not have been available. Private firms in that context would not have been able to build the necessary infrastructure. Customs would not have allowed the required inputs to come in at favorable rates if only isolated private entrepreneurs were doing the asking. In an ideal world, the government could have first privatized all banks and all infrastructure-related enterprises, and it could have fully liberalized foreign trade. Then the private sector might have responded on its own. That ideal world was close to reality in the late 1980s but not in the 1970s.

The case for an activist government industrial policy in Korea therefore does not rest initially on the presence of market failures, the usual valid economic argument for government intervention in the economy. The issue of market failures is relevant and will be dealt with. The activist government case instead rests on the fact that the Korean government had designed the rules of the game in such a way that only government could take the lead on projects of the magnitude contemplated in the HCI program.

Was Industrial Policy Efficient?

If, in the Korean context of the 1970s, an HCI program required an interventionist government, the question remains whether that intervention was handled efficiently. An active government role is the norm in the industrial programs of most developing countries, but only a few handle these interventions in a highly efficient manner. What was the case in the Republic of Korea with respect to the HCI program?

There are different levels on which the question of efficiency can be approached—for example, looking at the impact of the HCI effort on various indicators of the overall performance of the economy, in effect, a macro-approach to the efficiency question, or doing a detailed appraisal of the individual HCI projects, a micro-approach. In this study, both approaches were tried.

At the macrolevel, a definitive conclusion about the impact on the economy of the HCI program would have required a general equilibrium model that would have simulated Korea's development pattern in the absence of an HCI drive and would have compared that simulation with what actually occurred. The formidable data requirements of a reliable simulation of this sort, however, were beyond the scope of what was possible in this study. A number of partial aggregate indicators were looked at instead.

First, there was the question of whether Korean heavy and chemical industries grew much more rapidly than one would expect in a country at Korea's stage of development. Oh Won Chol felt that Korea in the early 1970s was in a position similar to that of Japan fifteen years earlier. The analysis in Chapter 4 suggests that that judgment was not far off the mark. Korea's heavy and chemical industries did grow to have a larger share in GNP than was true on average in all developing countries at Korea's level of per capita income. But Korea's shares were not unusual when one compares Korea with nations that had a comparable factor endowment, one with few natural resources, limited arable land, and a large, educated population. China is an example of a country that built up its heavy industry sector when per capita income was unusually low.

Did the HCI drive hurt Korea's export development? The HCI program in its early stages had many of the characteristics of import-substituting industrialization found elsewhere in the developing world. Import-substitution regimes tend to be associated with weak export performance. Was this true in Korea?

Certainly Korea's exports did not slow to a crawl in the 1970s as a result of the HCI program. In nominal U.S. dollar terms, exports between 1973 and 1980 grew at 27 percent a year. Although there was considerable inflation in these years due to the two OPEC oil price increases, Korean export growth in real terms was still very rapid. As a percentage of total world or Organization of Economic Cooperation and Development exports, Taiwan exports in both the light and heavy industry sectors grew more rapidly, particularly after 1978, than did the shares of Korea. Only after

1985 did Korea once again begin to catch up with Taiwan in this respect. It can be argued that the post-1985 acceleration in such Korean heavy industry exports as automobiles and steel would not have been possible without the earlier HCI program of the 1970s. But there was more than a ten-year lag between the beginning of the HCI effort and the payoff in accelerated heavy industry exports. And the acceleration after 1985 was aided by a number of exogenous changes that would have been difficult to foresee: the impact of American import quotas on Japanese automobiles or the effect of the Reagan budget deficits on the value of the yen, both with a major influence on Korea.

The large shift in investment funds into the HCI sector in the mid-1970s also led to a decline in the rate of return on capital in the HCI sector. Properly measured, a considerable gap opened up between the rate of return on capital in the HCI sector as compared to that in the light industry sector that had trouble finding adequate investment funds during the 1973–1978 period. The large-scale HCI investments also contributed to accelerating inflation at the end of the 1970s, although it would take a more systematic modeling effort to sort out the relative contributions of the HCI program and the OPEC oil price rise of 1979. Such a modeling effort is beyond the scope of this study.

When one turns to the microlevel appraisal of the HCI program and looks at the performance of individual enterprises, the picture is also mixed. Several of the enterprises, notably Pohang Iron and Steel (POSCO), have been clear successes. Others, notably Korean Heavy Industries and, until recently, Okpo Shipbuilding, have avoided bankruptcy only with large and continuing state subsidies. The performance of these latter two firms in particular has much to do with why many Korean economists have negative views of the whole HCI program.

A detailed social cost–benefit analysis of each of the HCI enterprises would be a massive undertaking, even if all of the necessary data were available, which they are not. Instead, in this study, detailed analyses were made of six enterprises that together represent most of the major sectors that were part of the HCI program. In addition, less systematic analyses were made of two particularly important heavy industries, POSCO and the Hyundai Motor Company, together with a review of the aluminum sector, shipbuilding, and automobile production. The cost-benefit calculations were done using both base-year prices, the price estimates when the project was undertaken, and current prices, later-year prices at a point after the project was completed and in production.

Two standards for measuring success were applied. One, the market-conforming test, considered the project a success if cost-benefit calculations indicated that the rate of return at both base-year and current prices was higher than the cost of capital. Three of the enterprises studied passed this test. The three others had high enough rates of return using base-year prices but did not meet the standard with current (later-year) prices. If the private sector had been in a position to make these same calculations instead of the government, the decision would have been to go ahead on all six. Thus, the successes and failures of the government in these six cases are similar to what one would have expected from private entrepreneurs in a free market setting.

The second non-market-conforming standard is a more rigorous test of what some analysts consider to be the advantages of a government-directed industrial policy. The assumption behind this second test is that market failures would have led private entrepreneurs to avoid certain projects that, once undertaken, would prove to have an actual rate of return well above the cost of capital. None of the six enterprises looked at systematically using cost–benefit techniques met this standard. The two important cases looked at less systematically due to lack of data, POSCO and Hyundai Motor Company, may have met this more rigorous standard. With regard to Hyundai Motor Company at least, there remains a question as to whether its subsequent success was the result of a well-thought-out industrial policy or simply good luck in the form of favorable exogenous shocks.

Where does this appraisal of the Korean HCI program end up? Some of these investments probably helped raise the rate of growth in GNP; others may have lowered that rate somewhat. Overall, Korea's GNP continued to grow rapidly throughout the 1970s and 1980s except over 1979–1981. But the negative shocks of 1979–1981 were not primarily the result of the HCI drive. Thus, Korea's heavy industries contributed more or less their share to what by any standards overall was an outstanding economic performance.

Did the government's industrial policy of the 1973–1978 period do better than what an unfettered market economy might have accomplished? The answer would appear to be no. Most of these projects would also have been attractive to a private entrepreneur in a free market setting. In Korea in the 1970s, of course, nothing remotely approaching a free market setting existed, so this standard is a hypothetical one. In Korea, as it actually operated in the 1970s, the government did a reasonably effective job of selecting and promoting heavy industries. Conceivably the private sector could have done as well or even a bit better, but not by any wide margin. Mistakes were made by the public industrial policy-makers. Korean Heavy Industries and Okpo Shipbuilding were major errors by any standard. But the private sector makes mistakes too.

Are there lessons in all this for other developing countries? Korea under President Park demonstrates that it is possible for a government that dedicates itself to promoting modern heavy industries to succeed if the critical inputs—skilled labor and management, for example—are available. But President Park's government was singlemindedly devoted to achieving rapid economic growth. Only the security of the state had a higher priority, and that security itself, in the eyes of the government, depended on continued accelerated development. Industrial policies carried out by governments not singlemindedly devoted to growth (President Marcos in the Philippines comes to mind) do not fare so well. Before a country can attempt to duplicate the Korean experience of the 1970s, it must first determine whether it can or even wants to duplicate the Korean government's dedication to economic growth as the overriding social objective.

Select Bibliography

Agarwala, Ramgopal. "Price Distortions and Growth in Developing Countries." *World Bank Staff Working Paper 575*. Washington, D.C.: World Bank, 1983.

Balassa and Associates. *The Structure of Protection in Developing Countries*. Baltimore: Johns Hopkins University Press, 1971.

Bank of Korea. *Economic Statistics Yearbook*. Seoul: Bank of Korea, various issues. (in Korean)

———. *Korean Economic Indicators*. Seoul: Bank of Korea, 1986. (in Korean)

Boltho, A. "Was Japan's Industrial Policy Successful?" *Cambridge Journal of Economics*, 9, (1985): 187–201.

Brown, G. T. *Korean Pricing Policies and Economic Development in the 1960s*. Baltimore: Johns Hopkins University Press, 1973.

Cho Yoon-je, and D. C. Cole. "The Role of the Financial Sector in Korea's Structural Adjustment." *Development Discussion Paper 230*. Cambridge: Harvard Institute for International Development, 1986.

Choi Byung-sun. "Institutionalizing a Liberal Economic Order in Korea: The Strategic Management of Economic Change." Ph.D. dissertation, Harvard University, 1987.

Chon, S. W. Executive vice president, Hyundai Motor Company. Interview. August 1989.

Chung So-Yong. Chairman, CORYO Research Institute (first senior secretary for economic affairs, Blue House, 1972–1979). Interview. July 1988.

Cole, D. C., and Yung-chul Park. *Financial Development in Korea, 1945–1978*. Cambridge: Council on East Asian Studies, 1983.

Dasgupta, P., S. Marglin, and A. Sen. *Guidelines for Project Evaluation*. Vienna: United Nations Industrial Development Organization, 1972.

Dertouzos, M., R. K. Lester, R. M. Solow, and the MIT Commission on Industrial Productivity. *Made in America: Regaining the Productive Edge*. Cambridge: MIT Press, 1989.

Dixit, A. K. "Trade Policy: An Agenda for Research." In P. R. Krugman, ed., *Strategic Trade Policy and the New International Economics*. Cambridge: MIT Press, 1986.

Economic Planning Board. *Handbook of Korean Economy, 1980*. Seoul: Economic Planning Board, 1980. (in Korean)

————. *Korean Economic Indicators*. Seoul: Economic Planning Board, 1986. (in Korean)

————. *Major Statistics of Korean Economy*. Seoul: Economic Planning Board, various issues. (in Korean)

————. *Report on Mining and Manufacturing Survey*. Seoul: Economic Planning Board, various years. (in Korean)

Enos, J. L., and W. H. Park. *The Adoption and Diffusion of Imported Technology*. New York: Croom Helm, 1988.

Frank, C. R., Kwang Suk Kim, and L. E. Westphal. *Foreign Trade Regimes and Economic Development: South Korea*. New York: National Bureau of Economic Research, 1975.

Government of the Republic of Korea. *Chunghwa-hak Kongophwa chongchaek sonohe ttayuh kongop kujo kaepyollon* (A theory of industrial structure reformation based on the declaration of the policies toward heavy chemical industrialization). Seoul: Government of the Republic of Korea, 1973. (in Korean)

————. *Comprehensive Stabilization Program*. Seoul: Government of the Republic of Korea, 1979. (in Korean)

————. *The First Five-Year Development Plan, 1962–1966*. Seoul: Government of the Republic of Korea, 1961. (in Korean)

————. *The Second Five-Year Development Plan, 1967–1971*. Seoul: Government of the Republic of Korea, 1966. (in Korean)

————. *The Third Five-Year Development Plan, 1972–1976*. Seoul: Government of the Republic of Korea, 1971. (in Korean)

Grossman, G. M. "Strategic Export Promotion: A Critique." In P. R. Krugman, ed., *Strategic Trade Policy and the New International Economics*. Cambridge: MIT Press, 1986.

Haggard, S., et al. *Macroeconomic Policy and Adjustment in Korea, 1970–1990*. Cambridge: Harvard University Press, 1994.

Han Duck-Soo. Director, Ministry of Trade and Industry. Interview. May 1990.

Han Jae-Yeul. Executive vice president, Korea Federation of Small Business. Interview. June 1988.

Han Seung Soo. Minister of trade and industry. Interview. May 1990.

Harberger, A. *Project Evaluation: Collected Papers*. Chicago: Chicago University Press, 1976.

————. "On the UNIDO Guidelines to Social Project Evaluation." In H. Schwartz and R. Berney, eds., *Social and Economic Dimensions of Project Evaluation*. Washington, D.C.: Inter-American Development Bank, 1977.

Hasan, P. *Korea: Problems and Issues in a Rapidly Growing Economy*. Baltimore: Johns Hopkins University Press, 1976.

Heavy Industry Promotion Committee. *Chung hwa-hak kongop paltalsa* (A history of the development of the heavy chemical industry, vol. 1). Seoul: Heavy Industry Promotion Committee, 1979. (in Korean)

Helmers, F. L. C. H. *Project Planning and Income Distribution*. Boston: Martinus Nijhoff Publishing, 1979.

Hong Sung-jua. President, Small and Medium Industry Promotion Corporation. Interview. July 1988.

Hong Won Tack. Professor of economics, Seoul National University. Interview. July 1988.

International Monetary Fund. *International Financial Statistics*. Washington, D.C.: World Bank, various issues.

Jenkins, G., and A. C. Harberger. "Cost-Benefit Analysis of Investment Decisions." Unpublished manuscript, 1988.

Jones, L. P. *Public Enterprise and Economic Development: The Korean Case*. Seoul: Korea Development Institute Press, 1976.

Jones, L. P., and Il Sakong. *Government, Business and Entrepreneurship in Economic Development: The Korean Case*. Cambridge: Council on East Asian Studies, 1980.

Karmokolias, Y. "Automotive Industry Trends and Prospects for Investment in Developing Countries." *IFC Discussion Paper 7*. Washington, D.C.: World Bank, 1990.

Kim Chulsu. Assistant minister for trade, Ministry of Trade and Industry. Interview. July 1988.

Kim Jung-ryom. *Thirty-Year History of Korean Economic Policy: A Memoir*. Seoul: Joong-ang Ilbo-san, 1990. (in Korean)

Kim Kwang Suk. *The Economic Effects of Import Liberalization and Industrial Adjustment Policy*. Seoul: Korea Development Institute Press, 1988.

Kim Kwang Suk, and M. Roemer. *Growth and Structural Transformation*. Cambridge: Harvard University Press, 1979.

Kim Mahn Je. (Former president of KDI, minister of finance and deputy prime minister). Interview. May 1990.

Kim Yong Hwan. Chairman, Central Policy Committee, New Democratic Party (Former director general, HCI Committee). Interview. June 1988.

Kim Young Tai. Assistant minister, International Policy Coordination Office, Economic Planning Board. Interview. March 1988.

Kissinger, H. *White House Years*. Boston: Little, Brown, 1979.

Koo Jay Y. Director, POHANG Iron and Steel Co., Ltd. Interview. August 1989.

Korea Auto Industries Cooperative Association. *20 Years of KAICA*. Seoul: KAICA, 1983. (in Korean)

Korea Exchange Bank. *Monthly Review* 10, no. 11 (November 1986): 4. (in Korean)

Korea Iron and Steel Association. *Steel Statistics Annual Report*. Seoul: KISA, various years. (in Korean)

Korean Shipbuilders' Association. *Shipbuilding Statistics Annual Report, 1984*. Seoul: KSA, 1984. (in Korean)

Kravis, I., A. Heston, and R. Summers. *World Product and Income: International Comparisons of Real Gross Product*. Baltimore: Johns Hopkins University Press, 1982.

Krueger, A. O. "Trade Policy as an Input to Development." *American Economic Review* 70, no. 2 (May 1980).

———. *The Developmental Role of the Foreign Sector and Aid*. Cambridge: Harvard University Press, 1979.

Krugman, P. "Targeted Industrial Policies: Theory and Evidence." In *Industrial Change and Public Policy*, proceedings of a symposium sponsored by the Federal Reserve Bank of Kansas City, Jackson Hole, Wyoming, August 24–26, 1983.

Kwack Taewon. *Depreciation and Taxation of Income from Capital*. Seoul: Korea Development Institute Press, 1985.

Lee Ik-Chi. Senior vice president, Hyundai Heavy Industry Co., Ltd. Interview. July 1988.

Lee Jong-Rie. Vice president, Burada Co., Ltd., and Myung Sung Industrial Co., Ltd. (worked at HCI Planning Agency). Interview. June 1988.

Leipziger, D. M., et al. *Korea: Managing the Industrial Transition*. 2 vols. Washington, D.C.: World Bank, 1987.

Luedde-Neurath, R. *Import Controls and Export-Oriented Development: A Reassessment of the South Korean Case*. Boulder, Colo.: Westview, 1986.

McKinnon, R. L. *Money and Capital in Economic Development*. Washington, D.C.: Brookings Institution, 1973.

Magaziner, I., and M. Patinkin. *The Silent War*. New York: Vintage Books, 1989.

Marglin, S. A. *Public Investment Criteria.* Cambridge: MIT Press, 1967.

Ministry of Trade and Industry. Internal Report. Seoul: Government of the Republic of Korea, 1980. (in Korean)

Nam Duck Woo. President, Korea Traders Association (former minister of finance, deputy prime minister, and prime minster). Interview. May 1990.

Nam Sang-woo. "Integrated Economic Stabilization Programs in Korea." Paper presented at the International Seminar on "The Process of Korea's Industrialization." Seoul, Korea, March 8–21, 1985.

Office of the Secretary to the President. *Collection of President Park Chung-hee's Speeches.* Vol. 5. Seoul: Daehan Gongron-sa, 1976. (in Korean)

Oh Won-Chul. Second senior secretary for economic affairs (Blue House, 1971–1979). Interview. June 1988.

Park Tae Joon. Chairman, Board of Directors, Pohang Iron and Steel Co., Ltd.; Member, National Assembly, Republic of Korea. Interview. August 1989.

Pepper, T., M. Janow, and J. Wheeler. *The Competition: Dealing with Japan.* New York: Praeger, 1985.

Public Information Department of Pohang Iron and Steel Corporation (POSCO). *POSCO's Present and Future.* Seoul: POSCO, April 1988. (in Korean)

Pyo Hak-kil. "Estimates of Capital Stock and Capital/Output Coefficients by Industries for the Republic of Korea (1953–1986)." *Korea Development Institute Working Paper 8810.* Seoul: Korea Development Institute Press, 1988.

Reynolds, B., ed. *Reform in China: Challenges and Choices.* Armonk, N.Y.: M. E. Sharpe, 1987.

Rhee Yung Whee, B. Ross-Larson, and G. Pursell. *Korea's Competitive Edge: Managing the Entry into World Markets.* Baltimore: Johns Hopkins University Press, 1984.

Sabin, L., and H. Kato. "Shadow Price Calculation and Application: A Case Study of Korea." *Development Discussion Paper 313.* Cambridge: Harvard Institute for International Development, 1989.

Schultze, C. L. "Industrial Policy: A Dissent." *Brookings Review* 2 (Fall 1983).

Shin Kook-Hwan. Director general, Trade Bureau, Ministry of Trade and Industry. Interview. March 1988.

Song, Y. R. Executive managing director, Corporate Planning Division, Samsung Electronics Co. Interview. March 1988.

Spencer, B. J., and J. A. Brander. "International R&D Rivalry and Industrial Strategy." *Review of Economic Studies* 50 (October 1983), 707–722.

State Statistical Bureau. *Statistical Yearbook of China, 1986.* Hong Kong: Economic Information and Agency, 1987.

Stern, J. "Korea's Industrial Policy and Changing Industrial Structure." *Development Discussion Paper 352*. Cambridge: Harvard Institute for International Development, July 1990.

Tower, E. "Industrial Policy in Less Developed Countries." *Contemporary Policy Issues* 4, no. 1 (January 1986).

United Nations. *Yearbook of International Trade Statistics*. New York: United Nations, various issues.

Westphal, L. E. "The Republic of Korea's Experience with Export-Led Industrial Development." *World Development* 6, no. 3 (1978): 350.

Westphal, L. E., and Kwang Suk Kim. "Korea." In B. Balassa et al., eds., *Development Strategies in Semi-Industrial Economies*. Baltimore: Johns Hopkins University Press, 1982.

World Bank. *Korea: Managing the Industrial Transition*. Washington, D.C.: World Bank, 1987.

———. *World Tables*. 3d ed. Washington, D.C.: World Bank, 1983.

Yoo Jung-ho. "Estimation of Some Disaggregate Export and Import Functions." *Korea Development Review* 6, no. 3 (Fall 1984). (in Korean)

Yun Jong-yong. Executive vice president, Samsung Electronics. Interview. August 1989.

Index